Proxmox Cookbook

Over 60 hands-on recipes to perform server virtualization and manage virtualized server solutions with Proxmox

Wasim Ahmed

BIRMINGHAM - MUMBAI

Proxmox Cookbook

First published: August 2015

Production reference: 1250815

Published by Packt Publishing Ltd.
Livery Place
35 Livery Street
Birmingham B3 2PB, UK.

ISBN 978-1-78398-090-1

www.packtpub.com

Credits

Author
Wasim Ahmed

Reviewers
Rudy Jauregui
Jorge Moratilla
Yacine Sebihi
Mark Verboom

Commissioning Editor
Kartikey Pandey

Acquisition Editor
Subho Gupta

Content Development Editor
Samantha Gonsalves

Technical Editor
Rahul C. Shah

Copy Editor
Sonia Michelle Cheema

Project Coordinator
Kinjal Bari

Proofreader
Safis Editing

Indexer
Monica Ajmera Mehta

Graphics
Jason Monteiro
Abhinash Sahu

Production Coordinator
Arvindkumar Gupta

Cover Work
Arvindkumar Gupta

About the Author

Wasim Ahmed, born in Bangladesh, is now a citizen of Canada and a veteran of the IT world. He first came into contact with computers in 1992, and since then, he's never looked back. Over the years, he has acquired an in-depth knowledge and understanding of network, virtualization, big data storage, and network security. By profession, Wasim is the CEO of an IT support and cloud service provider company based out of Calgary, Alberta. He provides his services to many companies and organizations on a daily basis. His strength is his experience, which he's gained from learning and serving clients regularly. He strives to find the most effective solution for a problem at the most competitive prices. He has built over 20 enterprise production virtual infrastructures from scratch using Proxmox and the Ceph storage system.

Wasim is well known for his reluctance to accept a technology based on its description alone, and putting it through rigorous tests to check its validity. Any new technology that his company provides goes through months of continuous testing before it is accepted. Proxmox has made the cut superbly.

I would like to thank all the staff at Proxmox for their support and dedication to the hypervisor community. I would also like to thank Packt Publishing for their vision of putting forward this one-of-a kind book on such a subject and their support through the journey of writing this book.

About the Reviewers

Rudy Jauregui is a site reliability engineer at Adyoulike, a French company providing the first native advertising platform for web editors around the world.

Being a Linux system administrator for important cloud hosting providers, he naturally specializes in DevOps engineering and is now working on large distributed infrastructures that receive a high amount of daily traffic. Since he's very passionate about open source and new technologies, he keeps trying new open source solutions, which are available on GitHub, and is convinced that open source technologies are the key to success in the IT world.

When on vacation, he likes to travel all around the world and meet different kinds of people in a bid to absorb their culture and knowledge. He has also become involved in skydiving and is trying to attain a B Certificate. You can follow him on Twitter at @rustx64.

Jorge Moratilla has a bachelor's degree in computer science and has worked for Internet companies since 1998. He has worked as a contractor for companies such as Sun Microsystems and Oracle. His passions are teaching and optimizing workloads of developers and production systems using automation techniques. He has worked at Sun Microsystems as a certified instructor and field engineer for several years. Jorge has a varied background and has worked with different products, such as Sun Solaris, Linux, LDAP services, and CheckPoint. Recently, he has worked with configuration management products, such as Puppet or Chef, on some assignments and has also taken part in Madrid DevOps (a group of technicians devoted to Continuous Deployment and DevOps culture) as a coordinator. He promotes the adoption of a culture of continuous improvement in enterprises and start-ups as the foundation for achieving great things. You can meet him at the talks and hangouts he organizes for the community.

Jorge has also reviewed *Configuration Management with Chef-Solo*, *Naveed ur Rahman*, *Packt Publishing*.

I would like to thank my wife, Nuria, and sons, Eduardo and Ruben, for being so understanding and supportive while I was reviewing this book. Also, I would like to thank my dear mom, Milagros, and dad, Toñi, who put in the effort of educating me. Finally, I would like to thank all those who have contributed to my personal and professional development through the years.

Yacine Sebihi is an IT consultant and has over 14 years of experience in Linux , open source, and virtualization. He holds certifications in Cisco Data Center, Linux RHEL, HP Storage SAN, and VMware. Currently, he's preparing for his exams (CCIE Data Center and VMware VCAP550-DCA) and is about to pursue his master's degree in expert cloud computing in France.

His personal blog can be found at `http://vdatacenter.info/`, where he writes technical articles and shares them with the IT world.. You can find out more about Yacine's technical skills and his personal details on his LinkedIn profile page at `https://www.linkedin.com/in/sebihiy`.

Mark Verboom has been adept at Unix since he first used it in 1992 (ULTRIX on VAX). With a BSc in software engineering and data communications, Mark has worked in numerous positions as a Unix administrator, consultant, and software engineer. He has branched out into areas, such as network design and administration, virtualization, security, and other non-IT fields, such as electronics and car fuel management systems. Because of this, his skills gradually became too broad to fit one job and led to him starting his own company in 2011, called Kram Solutions.

Outside of work, Mark has a keen interest in cars (modifying and upgrading them), audio books, and 3D printing.

I would like to thank Maika for her patience while reviewing this book.

www.PacktPub.com

Support files, eBooks, discount offers, and more

For support files and downloads related to your book, please visit www.PacktPub.com.

Did you know that Packt offers eBook versions of every book published, with PDF and ePub files available? You can upgrade to the eBook version at www.PacktPub.com and as a print book customer, you are entitled to a discount on the eBook copy. Get in touch with us at service@packtpub.com for more details.

At www.PacktPub.com, you can also read a collection of free technical articles, sign up for a range of free newsletters and receive exclusive discounts and offers on Packt books and eBooks.

https://www2.packtpub.com/books/subscription/packtlib

Do you need instant solutions to your IT questions? PacktLib is Packt's online digital book library. Here, you can search, access, and read Packt's entire library of books.

Why Subscribe?

- ▶ Fully searchable across every book published by Packt
- ▶ Copy and paste, print, and bookmark content
- ▶ On demand and accessible via a web browser

Free Access for Packt account holders

If you have an account with Packt at www.PacktPub.com, you can use this to access PacktLib today and view 9 entirely free books. Simply use your login credentials for immediate access.

Table of Contents

Preface

Proxmox is one of the biggest kept secrets in the world of virtualization. It stands tall with other major virtualization players, such as VMWare, Xen, Hyper-V, and so on. Since the first release of Proxmox in 2005, it has become the standard for open source hypervisors. It is loaded with great features, such as clustering, High Availability, major storage plugins, firewalls, full KVM/OpenVZ support, and a price that cannot be beaten by any other virtualization product in the industry. Proxmox provides a rock solid platform to build virtual environments that are scalable to any size and can be managed entirely from a single GUI. In a matter of minutes, a standard Proxmox cluster can be raised and brought into production without any licensing costs.

This book is written to get you familiar with Proxmox by following step-by-step procedures. The steps are broken down in as simple manner as possible, thereby allowing you to cook up a Proxmox cluster with minimal effort. This book can also be used as a quick reference to fall back on when working with a Proxmox hypervisor. Illustrations have been used wherever possible along with a hands-on approach that enables you to retain the knowledge you've acquired for a longer period of time. Different topics and features are categorized in different chapters, making this book an easy read.

Often, we lack a book that is a reference point to get things done quickly. Although there are other books on Proxmox written in greater detail, a book, such as this one, was needed so that you could be brought on board with regard to Proxmox in the least amount of time. Each chapter is written with the aim of doing more and reading less.

What this book covers

Chapter 1, *Installing Proxmox*, introduces Proxmox and its features. It also shows the types of hardware needed for a Proxmox node, the required repository, and how to install Proxmox in a few steps. At the end of the chapter, you will have a very basic Proxmox cluster up and running, which can be used throughout the book to practice the knowledge you've acquired.

Chapter 2, Getting to Know the Proxmox GUI, introduces the Proxmox graphical user interface (GUI) through illustrations and guides you through the entire menu system of Proxmox. Explanations of the functions of different categories of menus are also provided. Each menu item of different categories has been presented with visual figures along with a description of their functions.

Chapter 3, Cluster and VM Management, shows you how to create and configure a Proxmox cluster from the ground up. Topics such as virtual machine creation, migration, and cloning are also covered in this chapter. At the end of the chapter, you will be capable enough to manage virtual machines in a Proxmox cluster.

Chapter 4, Network Configurations, shows different network components and how to configure them in Proxmox. In this chapter, you will have a good understanding of how to a create virtual network within a Proxmox cluster and how all the components come together to form a complex network.

Chapter 5, Firewall Configurations, shows how to utilize the Firewall feature of Proxmox. Firewall is a fairly new feature that has enhanced Proxmox significantly. In this chapter, you will learn how to enable and configure a firewall for different entities, such as a data center, node, and VM.

Chapter 6, Storage Configurations, shows different storage plugin options that are available and how to attach them to a Proxmox cluster. Proxmox provides built-in plugins for a major storage type. In this chapter, you will learn how to attach a shared storage with Proxmox and configure it.

Chapter 7, Backup and Restore, shows you how to perform the backup and restore of a virtual machine in a Proxmox cluster. Backup is an important requirement of any network. This chapter shows you how to schedule regular backups, snapshots, and restore data in the event of a disaster.

Chapter 8, Updating and Upgrading Proxmox, shows you the upgrade process to keep a Proxmox node up to date at all times. Keeping a Proxmox node updated is important for an issue-free environment. In this chapter, you will learn the proper procedure to commit updates on a Proxmox node.

Chapter 9, Monitoring Proxmox, shows you the ways in which you can monitor Proxmox and Ceph clusters using the Zabbix and Ceph dashboards. The steps involved in configuring a host or virtual machine that needs to be monitored, are covered along with installation of the Ceph dashboard. At the end of this chapter, you will know how to monitor and configure notifications.

Chapter 10, Advanced Configurations for VMs, shows advanced configuration steps to add features such as sound, PCI passthrough, and more. Advanced configuration extends the ability of a VM beyond just the basics. This chapter shows steps to make this advanced configuration work seamlessly.

Chapter 11, The CLI Command Reference, shows you several lists of the most commonly used commands to manage different aspects of Proxmox, such as a cluster, storage, and so on. This is a reference chapter for quickly finding the most commonly used commands. Commands have been listed in different categories for an easy find.

What you need for this book

This book is designed with a hands-on approach in mind. Therefore, access to a Proxmox cluster or having enough hardware to build a cluster will greatly enhance the value of this book. A minimum of two nodes will be sufficient to practice all the steps described herein.

You will also need to download Proxmox VE 3.4 ISO images from the official Proxmox site. To set up a FreeNAS storage system reader, you will also need to download the ISO image of the FreeNAS 9.3 stable release from the official FreeNAS site. We have used PuTTY to log in to a Proxmox node through SSH, so, a copy of the PuTTY program is also needed. You can use any other SSH programs of your choice. All three of these files can be downloaded from the following links:

To download Proxmox, visit `http://proxmox.com/en/downloads/category/iso-images-pve`.

To download FreeNAS, visit `http://www.freenas.org/download-freenas-release.html`.

To download Putty, visit `http://www.chiark.greenend.org.uk/~sgtatham/putty/download.html`.

Who this book is for

This book is perfect for system administrators who want to learn how to implement and administer Proxmox VE environments. Since this book will not cover the basics of Proxmox, a basic understanding of virtualization and networking with the Proxmox VE is required.

Sections

In this book, you will find several headings that appear frequently (Getting ready, How to do it, How it works, There's more, and See also).

To give clear instructions on how to complete a recipe, we use these sections as follows:

Getting ready

This section tells you what to expect in the recipe, and describes how to set up any software or any preliminary settings required for the recipe.

How to do it...

This section contains the steps required to follow the recipe.

How it works...

This section usually consists of a detailed explanation of what happened in the previous section.

There's more...

This section consists of additional information about the recipe in order to make the reader more knowledgeable about the recipe.

See also

This section provides helpful links to other useful information for the recipe.

Conventions

In this book, you will find a number of text styles that distinguish between different kinds of information. Here are some examples of these styles and an explanation of their meaning.

Code words in text, database table names, folder names, filenames, file extensions, pathnames, dummy URLs, user input, and Twitter handles are shown as follows: "Once you have the information, simply run the `apt-get` command to install it through CLI."

A block of code is set as follows:

```
[OPTIONS]
enable: 1
policy_in: DROP

[RULES]
IN ACCEPT -p tcp -dport 22
IN ACCEPT -p tcp -dport 8006
```

When we wish to draw your attention to a particular part of a code block, the relevant lines or items are set in bold:

```
auto vmbr0
iface vmbr0 inet static
address 192.168.10.1
netmask 255.255.255.0
bridge_ports none
bridge_stp off
bridge_fd 0
```

Any command-line input or output is written as follows:

```
# cat /etc/apt/sources.list
deb http://ftp.ca.debian.org/debian wheezy main contrib
deb http://download.proxmox.com/debian wheezy pve-no-subscription
deb http://security.debian.org / wheezy/updates main contrib
```

New terms and **important words** are shown in bold. Words that you see on the screen, for example, in menus or dialog boxes, appear in the text like this: "After the installation is completed, eject the installation disk or the USB media, then click on **Reboot**."

Warnings or important notes appear in a box like this.

Tips and tricks appear like this.

Reader feedback

Feedback from our readers is always welcome. Let us know what you think about this book—what you liked or disliked. Reader feedback is important for us as it helps us develop titles that you will really get the most out of.

To send us general feedback, simply e-mail feedback@packtpub.com, and mention the book's title in the subject of your message.

If there is a topic that you have expertise in and you are interested in either writing or contributing to a book, see our author guide at www.packtpub.com/authors.

Customer support

Now that you are the proud owner of a Packt book, we have a number of things to help you to get the most from your purchase.

Errata

Although we have taken every care to ensure the accuracy of our content, mistakes do happen. If you find a mistake in one of our books—maybe a mistake in the text or the code—we would be grateful if you could report this to us. By doing so, you can save other readers from frustration and help us improve subsequent versions of this book. If you find any errata, please report them by visiting http://www.packtpub.com/submit-errata, selecting your book, clicking on the **Errata Submission Form** link, and entering the details of your errata. Once your errata are verified, your submission will be accepted and the errata will be uploaded to our website or added to any list of existing errata under the Errata section of that title.

To view the previously submitted errata, go to https://www.packtpub.com/books/content/support and enter the name of the book in the search field. The required information will appear under the **Errata** section.

Piracy

Piracy of copyrighted material on the Internet is an ongoing problem across all media. At Packt, we take the protection of our copyright and licenses very seriously. If you come across any illegal copies of our works in any form on the Internet, please provide us with the location address or website name immediately so that we can pursue a remedy.

Please contact us at `copyright@packtpub.com` with a link to the suspected pirated material.

We appreciate your help in protecting our authors and our ability to bring you valuable content.

Questions

If you have a problem with any aspect of this book, you can contact us at `questions@packtpub.com`, and we will do our best to address the problem.

1

Installing Proxmox

In this chapter, we are going to cover the following Proxmox basics:

- ▸ Hardware requirements
- ▸ Preparing for installation
- ▸ Installing Proxmox on a bare metal node
- ▸ Installing Proxmox on a Debian system
- ▸ A Proxmox subscription
- ▸ Disabling a Proxmox subscription
- ▸ Applying a Proxmox subscription
- ▸ Setting up a Proxmox package repository
- ▸ Seeking support

Introduction

The Proxmox **Virtual Environment (VE)** is an open source multinode clustered **hypervisor** built on Debian Linux, and is able to run on commodity hardware, thus eliminating any vendor lock ins. Proxmox is freely available without any features locked. However, a subscription type license is available to enable a enterprise repository to receive well-tested patches and updates. Subscriptions are recommended for a production-level Proxmox environment.

 A hypervisor is a software or firmware that creates a layer between native hardware and an operating system to form a virtual environment to create and run virtual machines. A hypervisor emulates the functions of physical hardware to enable virtual machines to see them as physical resources.

Proxmox can be configured to run a virtual environment of just a few nodes with virtual machines or an environment with thousands of nodes. Supporting both KVM and OpenVZ container-based virtual machines, Proxmox VE is a leading hypervisor today. Proxmox has an extremely vibrant community ready to provide help to any free Proxmox users. Also, the expert technical support team of Proxmox is equally capable of handling all corporate users with their mission critical virtual environment.

As mentioned earlier, Proxmox is a multinode environment, meaning that many nodes can form a single cluster where a virtual machine can be moved around to any node within the cluster, thereby allowing a redundant virtual environment. Through a robust **Graphical User Interface (GUI)**, the entire Proxmox cluster can be managed. As of Proxmox VE 3.4, only one cluster is manageable through the GUI.

Here are some of the notable features of the Proxmox VE:

- It provides a multinode cluster environment for virtualization. No single node acts as a master, thus eliminating single points of failure.

- It provides **High Availability (HA)** of virtual machines.

- It gives centralized web-based management and a single interface to manage an entire cluster.

- A console can be accessed through secured VNC, SPICE, and HTML5-based noVNC.

- It provides support for multiple authentication sources, such as local using **Pluggable Authentication Module (PAM)**, Microsoft ADS, and LDAP.

- A **Proxmox cluster file system (pmxcfs)** can be used to store configuration files for real-time replication on all nodes using **corosync** (`http://en.wikipedia.org/wiki/Corosync_%28project%29`).

- It provides role-based permission management for objects VMs, storages, nodes, pools, and so on.

- Unlike SOAP, REST is not a protocol but combination of various standards such as HTTP, JSON, URI and XML. Visit `http://www.restapitutorial.com` for information on REST based APIs.

- It provides a built-in powerful firewall for host nodes and virtual machines.

- It provides migration of VMs between physical hosts with or without shared storage.

- It supports mainstream storage types, such as Ceph, NFS, ZFS, Gluster, and iSCSI.

- It provides cluster-wide logging.

Hardware requirements

Proxmox can be installed on just about any commodity hardware, but in order to have a stable platform, some attention is required when selecting nodes. A setup selected for Proxmox learning can be underpowered and less expansive. While this setup is acceptable for very small environments and home usage, it will not be adequate for production-level setups where stability and redundancy is the minimum requirement.

Minimum hardware

Here are the minimum requirements to install Proxmox on a hardware node:

- **Processor**: Intel or AMD 64-bit
- **Motherboard**: Intel VT or AMD-V capable (not required for OpenVZ)
- **Memory**: 1 GB RAM
- **Network Interface Card (NIC)**: 1

Based on the minimum requirement of Proxmox, here are examples of Intel and AMD-based hardware configurations that are suitable for learning:

Processor → Requirement ↓	Intel	AMD
Processor/CPU	i3-4160 3.0 GHz	FX-4300 3.8 GHz
Motherboard	Asus B85M-D Plus 6 x SATA	Asus M5A78L-M/USB3 6 x SATA
Memory	Corsair 1 x 4 GB DDR3	Corsair 1 x 4 GB DDR3

Recommended hardware

To have a stable performing Proxmox cluster, here are the hardware configurations that are recommended:

- An Intel or AMD 64-bit processor
- An Intel VT or AMD-V capable Dual or Quad CPU motherboard
- 16 GB RAM memory
- Two Network Interface Card (NIC)
- RAID controller with **Battery Backup Unit (BBU)**
- **Solid State Drives (SSD)** for operating system or SSD for shared storage node
- Fencing hardware only if HA is needed

For more details on fencing and HA visit `https://pve.proxmox.com/wiki/Fencing`.

The following table lists the configurations of a server node that can be used in a production environment:

Requirement	Hardware
Processor/CPU	Intel Xeon E5-2630 v3 2.4 GHz
Motherboard	Intel S2600CP2 Dual LGA2011
Memory	Kingston 16 GB DDR3 Registered ECC
Power supply	Redundant

Note that the example configurations are for reference only. Your requirement will vary depending on the work load and expected performance. Adjust the hardware requirements accordingly by keeping in mind that in a hypervisor more core counts will increase performance of virtual machines rather than higher clock counts of a processor that is used. With a higher core count, more threads can be distributed among processors.

 It is worth mentioning here that it is better to select a CPU with a higher cache amount for a node with large amount of memory to minimize the main memory access and maximize the performance for each CPU cores.

Proxmox is a clustered hypervisor. In order to set up a cluster, a minimum of two nodes are required. For the purpose of following through this book, when selecting hardware, be sure to have enough components to set up two nodes.

 For more details on Proxmox, please visit `http://www.proxmox.com/`.

Although a Proxmox cluster can be set up with just two nodes, a minimum of three nodes are recommended for a production environment.

In a cluster, a quorum is established with a minimum of three votes. Each node is counted as single vote. The cluster health depends on this democratic system where the majority vote wins. So, in a two node cluster, when one node fails the other node can only cast one vote, creating an unresolved situation. With a three node cluster, when one node fails, the total vote from the remaining nodes is two out of possible three votes. Thus, the cluster operation continues. By any means, a two node cluster is not recommended for a production cluster. However, it is still possible to create using instructions by visiting `https://pve.proxmox.com/wiki/Two-Node_High_Availability_Cluster`.

Preparing for installation

Once the necessary hardware is assembled, in this recipe, we are going to see how to prepare ourselves before installing Proxmox.

Getting ready

We are going to use the Proxmox VE installation disk to install Proxmox. First, we need to prepare a disk with the Proxmox installation ISO image.

How to do it...

Here are the steps to install Proxmox:

1. Download the Proxmox ISO image by visiting `http://proxmox.com/downloads/category/iso-images-pve`.

2. Use a burning software to copy the ISO image on to a DVD disk.

3. Boot the physical node from the disk prepared from ISO to start the installation process.

There's more...

Some nodes may not have a ROM drive available to install from a disk. In such cases, it is possible to install Proxmox by transferring an ISO image onto a USB flash drive. Note that in order to boot from USB media, your motherboard must support the USB boot option. Check from the motherboard BIOS before proceeding to the following steps. If the motherboard does not support USB boot option, it may not also support an external USB ROM Drive. In this case, the best way to proceed is to install an ROM drive in the computer or use a newer motherboard if possible. Here are the instructions to transfer an ISO image to a USB and use it as bootable drive:

Use the following steps to do this on Windows:

1. Download the Proxmox ISO installation image from `http://proxmox.com/downloads/category/iso-images-pve`.

2. Rename the file extension of the downloaded ISO from `.iso` to `.raw`.

3. Download and install the USB image writing application from `https://github.com/downloads/openSUSE/kiwi/ImageWriter.exe`.

> In some Windows 7 versions, the preceding writer may not work. In such scenarios, download and install the **ImageUSB** from `http://www.osforensics.com/tools/write-usb-images.html`.

4. Using the preceding applications, copy the ISO image onto a USB drive.

5. Insert the USB media into the USB port of the physical node and boot from the USB media.

Use the following steps to do this on Linux:

1. Download the Proxmox ISO installation image from `http://proxmox.com/downloads/category/iso-images-pve`.

2. Insert the USB media into the USB port of the node and find out the device name of the drive using `#fdisk`. The name should be in the `/dev/XXX` format.

3. Use the following command to copy the ISO onto USB media. Use extra caution when using a device name in the following command. The wrong device name will destroy all the data on the device:

   `#dd if=<Proxmox ISO file> of=/dev/XXX bs=1M`

4. Reboot the node from the USB media to start the installation.

Installing Proxmox on a bare metal node

The Proxmox installation process is guided by a fully graphical interface through various prompts. In this recipe, we are going to follow through creating our first Proxmox node.

Getting ready

Power up and boot the physical node using the installation disk or the USB media we created in the preceding recipe. The following screenshot is how the screen looks after the boot:

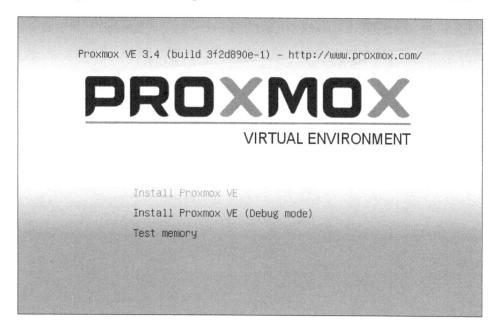

How to do it...

1. At the main installation window after the booting process press *Enter* to start the installation.

2. On the **End User License Agreement** (**EULA**) screen click on **Agree**.

3. In this step, we have chosen the drive to install the hypervisor on. From Proxmox VE 3.4, a new feature to change the filesystem has been added. After selecting **Target Harddisk** from the drop-down menu, select **Options** to open the **Filesystem** selection dialog box. The following screenshot shows the drive selection screen with the **Filesystem** dialog box open:

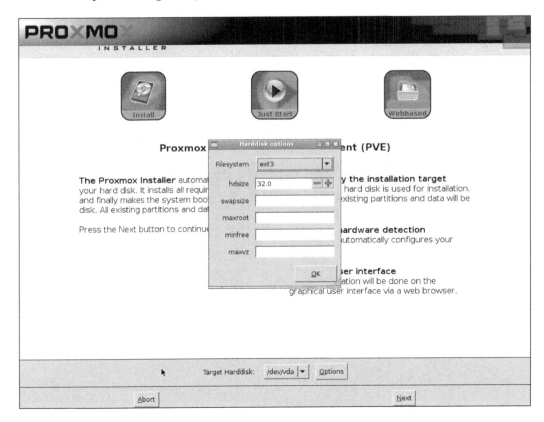

4. From the **Filesystem** drop-down menu, select the desired filesystem. Select the desired filesystem size in **hdsize**. In version 3.3, support for the **ext3**, **ext4**, and **ZFS** filesystems have been added. Add additional information, such as the **swapsize**, **maxroot**, **minfree**, and **maxvz** values as required or leave them blank to continue with default, then click on **Next**. The following table shows the functions of these four options. These values are usually alternatives to each other, meaning if values are entered for one of these options, values for other options are automatically calculated:

Option	Function
swapsize	This defines the size of a swap partition. There are complex formulas to calculate this value. However, it is generally left as the default value.
maxroot	This refers to the maximum size the root partition should be.
minfree	This refers to the minimum free space to allocate for a pve partition.
maxvz	This refers to the maximum space to allocate to locally store VMs. The default path for local VM storage is `/var/lib/vz`.

The following screenshot shows the filesystem that is supported after clicking on the drop-down menu:

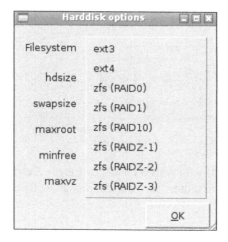

5. After selecting the drive for installation, we now have to select localization information, such as **Country**, **Time Zone**, and **Keyboard Layout** based on the desired language. Then, click on **Next**. The following screenshot displays the localization screen:

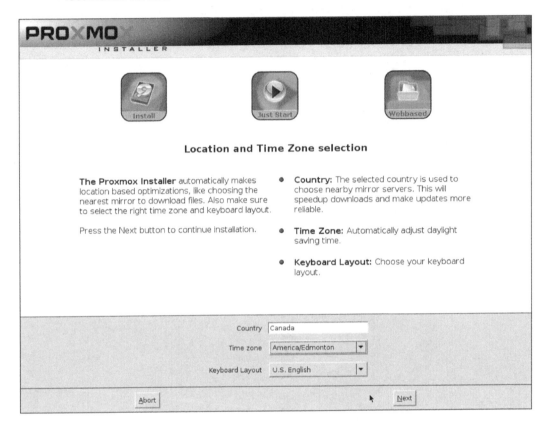

6. Type in and confirm the password for the root login. Then, enter an e-mail address where all the Proxmox cluster notifications will go to. Click on **Next**.

7. In this step, we need to enter the hostname and network information, such as **IP Address**, **Gateway**, **DNS Server**, and so on. Enter the necessary information for your environment, then click on **Next**. The following screenshot shows the network information screen:

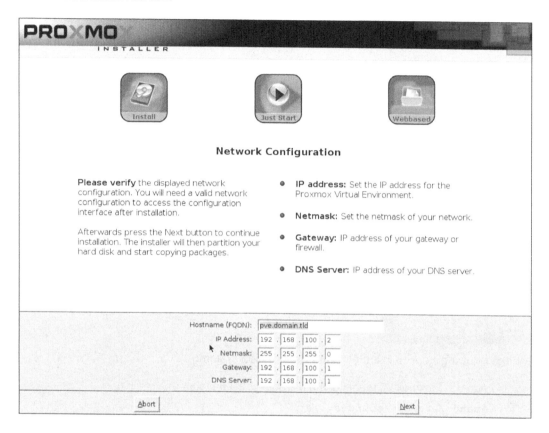

8. At this point, all the necessary information has been collected and the main installation has been started. After the installation is completed, eject the installation disk or the USB media, then click on **Reboot**.

There's more...

Follow steps 1 to 7 to set up the second node. A minimum of two nodes are required to form a Proxmox cluster. More information on cluster configurations is available in *Chapter 3, Cluster and VM Management*.

Installing Proxmox on a Debian system

Although installation of Proxmox on a native bare metal node is recommended, at times, it may be necessary to install Proxmox on an existing Debian node. In this recipe, we will see how to install the Proxmox VE on Debian. Note that Proxmox can only be installed on 64-bit hardware and a 64-bit operating system.

Getting ready

Install Debian from instructions from the official Debian site at `http://www.debian.org`. Prior to installing Proxmox on the Debian node, ensure that the hostname can be resolved. Check the hostname using the following command:

`#nano /etc/hosts`

It should have these entries:

```
127.0.0.1 localhost.localdomain localhost
172.16.0.71 pmx1.domain.com pmx1 pvelocalhost
```

If the entries are missing, type in the proper IP address associated with the hostname of the node. The `pvelocalhost` entry must be present at the end of the line.

How to do it...

Use the following steps to install Proxmox on a Debian system:

1. Add the Proxmox VE repository in the source list as follows:

   ```
   #nano /etc/apt/sources.list
   deb http://ftp.ca.debian.org/debian wheezy main contrib

   #PVE repository for installation
   deb http://download.proxmox.com/debian wheezy pve

   #PVE security updates
   deb http://security.debian.org/ wheezy/updates main contrib
   ```

Due to a bug in the Debian OS, `apt-get` may display an error of not finding `/binary-i386` with a `Unable to find expected entry 'pve/binary-i386/packages'` error message. The error may occur even though it is a 64-bit Debian installed operating system. In such cases, change the PVE repository entry to the following:

`deb [arch=amd64] http://download.proxmox.com/debian wheezy pve`

2. Add the Proxmox VE repository key using the following command:

   `#wget -O-http://download.proxmox.com/debian/key.asc | apt-key add -`

3. Update the repository using the following command:

   `#apt-get update`

4. Update the operating system using the following command:

   `#apt-get dist-upgrade`

5. Install the Proxmox VE Kernel:

   `#apt-get install pve-firmware pve-kernel-2.6.32-37-pve`

6. Install Kernel headers:

   `#apt-get install pve-header-2.6.32-37-pve`

7. Be sure to select the Proxmox VE Kernel on the boot loader grub2.

8. Reboot the node to activate the new Proxmox VE Kernel.

9. Verify the running kernel to ensure that the proper Proxmox VE Kernel is loaded:

   `#uname -a`

10. Check the grub2 config using following command:

    `#update-grub`

11. Install the Proxmox VE packages:

    `#apt-get install Proxmox-ve-2.6.32 ntp ssh lvm2 postfix ksm-control-daemon vzprocps open-iscsi bootlogd`

12. During installation, accept suggestions to remove **Exim** and set up **Postfix**. Exim can be installed later if required.

13. Reboot the node after the Proxmox VE installation is done.

There's more...

Follow steps 1 to 13 to set up a second node. A minimum of two nodes are required to form a Proxmox cluster. We will take a good look at the Proxmox GUI in *Chapter 2, Getting to know the Proxmox GUI.*

A Proxmox subscription

The Proxmox VE itself is free. There are absolutely no costs involved in simply downloading the ISO image and installing a fully-functional Proxmox cluster without paying for a license or subscription. However, there is a Proxmox subscription option available to support the project, which enables enterprise repository. There are no feature differences between the Free and Subscription versions of Proxmox. Both are exactly the same. The difference is between the type of releases, updates, and patches they receive.

 Packages from the enterprise repository go through an extra layer of scrutiny and testing. Thus, a subscription is recommended for a production-level Proxmox VE.

This not to be confused with the fact that a Proxmox cluster is built with no subscription and is not stable enough to use. New packages are usually released through a no-subscription repository first. Same packages are pushed through the Enterprise repository at a later time. This delay allows the Proxmox team to pin point and fix any lingering bugs or defects in the package. In a cluster running mission critical virtual machines may face unacceptable downtime due to the bug, which will not affect a smaller environment that is able to sustain downtime.

There are four levels of subscription at various price points, such as **COMMUNITY**, **BASIC**, **STANDARD**, and **PREMIUM**. For more information on the Proxmox subscription, visit `https://www.proxmox.com/proxmox-ve/pricing`.

Disabling a Proxmox subscription

A fresh installation of the Proxmox VE without subscriptions will display a message upon login to Proxmox GUI, as shown in the following screenshot:

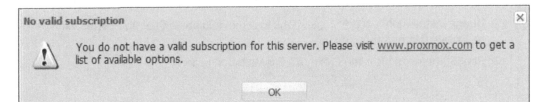

This is because an enterprise repository is enabled by default. If you decide not to get any Proxmox subscriptions and continue using the fully Free version, you will have to disable the enterprise repository.

Getting ready

Login to the Proxmox node through a console or SSH. An enterprise repository can only be disabled through CLI.

How to do it...

The enterprise repository is listed in `/etc/apt/sources.list.d/pve-enterprise.list`. We have to comment out the line to disable the repository:

```
# nano /etc/apt/sources.list.d/pve-enterprise.list
```

```
#deb https://enterprise.proxmox.com/debian wheezy pve-enterprise
```

Add the Proxmox No-Subscription repository as follows:

```
# nano /etc/apt/sources.list
```

```
deb http://download.proxmox.com/debian wheezy pve-no-subscription
```

How it works...

No restart of services or reboot is required to apply the changes. Log out from the Proxmox GUI and log back in to see if the changes were applied correctly. The "no subscription" message box should not pop-up after login. Subscriptions can be managed from the Proxmox GUI under the **Subscription** tab. Here is a screenshot of a nonsubscribed Proxmox node:

Applying a Proxmox subscription

If you choose to get a Proxmox subscription of any type, a subscription key must be uploaded into the Proxmox node to activate it. The subscription key is sent by e-mail after successful payment. The key can be uploaded through the Proxmox GUI.

Getting ready

Login to the Proxmox GUI by accessing the link through a browser and enter the admin login credentials. The default username is root and the password is the same as was entered during installation: `https://<pmx_node_IP>:8006`.

How to do it...

1. After logging into the Proxmox GUI, click on the node that the subscription is going to be applied to.

2. Click on the **Subscription** tab.

3. Click on the **Upload Subscription Key** button to open the key dialog box, as shown in the following screenshot:

4. Copy/paste the subscription key from the e-mail received from Proxmox in the key box, then click on **Ok**.

5. Click on **Check**. At this moment, the key will be verified with Proxmox to check the validity. After the activation is completed, it should look like the following screenshot:

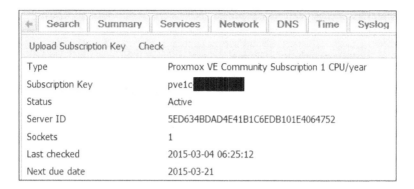

There's more...

If a wrong subscription key has been entered, then the display should resemble the following screenshot:

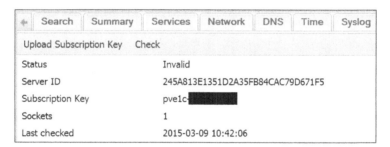

In such cases, simply upload the correct key to activate again. You may also see the key invalid notice when the key has already been activated for another node, which is no longer in service. In such cases, contact Proxmox or other third-party license providers that the license was purchased from to request reissuing of the same license. Then, simply click on the **Check** button to reactivate the key. Each key is hard coded to each server ID. The key needs to be reissued by Proxmox in order to use it.

Please keep in mind that once a key is reissued, it will no longer work on the previous node it was activated for. If you have asked for reissue a license by mistake, request to reissue again and click on the **Check** button on the previous node.

Setting up a Proxmox package repository

The Proxmox VE offers three main repositories:

Repository	Subscription	Usage
Enterprise	Required	This is primarily used in the production of the Proxmox node. Packages in this repository go through additional scrutiny, bug fixes, and testing.
No-Subscription	Not required	This is used in learning, training, and home Proxmox cluster nodes. Packages in this repository go through initial bug fixes and are stable enough to be referred as the final release.
Test	Not required	This is used for the testing and development of Proxmox only. Packages in this repository are usually the very latest and are still going through final phases of the release cycle, such as beta testing and release candidate. Packages in this repository may contain a number of bugs and issues. Users of this repository are encouraged to share bug reports with developers.

The location and content of the **Enterprise Repository** source file is as follows:

```
#cat /etc/apt/sources.list.d/pve-enterprise.list
deb https://enterprise.proxmox.com/debian wheezy pve-enterprise
```

The location and content of the **No-Subscription Repository** source file is as follows:

```
#cat /etc/apt/sources.list
deb http://ftp.ca.debian.org/debian wheezy main contrib
deb http://download.proxmox.com/debian wheezy pve-no-subscription
deb http://security.debian.org / wheezy/updates main contrib
```

Proxmox offers a **Test Repository** to allow users to try out new features or packages. As the name implies, the Test Repository should only be used for testing. All the new features of Proxmox are released in the Test Repository before they are available for the No-Subscription and Enterprise repositories. Packages in the Test Repository are not well-tested and may contain bugs. For this reason, the repository should never be used in a production-level cluster. The Test Repository is not enabled by default.

Getting ready

Log in to the Proxmox node through a console or SSH. The repository source file needs to be edited through CLI to enable the Test Repository.

How to do it...

Use the following steps to set up the Proxmox package repository:

1. Open the repository source file using any favorite text editor:

   ```
   #nano /etc/apt/sources.list
   ```

2. Make the necessary changes to make the entries look similar to the following:

   ```
   deb http://ftp.debian.org/debian wheezy main contrib
   deb http://download.proxmox.com/debian wheezy pvetest
   deb http://security .debian.org/ wheezy/updates main contrib
   ```

3. Save the file and exit the editor.

4. Run the following command to update the repositories:

   ```
   #apt-get update
   ```

How it works...

Usually, the announcement of the availability of a new package is made on the official Proxmox forum (`http://forum.proxmox.com`). The name of the package or the version information is included in the announcement. If you want to find information on a package, simply ask for it on the forum. Once you have the information, simply run the `apt-get` command to install it through CLI:

```
#apt-get install <package_name>
```

There's more...

Besides Enterprise, No-Subscription, and Test repositories there are two repositories that are outdated and are no longer supported or updated:

- **Outdated stable repository (pve)**: This repository has stopped receiving updates after the initial release of Proxmox VE 3.1:

  ```
  /etc/apt/sources.list
  deb http://ftp.debian.org/debian wheezy main contrib
  deb http://download.proxmox.com/debian wheezy pve
  deb http://security .debian.org/ wheezy/updates main contrib
  ```

If you're upgrading from Proxmox VE 2.x to 3.x, the second entry in `/etc/apt/sources.list` needs to be changed from `wheezy pve` to `wheezy pve-no-subscription`.

▶ **Outdated Proxmox VE 2.x stable repository (squeeze pve)**: In order to have a stable Proxmox node, it is highly recommended to upgrade and update to the latest stable release of the Proxmox VE.

`/etc/apt/sources.list`

`deb http://ftp.debian.org/debian squeeze main contrib`

`deb http://download.proxmox.com/debian squeeze pve`

`deb http://security.debian.org/ squeeze/updates main contrib`

Seeking support

As mentioned in the beginning of this chapter, Proxmox has a vibrant community of users ready to provide help to anybody in need. There are several ways that a new Proxmox user can seek help and support to learn and extend knowledge of the Proxmox VE:

Help and support	Free/subscription
Forum	Free
Wiki/Documentation	Free
Customer portal and tickets	Requires subscription
Proxmox Mailing list	Free
Proxmox Bug tracker	Free

The forum

The official forum of Proxmox is a gathering place for newbies or experts alike to receive or provide help from the Proxmox community. It is also a vast information resource of past issues and solutions to many problems. A few of the Proxmox staff also spend a significant amount of time in this forum to offer help outside their job responsibilities. There is an array of Proxmox experts willing to help out without expecting anything in return. This is the only place for Free and Community-level subscriptions for Proxmox users to seek support. Visit `http://forum.proxmox.com` to access the official Proxmox forum.

Wiki/Documentation

The Proxmox Wiki site contains a wealth of information on installation, configuration, and the management of Proxmox clusters. All documentation is written in a very easy to understand form with as many illustrations as possible. The use of the Proxmox Wiki page is completely free and requires no registration. Visit `https://pve.proxmox.com/wiki/Main_Page` for the official Proxmox documentation.

Customer portals and tickets

A customer portal is only available for basic, standard, and premium subscription-level users. Supports tickets must be opened through a customer portal by visiting `https://my.proxmox.com/` to receive technical support directly from the Proxmox staff.

Depending on the subscription level, a number of tickets that can be opened varies. Responses are guaranteed within one business day. See the different support levels for subscriptions by visiting `https://www.proxmox.com/proxmox-ve/pricing`.

Proxmox mailing lists

There are two different mailing lists available from Proxmox:

- **User mailing list**: This mailing list is targeted at general Proxmox users to ask technical questions (`http://pve.proxmox.com/cgi-bin/mailman/listinfo/pve-user`).
- **Developer mailing list**: This mailing list is for developers who are interested in participating in code-related commits and developmental related questions (`http://pve.proxmox.com/cgi-bin/mailman/listinfo/pve-devel`).

The Proxmox bug tracker

The Proxmox bug tracker is available to submit and review any bugs found in Proxmox during day-to day-use (`https://bugzilla.proxmox.com/`). It can also be used to submit new feature requests. Not all features get added to Proxmox, but developers of Proxmox are very forward thinking and apply time appropriate and main stream features to make the Proxmox VE even better.

 The Proxmox bug tracker is NOT to be used to ask technical questions or to seek any sort of support.

2
Getting to Know the Proxmox GUI

In this chapter, we will cover the following topics:

- ▶ Accessing the Proxmox GUI
- ▶ Viewing styles
- ▶ Accessing datacenter-specific menus
- ▶ Accessing node-specific menus
- ▶ Accessing KVM-specific menus
- ▶ Accessing OpenVZ-specific menus

Introduction

This chapter is about getting to know the robust menu system available in Proxmox VE. We will get to see the Proxmox **Graphical User Interface** (**GUI**) where most of the management occurs in a graphical environment. Apart from some advanced configuration through CLI, such as Ceph cluster creation and container UBC configuration, most of the administrative tasks can be performed through the Proxmox GUI.

Accessing the Proxmox GUI

Proxmox GUI is a web-based management control panel, which can be accessed through any major web browser. In this recipe, we are going to see how to access both the desktop and mobile Proxmox GUI through a web browser.

Getting ready

This chapter assumes that you, the reader, have access to a Proxmox cluster to follow along. Refer to *Chapter 1, Installing Proxmox*, in this book to quickly set up a basic Proxmox node.

How to do it...

The Proxmox VE comes equipped with a web-based management system from where almost all aspects of a cluster or a single node can be controlled. The web GUI is accessible immediately after Proxmox is installed on a hardware platform. Use the following steps to access the Proxmox GUI:

1. Type this URL into any browser to access the GUI with the format as:
    `https://<any_node_ip/hostname>:8006`.

     As of Proxmox VE 3.3, a mobile interface for the GUI is also available. Most mobile devices, such as tablets and smartphones, will automatically detect mobile access and redirect the previous link to the mobile optimized GUI. In case it does not autodetect, manually type `https://<any_node_ip/hostname>:8006?mobile=1` to access the mobile Proxmox GUI.

    While accessing the mobile site of the GUI, keep in mind that as of Proxmox VE 3.4, the level of administrative tasks that can be performed are still very limited. In later versions, more features will be added.

    The first step after accessing the web GUI is to enter login information.

2. Use the default `root` username and the password you have selected during the installation process of Proxmox to log in. The **Realm** field should be left as the default **Linux PAM standard authentication**:

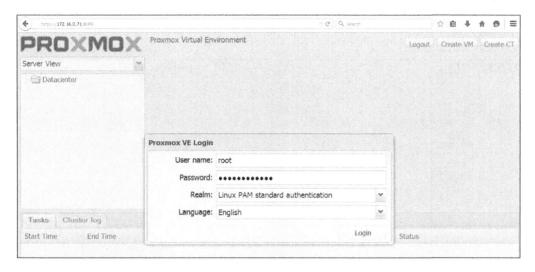

How it works...

The Proxmox GUI is a very powerful web-based management system. Apart from some advanced configurations, such as **Infiniband**, Ceph cluster creation, and so on, a Proxmox user can perform almost all day-to-day activities from this GUI. The Proxmox GUI listens on port 8006. If you access the GUI for a cluster from a remote location, be sure to open a port forwarding for port 8006. On occasions when a **Command Line Interface** (**CLI**) is needed, it can even be accessed through **Shell** from the GUI. Refer to the *Node management menu* subsection under the *How it works...* subsection of the *Accessing node-specific menus* recipe later on in this chapter for details on the **Shell** access option.

Based on resources being managed such as nodes, VMs, storages, and so on, Proxmox GUI shows specific menus in tabbed format.

We will look into these menus as they appear while managing individual resources. Some of the menus are very specific to their respective resources. Here is a list of resource-specific menus available through the Proxmox GUI:

- ▸ Datacenter
- ▸ Node
- ▸ Storage
- ▸ KVM virtual machine
- ▸ OpenVZ container

Let's now take a look how the GUI looks like upon login. The following screenshot shows the GUI for Proxmox VE 3.4:

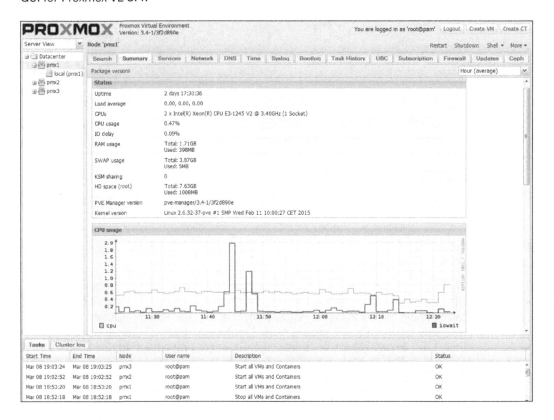

As we can see from the preceding screenshot, a Proxmox GUI not only presents all the menus in a very user-friendly manner, but also shows real-time information about running nodes and VMs. The Proxmox GUI has an interactive tabbed style menu system, which means that it changes based on the area you are managing. For example, when we click on **Datacenter**, the tabbed menu looks like the following screenshot:

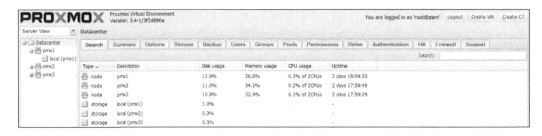

If we now click on a node, the tabbed menu appears as shown in the following screenshot and an additional clickable menu appears to manage physical nodes, such as **Restart**, **Shutdown**, **Shell**, and **More** along with the real-time status of the node itself. The **More** button has been added from Proxmox VE 3.4. If you have an older version of Proxmox, you will not see this additional button.

Finally, when we click on a particular VM, the tabbed menu changes along with additional information, such as status and resource usage by this VM, as we can see from the following screenshot:

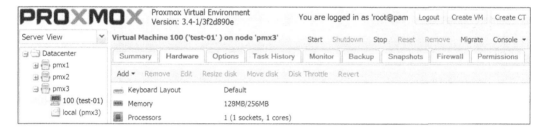

As we can see, the Proxmox GUI is indeed a robust centralized management system, yet very simple to get acquainted with. We are now going to dig deeper into the Proxmox GUI by looking at each area of the GUI individually.

Viewing styles

In this recipe, we are going to see different viewing styles available in the Proxmox GUI.

Getting ready

We will start by logging in as a root user.

How to do it...

By default, the GUI is open with **Server View**. By clicking on the drop-down menu, as shown in the following figure, we can see the other types of views available:

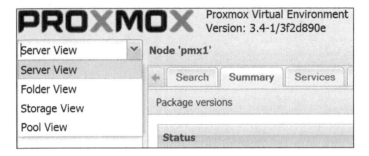

Other view styles available to us are **Folder View**, **Storage View**, and **Pool View**.

How it works...

There are four viewing styles available in the Proxmox GUI:

- ▶ **Server View**
- ▶ **Folder View**
- ▶ **Storage View**
- ▶ **Pool View**

Displaying Server View

This is the most commonly used view among Proxmox users and is also used as a default in the GUI. The **Server View** viewing style displays all nodes individually along with their storages and any VMs or containers in them. With this view, it is easy to see which VM belongs to which node. As we can see from the following screenshot, with **Server View** it is easy to manage node by node:

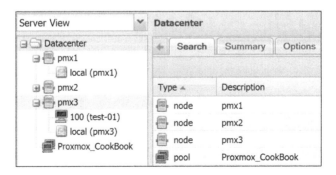

Displaying Folder View

This view takes a categorized folder approach to display all nodes and resources. Each type of resource is treated as a different folder. The same type of resources are put into their respective folders. We can see from the following screenshot how all the nodes are in the Nodes List folder, all the storages are in the Storage List folder, and so on:

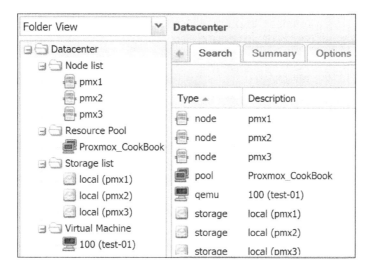

Although it is the second most used view style, one major drawback is the lack of ability to differentiate which VM belongs to which node since the Virtual Machine folder lists all the virtual machines within the cluster. In some cases, this can also be an advantage when unsure of which node a VM belongs to. This view allows us to quickly find a VM without searching. This is specially needed when you're trying to migrate a VM from one node to another. However, for the most part, it is an excellent view style when only one type of resource is to be managed.

Displaying Storage View

As the name implies, this view only displays the storage available for all the nodes. It strips all other resources from the display, such as virtual machine, nodes, and so on, except for the storages. This is a useful view when different nodes have different storages. In Proxmox, it is possible to assign a particular storage to a particular node without having it available cluster-wide from all nodes. For a storage manager assigned with tasks to manage storage systems for a virtual environment, **Storage View** can be a very useful tool. This is how **Storage View** looks through the Proxmox GUI:

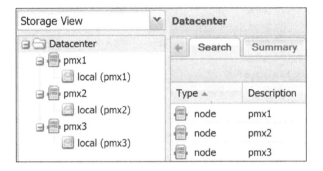

Displaying Pool View

This is an excellent view style to manage pools in Proxmox. Pools are nothing but grouping certain resources together for the sole purpose of easier manageability. For example, if there are multiple clients or customers on a cluster and each client has their own set of VMs storages, it is easier to manage resources client by client through pools. In the following screenshot, there is a pool named **Proxmox_CookBook**, which has a KVM virtual machine and an `nfs` shared storage. If we are to manage just this client, it would be much easier to go to `Pool View` and manage just the VM and storage that belong to this client.

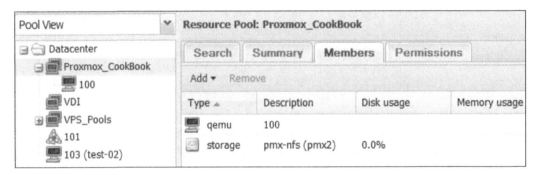

Accessing datacenter-specific menus

These are cluster-wide menus that do not pertain to any specific node or VM, such as users, backup, storage, and so on. Here are datacenter-specific menus:

- ▸ **Search**
- ▸ **Summary**
- ▸ **Options**
- ▸ **Storage**
- ▸ **Backup**
- ▸ **Users**
- ▸ **Groups**
- ▸ **Pools**
- ▸ **Permissions**
- ▸ **Roles**
- ▸ **Authentication**
- ▸ **HA**
- ▸ **Firewall**
- ▸ **Support**

Getting ready

Let us view a datacenter-specific menu by clicking on **Datacenter** from the viewing tree on the left-hand side of the GUI. Here is a screenshot of how the tabbed menu looks when **Datacenter** is selected:

How to do it...

Click on **Datacenter** from left navigation window, then click on the appropriate menu from the tabbed menu.

How it works...

Here are the details of each menu and their functions.

Datacenter | Search menu

This menu is for exactly what the name implies: to search for specific resources, such as nodes, VMs, pools, and so on. Type in the keyword in the search box, as shown in the following screenshot:

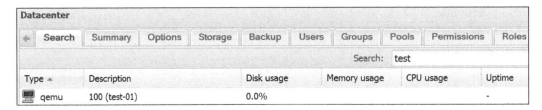

The search box searches both the **Type** and **Description** column of the display. In the previous example, we typed `test`, which is the name a virtual machine in node #3 in the cluster. If we only wanted see all the nodes, we could type `node` in the search box. Or, to see all the pools, we could type `pool` in the search box. This **Search** option can save lot of time in a large environment with hundreds of VMs and nodes.

Datacenter | Summary menu

This menu only shows all the nodes in the cluster being managed and information pertaining to a node, such as **Name**, cluster **ID**, online/offline, Proxmox subscription level, fenced, IP address, and cluster service. Here is a screenshot of a test cluster prepared for the purpose of writing this chapter:

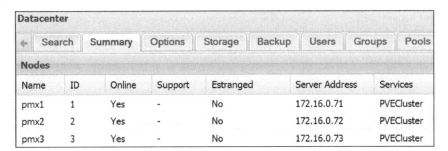

The following image demonstrates the **Summary** page with **Proxmox Community Subscription** (`https://www.proxmox.com/proxmox-ve/pricing`) enabled:

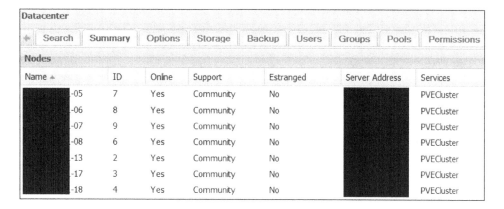

Datacenter | Options menu

From this menu, we can set up a default keyboard layout for the GUI, HTTP proxy, default consoles (Java VNC, SPICE, and HTML5-based noVNC), and an e-mail "from" address.

When using Java-based VNC, it is necessary to install Java and configure Java security to allow the VNC console. The latest version of Java can be downloaded from `https://java.com/en/download/`.

To access a SPICE-based console, SPICE or Virt Viewer needs to be installed. The SPICE download is available for both Linux and Windows-based platforms, which can be download from `http://www.spice-space.org/download.html`.

The noVNC console is based on HTML5, which only requires the latest version of browsers and no Java plugins.

The default console viewer allows us to set the default console type. As of Proxmox 3.3 and later, HTML5 or noVNC is the default console viewer. Here is a screenshot of the **Options** menu under **Datacenter**:

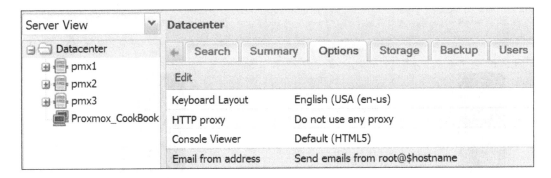

 To learn more about noVNC, visit `http://kanaka.github.io/noVNC/`, and for SPICE, visit `http://www.spice-space.org/home.html`.

Datacenter | Storage menu

This is the menu where we add storages to the Proxmox cluster. As of Proxmox VE 3.4, Proxmox supports LVM, NFS, iSCSI, GlusterFS, RBD, and ZFS storage types. A storage is used to store VM disk images, ISO templates, and back files. To learn details about how to add each storage, refer to *Chapter 6, Storage Configurations*. Here is a screenshot of the **Storage** menu for a test cluster:

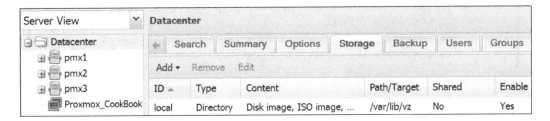

From the preceding screenshot, we can see that there are three storages that are currently set up for the test cluster. The storage display shows the following information:

Column name	Description	Available options
ID	This refers to the identification name of the storage.	This refers to alphanumeric, - and _ string options only. The first digit must be an alphabet.
Type	This refers to the storage type, such as Local, NFS, ZFS, and so on.	This refers to local, LVM, NFS, iSCSI, GlusterFS, RBD, and ZFS.

Column name	Description	Available options
Content	This refers to the types of data the storage can store.	This refers to a disk image, ISO image, OpenVZ template, VZDump Backup file and OpenVZ Container.
Path/Target	This shows the path where a storage is mounted on a Proxmox node.	By default, a local storage is mounted on `/var/lib/vz` and shared storage on `/mnt/pve/<storage_id>`.
Shared	This displays whether the storage is available to all nodes or to a specific node.	**Yes** **No**
Enable	This displays whether the storage is enabled or disabled.	**Yes** **No**

To remove or edit storage, simply click on **Storage**, then select **Remove** or **Edit**. To add a new storage, click on **Add**, then select a storage type.

Datacenter | Backup menu

This menu is used to configure a backup schedule for virtual machines in a Proxmox cluster. As of Proxmox VE 3.3, only a weekly backup schedule is possible. For details of how to create backup schedules, please refer to *Chapter 7, Backup and Restore*. Here is a screenshot of the Proxmox **Backup** menu:

The backup menu displays scheduled backups in the following format:

Column name	Description
Node	This refers to the node that contains the selected virtual machines to be backed up.
Day of week	This refers to the days of the week when backups will be performed.
Start Time	This refers to the time when scheduled backups will start.
Storage	This refers to the storage where will backups will be stored.
Selection	This refers to the IDs of virtual machines scheduled to be backed up.

Column name	Description
Send email to	This refers to the admin e-mail address where automated e-mails will be sent.
Email notification	This refers to the drop-down menu to select when the system should e-mail. We have the option to receive e-mails for all tasks or e-mails only if there are issues, such as a failed backup.
Compression	This refers to the drop-down menu to select for compression types. The **None** Option will use no compression, thus the backup files will take the actual size of the virtual disk image file. The LZO compression is a balance between speed and compression ratio. It is also the faster backup method. The GZIP compression will use the highest compression possible while consuming more CPU and memory resources of a node.

It is also possible to schedule daily backupa. Simply select all days of the week to schedule a daily backup. Here is a screenshot of the **Backup Job** creation window:

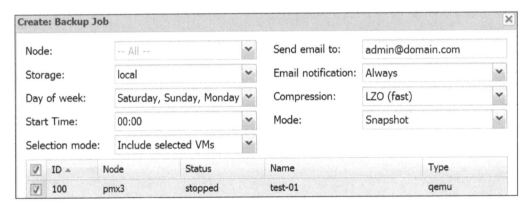

To remove or edit a backup schedule, simply select the backup task and click on the **Remove** or **Edit** button. To **Add**, **Remove**, and **Edit** a backup schedule, select the respective button from the **Backup** menu as shown in the following screenshot:

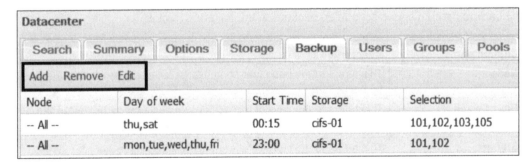

Datacenter | Users menu

This is the menu used to create, edit, remove, or change passwords for new or existing users in a Proxmox cluster. Note that in order to put a user to a particular group, the group must be created through the **Groups** menu before creating a user. This user menu is only to create a user. Permissions for the group must be changed from the **Permissions** menu. Here is a screenshot of the **Users** menu:

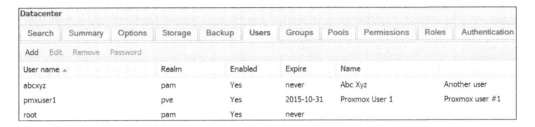

User name ▲	Realm	Enabled	Expire	Name	
abcxyz	pam	Yes	never	Abc Xyz	Another user
pmxuser1	pve	Yes	2015-10-31	Proxmox User 1	Proxmox user #1
root	pam	Yes	never		

To create a new user, simply click on **Add** and fill in the information as required, as shown in the following screenshot:

As of Proxmox VE 3.4, **Two-factor Authentication** (**TFA**) is supported. Currently, only OATH and Yubico-based TFA are available. In the user creation windows, fill in **Key ID** provided by the TFA provider.

 For details on OATH-based TFA, visit `http://www.openauthentication.org`. For a Yubico-based TFA, visit `http://www.yubico.com`.

Note that there is no **Password** entry box in the user creation window when **Linux PAM standard authentication** is selected. The **Password** entry box is available on a user creation window when creating users under **Proxmox VE authentication server**. To add or change password for a user, select an already created user, then click on **Password** from the menu.

Datacenter | Groups menu

This is the menu to create, edit, or remove user **Groups** in the Proxmox cluster. Users can be put in different groups depending on various levels of permission and access. Here is a screenshot of the **Group** menu with two groups already created. A freshly installed Proxmox cluster does not have any groups created:

To create a new group, click on **Create**, then enter **Name** and **Comment** as groups. Spaces and special characters are not allowed as group names.

Datacenter | Pools menu

This is the menu to manage **Pools** in a Proxmox cluster. Pools in Proxmox are nothing but a collection of resources, such as virtual machines or storages. For example, all the resources belonging to a particular client or customer named ABC in the cluster can be put in a single pool named ABC for easier navigation and management. It is especially useful in a large environment where hundreds of virtual machines exist and belong to multiple clients. Here is a screenshot of the **Pools** menu in Proxmox:

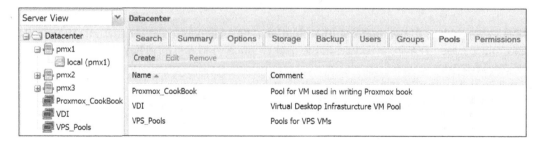

To create a new pool, click on **Create**, then fill in **Name** and **Comment** about the pool.

Once a pool is created, the name of the pool cannot be changed at a later time. Only the description of the pool can be changed.

To add resources to the pool, select the pool from the **Server View** tree, then click on **Add** under the **Members** menu as shown in the following screenshot:

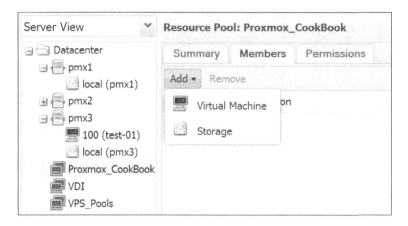

Datacenter | <Pool_name> | Members tab

When a pool name is selected from **Server View** or **Pool View**, the **Members** tab under the pool view lists all the resources added to the pool and their resource consumption, such disk, memory, CPU usage, and uptime of virtual machines. This is also where new items get added to the pool, as shown in the previous section.

Datacenter | <Pool_name> | Permissions tab

The **Permissions** tab under the Pool View displays users or groups allowed to manage or access the pool and their assigned role. In our **Proxmox_CookBook** pool, the **Authors** group is given permission to administer virtual machines in the pool:

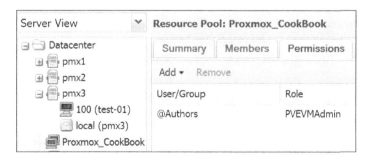

Datacenter | Permissions menu

This is the menu used to assign specific permissions to a particular user or group in the cluster. This display shows all the permissions assigned anywhere in the cluster, such as pools, virtual machines, storage, and any other resources available through the Proxmox cluster.

 Note that any **Permissions** menu in the Proxmox GUI does not have any **Edit** option. If any changes are needed, the permissions must be removed and recreated again.

Here is a screenshot of the **Permissions** menu through the GUI:

Datacenter | Roles menu

The **Roles** menu shows all the default Proxmox roles and their available privileges. These roles cannot be deleted nor can they be edited. Each role has different privileges or access levels for different entities in a Proxmox cluster. For example, roles are added to a **User/Group** through the **Datacenter | Permissions | Add** button.

Datacenter | Authentication menu

The **Authentication** menu displays the login **Realm** information available for users to log in. Proxmox stores all user attributes in the /ets/pve/user.cfg directory path. No password is stored in this file; instead, a different realm is used to verify user passwords. Two realms, **pam** and **pve**, are created by default and cannot be deleted or edited, as shown in the following screenshot:

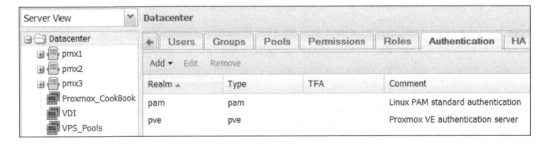

Pluggable Authentication Module (**PAM**) is a Linux-based centralized authentication system that uses pluggable and modular architecture, providing operating system-wide common authentication schema. In contrast, the **Proxmox VE** (**PVE**) authentication stores password in /etc/pve/priv/shadow.cfg, which are encrypted using the SHA-256 hashing. This is the preferred authentication when creating general users besides administrative users. This way, the user only gains access to Proxmox and not the other parts of an operating system.

As of Proxmox VE 3.4, we can also use the Active Directory Server and the LDAP server as authentication realms. Click on **Add**, then select the appropriate server available to create a new login realm:

Datacenter | Authentication | Add | Active Directory Server menu

If there is a Windows-based Active Directory Server or a LDAP server in a network, we can create a new login realm to authenticate it. To create a new authentication realm, click on **Add** and select the appropriate server. Then, fill in the required server information for a new login realm. This screenshot shows the Active Directory Server authentication creation windows:

This screenshot shows the LDAP server authentication creation window:

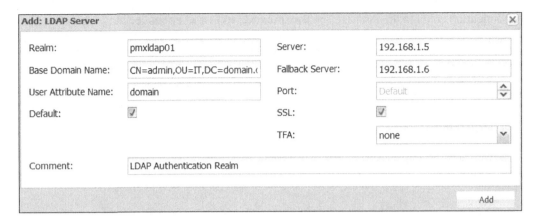

As of Proxmox VE 3.4, both the Active Directory and LDAP server authentications supports **Two-factor Authentication** (**TFA**). Currently, OATH and Yubico TFA are supported. Select the appropriate TFA option from the new realm creation window as shown in the following screenshot:

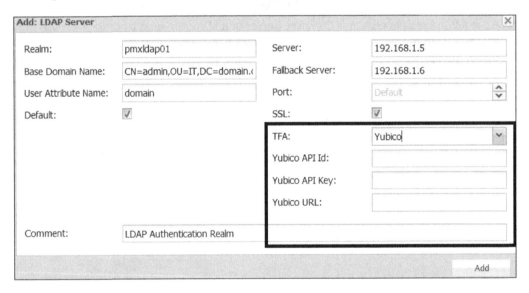

Datacenter | HA menu

This is the menu used to set up **High Availability** (**HA**) in a Proxmox cluster. HA is an enterprise feature where it provides redundancy during node failure. Any VM configured with HA is automatically moved and restarted in the next available node when the owner node of the VM fails for any reason. The HA menu displays an existing cluster configuration and allows a user to enable HA for a VM or container. Here is a screenshot of the Proxmox **HA** menu with a default cluster configuration:

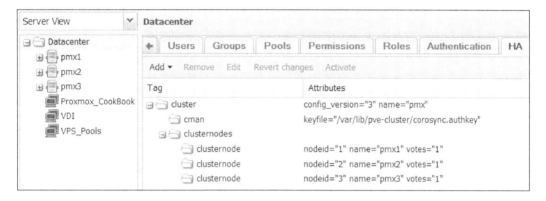

By default, only the **Add** menu tab under the Proxmox **HA** menu is enabled. Other menu options appear as we make changes to the HA configuration by adding or removing resources, such as a VM or container. Here is a table of available menu options and their functions:

Menu options	Functions
Add	This refers to adding resources, such as VM/Container and failover domain, to a HA configuration.
Remove	This refers to removing a resource from a HA configuration.
Edit	This refers to editing an HA configuration for a resource.
Revert Changes	This refers to undoing an HA configuration to the last changes.
Activate	This activates any changes made to a HA configuration. All changes must be activated.

We will look into HA configuration in *Chapter 4, Network Configurations*.

Datacenter | Firewall menu

A firewall is a new feature added to Proxmox from version 3.3. It is an excellent feature to provide firewalling option to specific nodes or virtual machines. Node or host-specific firewall rules apply to all virtual machines within a node, while VM-specific firewall rules apply to a particular VM. By default, the **Firewall** feature is disabled. We will look into Firewall configurations in *Chapter 5, Firewall Configurations*. Here is a screenshot of the **Firewall** menu in the Proxmox GUI:

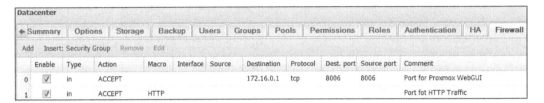

Prior to the **Firewall** feature addition, adding a virtualized firewall or manually adding iptable rules directly into interfaces or virtual machines were the ways to protect a VM or node from being compromised. Integrated graphical firewall features alleviate the complexity of manual rule entry and the overhead of managing separate virtualized firewalls. A datacenter **Firewall** menu has five additional submenus, such as **Rules**, **Security Group**, **Alias**, **IPset**, and **Options**.

Datacenter | Firewall | Rules menu

This is the default display for the **Datacenter | Firewall** menu. This displays all the datacenter created firewall rules affecting all virtual machines in a cluster.

Datacenter | Firewall | Security Group menu

This firewall menu allows the creation of a group of firewall rules that can be assigned to multiple virtual machines with similar roles, such as e-mail servers, web servers, and so on. Security groups can be assigned to a particular rule from the **Rules** menu. The following screenshot shows two security groups for mail and web servers:

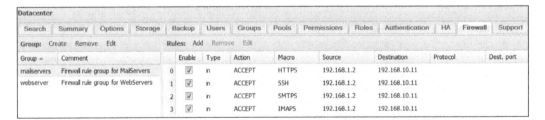

Datacenter | Firewall | Alias menu

This menu is to create aliases that can be associated to the IP addresses of a cluster network. These aliases can then be called from firewall rules or IP definitions. The following screenshot shows two aliases created for `Client-ABC` and `Client-XYZ`:

Datacenter | Firewall | IPSet menu

This menu allows us to group multiple networks or hosts together and easily call them from the firewall rule properties. In the following example, we have created an **IPSet** for a cloud storage access for `client-abc`, `client-xyz` and one additional subnet:

Datacenter | Firewall | Options menu

This menu allows us to enable/disable datacenter-wide firewalls and change the behavior of I/O policies. The following screenshot shows that the firewall rules are turned off for **Datacenter**, all incoming connections are to be dropped, and outgoing connections are to be accepted:

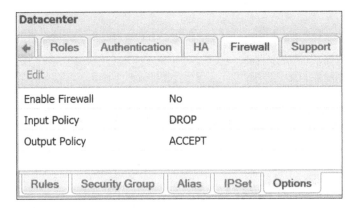

Datacenter | Support menu

This is an informational menu only to display the Proxmox VE subscription level, **Documentation**, and **Bug Tracking** link, as shown in the following screenshot:

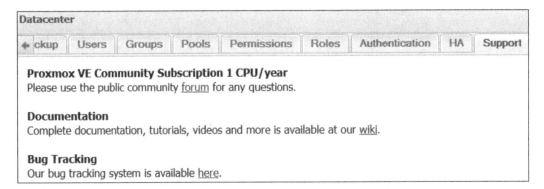

Accessing node-specific menus

These tabbed menus are only available when a node is selected. Here are the menus only accessible when a node is selected:

- **Search**
- **Summary**
- **Services**

- ▸ **Network**
- ▸ **DNS**
- ▸ **Time**
- ▸ **Syslog**
- ▸ **Bootlog**
- ▸ **Task History**
- ▸ **UBC**
- ▸ **Subscription**
- ▸ **Firewall**
- ▸ **Updates**
- ▸ **Ceph**

Getting ready

Any changes in a node-specific menu only affect the node itself and not the other nodes or the cluster itself.

How to do it...

Click on a specific node from the left navigation window to make the node-specific tabbed menu visible.

How it works...

Here are the details of each menu and their functions.

Node | Search menu

The function of this menu is same as the **Datacenter** | **Search** menu. It allows for the searching of resources, such as a VM or storage within the node.

Node | Summary menu

This menu displays the node status, such as node hardware information and resources, such as CPU, memory, and network bandwidth usage. Here is a screenshot of one of the nodes in our test cluster:

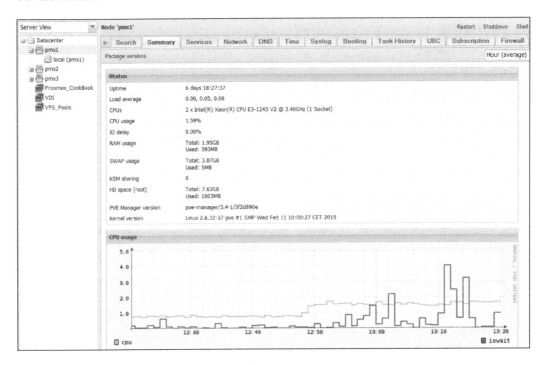

Node | Services menu

This menu displays running services on the node. Services can be **Start**, **Stop**, and **Restart** through this menu, as shown in the following screenshot:

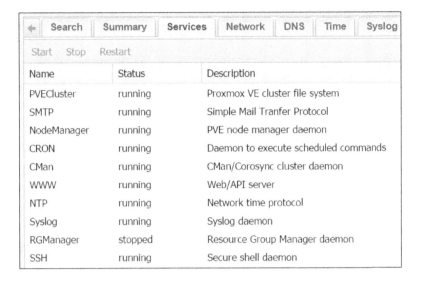

Name	Status	Description
PVECluster	running	Proxmox VE cluster file system
SMTP	running	Simple Mail Tranfer Protocol
NodeManager	running	PVE node manager daemon
CRON	running	Daemon to execute scheduled commands
CMan	running	CMan/Corosync cluster daemon
WWW	running	Web/API server
NTP	running	Network time protocol
Syslog	running	Syslog daemon
RGManager	stopped	Resource Group Manager daemon
SSH	running	Secure shell daemon

Node | Network menu

This menu is used to configure and manage network interfaces installed in the node. We can create, revert changes, edit, and remove network configurations through this menu. Any changes made through this GUI menu will require a node reboot. Changes made here temporarily are written in /etc/network/interfaces.new. During reboot, all changes get transferred permanently to /etc/network/interfaces. We will see this menu in detail in *Chapter 4, Network Configurations*. Here is a screenshot of the **Network** menu:

Name ▲	Type	Active	Autostart	Ports/Slaves	IP address	Subnet mask	Gateway
eth0	Network Device	Yes	No				
vmbr0	Linux Bridge	Yes	Yes	eth0	172.16.0.71	255.255.252.0	172.16.3.254

Node | DNS menu

We can configure a DNS server for the node through this menu.

Node | Time menu

This menu is to configure the time zone and adjust the time for the selected node.

Node | Syslog menu

This menu displays a running system log in real time. During any node or VM-related issue, it helps to check out **Syslog** for any anomalies.

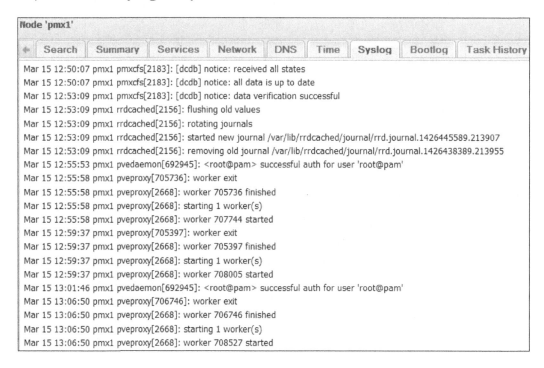

Node | Bootlog menu

This menu displays the log created during a boot. We can spot any issue that has occurred during a node reboot through this menu. Here is a screenshot of the menu displaying the log of a clean reboot:

Node | Task History menu

This menu displays all the tasks performed by a user or a schedule through the WebGUI or a command-line interface. We can drill into details of a task by clicking on the **View** option, which becomes available upon clicking on a task, as shown in the following screenshot:

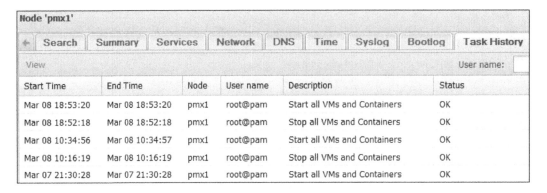

Start Time	End Time	Node	User name	Description	Status
Mar 08 18:53:20	Mar 08 18:53:20	pmx1	root@pam	Start all VMs and Containers	OK
Mar 08 18:52:18	Mar 08 18:52:18	pmx1	root@pam	Stop all VMs and Containers	OK
Mar 08 10:34:56	Mar 08 10:34:57	pmx1	root@pam	Start all VMs and Containers	OK
Mar 08 10:16:19	Mar 08 10:16:19	pmx1	root@pam	Stop all VMs and Containers	OK
Mar 07 21:30:28	Mar 07 21:30:28	pmx1	root@pam	Start all VMs and Containers	OK

Node | UBC menu

This menu displays the **User Bean Counters** (**UBC**) values for all the containers in the node. Without the OpenVZ containers in the cluster, this display is usually is empty. More details on **UBC** can be found in *Chapter 3, Cluster and VM Management*.

Node | Subscription menu

This menu displays the subscription information applied to the node. We can also apply the subscription license and activate it through this menu:

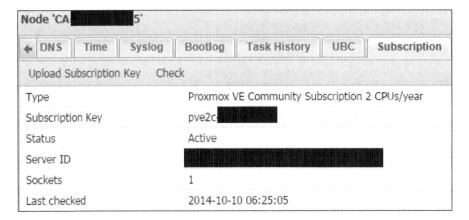

Type	Proxmox VE Community Subscription 2 CPUs/year
Subscription Key	pve2c‑
Status	Active
Server ID	
Sockets	1
Last checked	2014-10-10 06:25:05

Node | Firewall menu

This menu is used to configure node-wide firewall rules, which apply to all VMs within the same node. The **Firewall** menu for nodes have three additional submenus: **Rules**, **Options**, and **Log**.

Node | Firewall | Rules menu

As with the firewall **Rules** menu for **Datacenter**, a node-specific firewall **Rules** menu also displays all rules created in the node, as shown in the following screenshot:

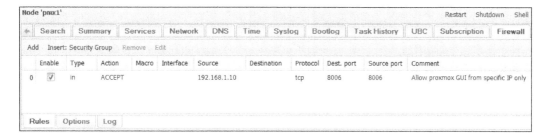

Node | Firewall | Options menu

This menu shows the options available for node-specific firewalls. Options, such as enable/disable firewall, **SMURFS filter** (packets with a broadcast address as the source), **TCP flags filters**, logs, and so on, can be edited through this menu. Simply click on a line item and then click on **Edit** to change. The following screenshot shows the **Options** menu for the pmx01 node in our test cluster:

Node | Firewall | Log menu

This menu shows log entries created by firewall activity in a node.

Node | Updates menu

This menu displays the updates available for operating systems of the node. We can also apply an update and check the change logs of a package from this menu. The Proxmox VE automatically checks for updates. If you manually want to check, click on **Refresh**. To upgrade or update through Proxmox GUI, click on **Upgrade**. The upgrade console will start with a default console, which is noVNC. To view the console using VNC or SPICE, click on the **Upgrade** drop-down menu and select the desired upgrade **Shell** console. Here is a screenshot of the **Updates** menu with some available updates ready to be applied:

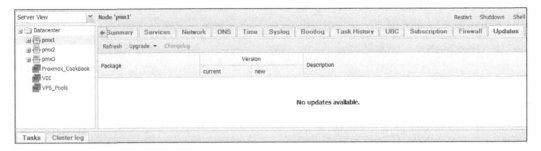

Node | Ceph menu

This menu is to manage a Ceph storage system. If Ceph is not setup in the cluster, it will cause errors when accessing the **Ceph** menu since Ceph will try to find a Ceph configuration file, which will not exist till Ceph cluster is created.

Ceph is one of the enterprise class distributed storage systems with built-in redundancy and IS able to scale out several petabytes. If you are new to Ceph, visit the official Ceph site at `http://ceph.com/`. For more information, also refer to *Chapter 6, Storage Configurations*. As of Proxmox VE 3.3, it is possible to install Proxmox and Ceph on the same node, allowing the consolidation of nodes and eliminating the need to have separate nodes for the Ceph storage.

Ceph can easily be installed on commodity hardware and is managed through the Proxmox GUI. For a production environment, it is recommended to use separate nodes for Ceph storage so that VMs and Ceph storage do not share the same resources. For a small environment of several terabytes storage, Proxmox and Ceph can be used together so long as the Proxmox node has enough resources without starving any VM during peak usage. Here is a screenshot of the Ceph menu with Proxmox and Ceph on same node in a production cluster:

The Proxmox Ceph menu enables some more additional tabbed menus to manage a Ceph cluster.

 Do not worry if you are not familiar with keywords used in a Ceph cluster, such as **Monitor**, **OSD**, CRUSH map, and so on. We will look into Ceph in greater detail in *Chapter 6, Storage Configurations*.

Node | Ceph | Status menu

This menu shows the current Ceph cluster's health status at a glance. Any issues in the cluster can be quickly spotted through this **Status** menu.

Node | Ceph | Config menu

This is a display only menu that shows the content of the current Ceph cluster configurations. Any necessary changes to this file can be made through CLI by editing the /etc/pve/ceph. conf configuration file.

Node | Ceph | Monitor menu

This menu is used to manage the Ceph Monitors in the cluster. The menu allows us to **Start**, **Stop Create**, or **Remove** Ceph Monitors. For information on Ceph Monitors, refer to *Chapter 6, Storage Configurations*. Here is a screenshot of configured monitors in our test cluster:

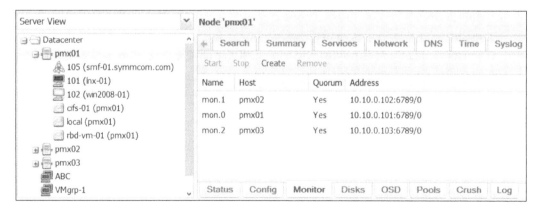

Node | Ceph | Disks menu

This menu is to create Ceph Object Storage Daemons (OSDs). Refer to *Chapter 6, Storage Configurations*, for details on OSD.

Node | Ceph | OSD menu

This menu is to manage Ceph OSDs once they are created through the **Disks** menu. We can **Start**, **Stop**, **Remove**, **Online**, and **Offline** an OSD through this menu.

Node | Ceph | Pools menu

This menu is to manage Ceph storage pools. We can **Create** and **Remove** pools through this menu. Pools in Ceph allows to create separate storages within a Ceph cluster.

Node | Ceph | Crush menu

This is a view-only menu that displays CRUSH map currently in use within a Ceph cluster. A **Controlled Replication Under Scalable Hashing Map** (**CRUSH map**) is the heart of a Ceph cluster. A CRUSH map directs where and how an object is stored within the cluster. We will look into CRUSH map in detail in *Chapter 6, Storage Configurations*.

 In order to configure a Ceph cluster beyond default and make it adaptable to just about any size or nature of environment, a good understanding of a CRUSH map is necessary.

Node | Ceph | Log menu

This menu displays a Ceph log in real time of all the read/write occurring in the cluster.

Node management menu

This menu allows node-specific management tasks, such as **Restart**, **Shutdown**, **Shell** access, and **Start/Stop** VMs. Here are four options are available for this menu:

- ▶ **Restart**: We can restart the node by clicking on **Restart**.
- ▶ **Shutdown**: We can shutdown a node gracefully with this option.
- ▶ **Shell**: We can access **Shell** of the node through this drop-down menu. We can select console types, such as **noVNC**, **VNC** and **SPICE**, from the drop-down option.
- ▶ **More**: This menu allows **Start**, **Stop**, and **Migrate** of all virtual machines in the node. This is a useful menu option for a node with a large number of VMs.

Accessing KVM-specific menus

These menus are available when a KVM-based virtual machine is selected on the Proxmox GUI. Any changes made through these tabbed menus affect the VM directly. The available tabbed menu for VMs are shown in the following screenshot:

Here are the menus only accessible when a KVM-based VM is selected:

- **Summary**
- **Hardware**
- **Options**
- **Task History**
- **Monitor**
- **Backup**
- **Snapshots**
- **Firewall**
- **Permissions**

Getting ready

Any changes in a KVM-specific menu only affect the KVM VM itself and not the other VMs.

How to do it...

Click on a KVM-based virtual machine from the left navigation window to make the node-specific tabbed menu visible.

How it works...

Here are the details of each menu and its functions.

KVM | Summary menu

This menu displays the VM information and resource status. Additionally, there is a **Notes** box in the VM summary page to enter VM-specific information by a user. Here is a screenshot of the **Summary** page with some notes added:

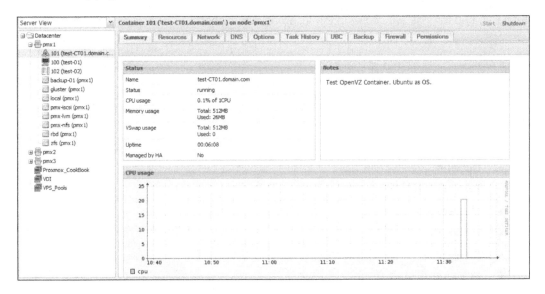

KVM | Hardware menu

This menu displays virtualized hardware information and the resource status for a VM. We can allocate and change specifications, such as **Keyboard Layout**, amount of memory, number of CPU cores, add/remove virtual disk image, and so on.. Here is a screenshot of the **Hardware** menu tab of a KVM-based virtual machine:

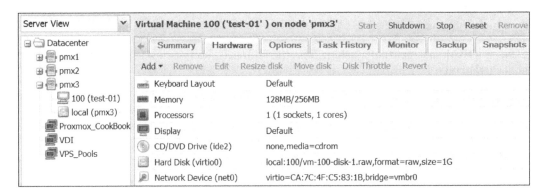

KVM | Options menu

This is the **Options** menu for a VM to rename a VM, change the start or shutdown behavior, enable hotplugging, and more. Here is a screenshot of the **Options** menu for a VM:

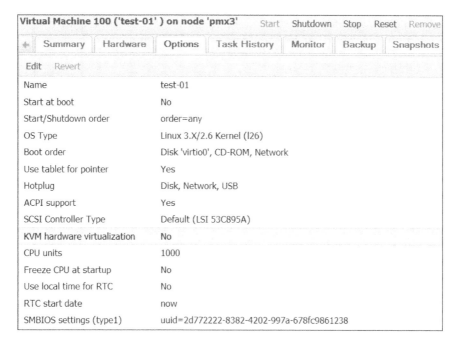

Name	test-01	
Start at boot	No	
Start/Shutdown order	order=any	
OS Type	Linux 3.X/2.6 Kernel (I26)	
Boot order	Disk 'virtio0', CD-ROM, Network	
Use tablet for pointer	Yes	
Hotplug	Disk, Network, USB	
ACPI support	Yes	
SCSI Controller Type	Default (LSI 53C895A)	
KVM hardware virtualization	No	
CPU units	1000	
Freeze CPU at startup	No	
Use local time for RTC	No	
RTC start date	now	
SMBIOS settings (type1)	uuid=2d772222-8382-4202-997a-678fc9861238	

KVM | Task History menu

Similar to the **Task History** of nodes, this VM-specific menu shows **Task History** only for the selected VM, whereas the **Task History** of nodes shows tasks for all the VMs in the node.

KVM | Monitor menu

This menu provides a console for interacting with a VM through various commands that are entered through the Proxmox GUI. By typing `help` or `?` we can view the available commands to be performed to inspect and control different areas of a running virtual machine. Here is a screenshot of the output of four commands: `info name`, `info version`, `info status`, and `info registers`, which can be seen through the **Monitor** menu:

To find out all the available commands through the **Monitor** menu, simply type `help` in the input box of the **Monitor** menu.

For more info on the VM Monitor, visit `http://en.wikibooks.org/wiki/QEMU/Monitor`.

KVM | Backup menu

This menu is used to manage backup files for a virtual machine. It is also used to manually backup a virtual machine without a schedule. The backups performed through this menu are only for full VM backups. This screenshot shows the **Backup** menu for VM 100 with one backup file:

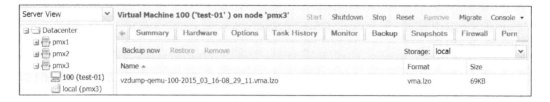

To perform a backup, click on **Backup now** to open a backup window. Select the destination backup storage, backup mode and the compression type. Then, click on the **Backup** button to start the backup process. Here is a screenshot of the **Backup** creation window after clicking on the **Backup now** menu:

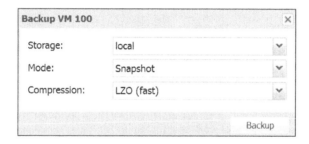

To restore a backup, select a backup file, then click on **Restore** to open the restore window, as shown in the following screenshot:

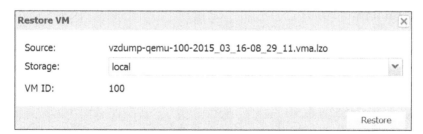

To remove unneeded backup files, simply select them from the backup file list and click on **Remove**. As of Proxmox VE 3.4, there are three backup modes available:

1. **Snapshot**: This refers to a live backup without shutting down a VM. It requires minimal downtime.

2. **Suspend**: This refers to a VM that is suspended or frozen before commencing the backup. It requires moderate downtime.

3. **Stop**: This refers to a VM that is fully stopped or shutdown before the backup and automatically started after the backup is completed. It requires significant downtime.

KVM | Snapshots menu

This is the menu used to create snapshots of a virtual machine. Snapshots are simply images of a point in time of the virtual machine. This allows us to revert back to the earlier stage of the VM in case of misconfiguration or a bad software install on the VM. Do not substitute full backups with snapshot because snapshots do not do full backups of a VM. When performing a full backup on a VM with snapshots, all the snapshot images are excluded from the backup. This menu is also used to rollback a VM and remove or edit already created snapshots. Refer to *Chapter 7, Backup and Restore*, to learn about the snapshots of VM.

Note the difference between VM **Snapshots** and the **Snapshot** option of **Backup**. They are two completely different features. The **Snapshot** backup does a full backup of a VM without shutting down, whereas **Snapshots** freezes the state of a VM to revert back later if needed.

KVM | Firewall menu

This menu allows us to set firewall rules for individual virtual machines. Any rules created through this menu only affect the VM it was created for. This firewall menu also has submenus: **Rules**, **Alias**, **IPset**, **Options**, and **Log**. The functions of these submenus are identical to the ones for node and datacenter-specific firewalls. Refer to *Chapter 5, Firewall Configurations*, for details on creating firewall rules.

KVM | Permissions menu

This menu allows the setting or removal of access permissions for the virtual machine that is selected. Refer to the *Accessing datacenter-specific menus* recipe earlier in this chapter for the **Users**, **Groups**, and **Roles** options. This screenshot shows two access permissions given to a user and a group with different levels of access rights:

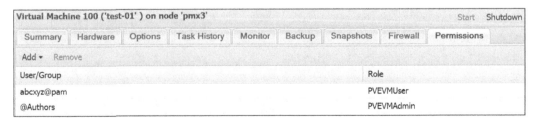

Accessing OpenVZ-specific menus

These menus are available when an OpenVZ-based container is selected on the Proxmox GUI. Any changes made through these tabbed menus affect the container directly. Refer to *Chapter 3, Cluster and VM Management*, to learn how to create OpenVZ containers. Here is a screenshot of available menus for OpenVZ containers:

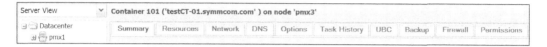

Here are the menus only accessible when an OpenVZ-based container is selected:

- **Summary**
- **Options**
- **Task History**
- **UBC**
- **Backup**
- **Firewall**
- **Permissions**

Getting ready

Any changes in a node-specific menu only affect the node itself and not the other nodes or the cluster itself.

How to do it...

Click on a OpenVZ container virtual machine from the left navigation window to make the container-specific tabbed menu visible.

How it works...

Here are the details of each menu and their functions.

OpenVZ | Summary menu

This menu shows **Status**, configuration information, and **Notes** for selected OpenVZ containers as shown in the following screenshot:

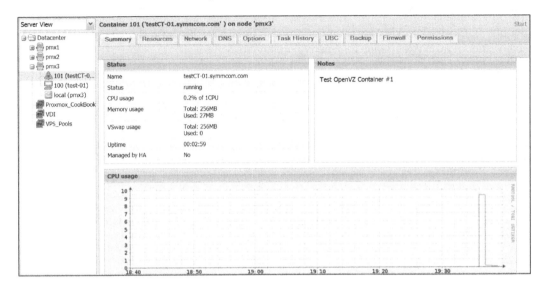

OpenVZ | Resources menu

Resources, such as CPU cores, memory swap, and disk sizes can be configured through this menu. This screenshot shows the resources allocated for the 101 container:

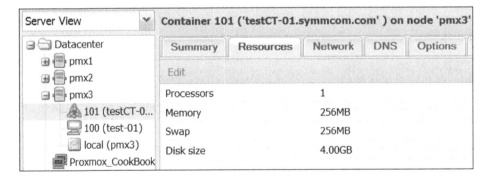

OpenVZ | Network menu

This menu allows adding additional IP addresses or network devices to containers. This screenshot shows how container `101` is configured to a virtual network interface:

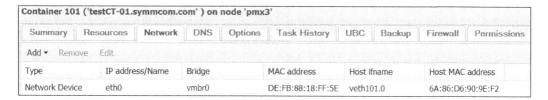

Container 101 ('testCT-01.symmcom.com') on node 'pmx3'									
Summary	Resources	Network	DNS	Options	Task History	UBC	Backup	Firewall	Permissions
Add ▾ Remove Edit									

Type	IP address/Name	Bridge	MAC address	Host ifname	Host MAC address
Network Device	eth0	vmbr0	DE:FB:88:18:FF:5E	veth101.0	6A:86:D6:90:9E:F2

OpenVZ | DNS menu

This menu allows the DNS server configuration of the container.

OpenVZ | Options menu

Options, such as auto boot with node reboot, name of template in use for the container, storage where the container is located, and assigned CPU units, are available through this menu. This screenshot shows the options currently set for the container `101`:

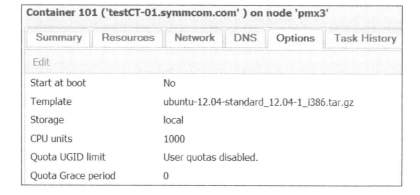

Container 101 ('testCT-01.symmcom.com') on node 'pmx3'					
Summary	Resources	Network	DNS	Options	Task History
Edit					

Start at boot	No
Template	ubuntu-12.04-standard_12.04-1_i386.tar.gz
Storage	local
CPU units	1000
Quota UGID limit	User quotas disabled.
Quota Grace period	0

OpenVZ | Task History menu

This menu displays all the tasks performed for the selected container.

OpenVZ | UBC menu

This menu displays the values for **User Bean Counters** (**UBC**) for a selected container. UBCs are set of limits set per container to guarantee the proper functioning of the container. This menu is for display only and no changes can be made here. All additional configurations of these values can be made through CLI by editing the container configuration file. This screenshot shows the UBC values for the `101` container:

Container 101 ('testCT-01.symmcom.com') on node 'pmx3'							
Summary	Resources	Network	DNS	Options	Task History	UBC	Backup

Resource ▲	Held	Maxheld	Barrier	Limit	Failcnt
dcachesize	2MB	2MB	58MB	64MB	0
dgramrcvbuf	0	0	-	-	0
kmemsize	4MB	5MB	116MB	128MB	0
lockedpages	0	0	128MB	128MB	0
numfile	281	345	-	-	0
numflock	4	7	-	-	0
numiptent	20	20	-	-	0
numothersock	18	39	-	-	0
numproc	17	48	-	-	0
numpty	0	1	-	-	0
numsiginfo	0	27	-	-	0
numtcpsock	6	7	-	-	0
oomguarpages	6MB	7MB	0	-	0
othersockbuf	23KB	120KB	-	-	0
physpages	27MB	36MB	0	256MB	0
privvmpages	12MB	22MB	-	-	0
shmpages	1MB	1MB	-	-	0
swappages	0	0	0	256MB	0
tcprcvbuf	96KB	112KB	-	-	0
tcpsndbuf	102KB	119KB	-	-	0

OpenVZ | Backup menu

The **Backup** menu for the container is identical to KVM-based virtual machines including **Snapshot**, **Suspend**, and **Stop** backup options. All manual backups, restore, or removal of container backup files can be done through this menu.

OpenVZ | Firewall menu

The **Firewall** menu for container is also identical to the **Firewall** menu for KVM. Refer to the *KVM | Firewall menu* subsection under the *Accessing KVM-specific menus* recipe earlier in this chapter. Refer to *Chapter 5, Firewall Configurations*, to learn to create firewall rules.

OpenVZ | Permissions menu

The **Firewall** menu for a container is also identical to the **Firewall** menu for the KVM. Refer to the *KVM | Permissions menu* subsection under the *Accessing KVM-specific menus* recipe, earlier in this chapter.

3
Cluster and VM Management

In these chapter, we will cover the following topics:

- ▶ Creating a Proxmox cluster
- ▶ Adding nodes to a cluster
- ▶ Removing nodes from a cluster
- ▶ Rejoining a removed node into a cluster
- ▶ Understanding the Proxmox cluster filesystem
- ▶ Managing the ISO and OpenVZ templates
- ▶ Creating a KVM-based virtual machine
- ▶ Creating an OpenVZ container
- ▶ Migrating a virtual machine
- ▶ Cloning a virtual machine
- ▶ Managing a virtual disk image
- ▶ Managing OpenVZ containers
- ▶ Understanding OpenVZ user bean counters

Introduction

A cluster is a sum of multiple computer nodes connected together through networking. One of the many advantages of clustering is that it moves virtual machines to different nodes as the need arises while providing the maximum uptime. A cluster also allows centralized management of all member nodes and virtual machines within the nodes. Although nodes in a cluster work together, it does not provide HA out of the box. In order to have a fully automated HA, we will have to configure it first. More on HA configuration can be found in *Chapter 4, Network Configurations*. Proxmox clusters use a few specific ports for various functions. It is important to ensure that these ports are accessible and not blocked any firewalls. This table shows the ports and their functions:

Port	Function
TCP 8006	Proxmox WebGUI
TCP 5900-5999	VNC Console access
TCP 3128	SPICE Console access
TCP 22	SSH access
UDP 5404, 5405	CMAN multicast when using cluster configurations

The following diagram shows a basic Proxmox cluster diagram with three Proxmox nodes:

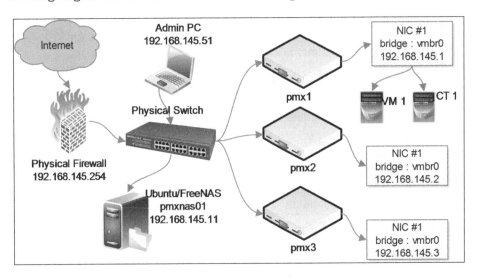

In the preceding network diagram, there are all three Proxmox nodes. Firewalls, NFS-based shared storage, and a computer for administrative task are connected to a **physical switch**. The Proxmox node 1 contains one KVM-based virtual machine and one OpenVZ container. Each of the virtual machines are connected to the node with a bridge named vmbr0. Each of these bridges are linked with the physical network interface of each Proxmox node. Of course, this is an overly simplified diagram of how different components comes together in a cluster.

More on the networking components can be found in *Chapter 4, Network Configurations*. In this chapter, we are going to learn about basic cluster configurations and virtual machine management in the Proxmox VE cluster.

Creating a Proxmox cluster

A cluster is not automatically created on a freshly installed Proxmox node. It must be created through a CLI from any Proxmox node that is going to be a part of the cluster. After the cluster is created and nodes are the added to the cluster, the bigger part of the management can be done through the GUI.

Getting ready

Login to a Proxmox node as the root through SSH or the Proxmox GUI | **Shell** option, as shown in the following screenshot:

How to do it...

1. To create a new cluster, use the following command format:

    ```
    # pvecm create <cluster_name>
    ```

    For our example, in the Proxmox environment, we are going to create a cluster named pmx:

    ```
    #pvecm create pmx
    ```

2. After running the cluster creation command, verify that is it created using the following command:

```
#pvecm status
```

The command should display information similar to the following code:

```
Version: 6.2.0
Config Version: 1
Cluster Name: pmx
Cluster Id: 786
Cluster Member: Yes
Cluster Generation: 51
Membership state: Cluster-Member
Nodes: 1
Expected votes: 3
Total votes: 3
Node votes: 1
Quorum: 1
Active subsystems: 5
Flags:
Ports Bound: 0
Node name: pmx1
Node ID: 1
Multicast addresses: 239.192.3.21
Node addresses: 172.16.0.71
```

How it works...

The cluster creation command creates a configuration file in the `/etc/pve/cluster.conf` directory path. The content of the configuration file should look similar to the following screenshot:

```
  GNU nano 2.2.6                    File: /etc/pve/cluster.conf

<?xml version="1.0"?>
<cluster config_version="3" name="pmx">

   <cman keyfile="/var/lib/pve-cluster/corosync.authkey"/>

   <clusternodes>
   <clusternode name="pmx1" nodeid="1" votes="1"/>
   </clusternodes>
</cluster>
```

As we add more nodes to the cluster, this configuration file will be automatically updated with the node information. It is important to note the syntax, which is `config_version`. If you are manually editing this configuration file, be sure to change the version number incrementally. When the cluster configuration is performed through the CLI, this version number gets autoupdated.

 In most cases, there is no need to manually adjust the configuration. On rare occasions, this may be necessary, such as restoring the configuration file from a backup to recover a damaged cluster.

There's more...

When we add some nodes into the cluster, we will review the cluster configuration again to see the changes. This is also the configuration file we will make changes to when configuring the Proxmox HA.

See also

▶ We will look into the Proxmox HA in *Chapter 4, Network Configurations*

Adding nodes to a cluster

After the cluster is created, we have to add additional nodes to complete the cluster role. A Proxmox cluster requires a minimum of three nodes for proper cluster creation. With three nodes, a **quorum** is possible, which allows clusters to be online and function properly. It is also possible to create a cluster with only two nodes, but it's not recommended. With only two nodes, a majority vote is not possible for cluster election. For learning purposes or for a very small virtual environment, a two node cluster is an option.

Getting ready

The task of adding nodes also needs to be accomplished through the CLI. As of Proxmox VE 3.4, it is not possible to add nodes to a cluster through the Proxmox GUI. Check to ensure that the time and date are synchronized between nodes. The process of cluster creation uses the **cryptograph** method, and it is important that all nodes have same time and date.

How to do it...

Use the following steps, to add nodes to a cluster:

1. Log in as the root to the node to be added through SSH or the Proxmox GUI | **Shell**.

2. From the node to be added, run the following command:

   ```
   #pvecm add <existing_node_in_cluster>
   ```

> An existing node could be any node already added to the cluster or the very first node where the cluster was created if there are no other additional nodes. In a Proxmox cluster, there is no master or slave hierarchy. All nodes participate in the cluster equally.

3. In our example cluster, we are going to add the pmx2 and pmx3 nodes in the cluster by running the following command from both the nodes:

   ```
   #pvecm add 172.16.0.71
   ```

4. Our example `pmx` cluster now has three nodes. We can verify it through the following command, which shows a list of nodes in the cluster:

`#pvecm nodes`

The command displays information, as shown in the following screenshot:

```
root@pmx1:~# nano /etc/pve/cluster.conf
root@pmx1:~# pvecm nodes
Node   Sts   Inc    Joined                      Name
    1    M    1876   2015-07-22 22:04:14     pmx1
    2    M    1876   2015-07-22 22:04:14     pmx2
    3    M    1876   2015-07-22 22:04:14     pmx3
root@pmx1:~#
```

How it works...

After adding the nodes the cluster configuration file in `/etc/pve/cluster.conf`, it should look similar to the following screenshot:

```
  GNU nano 2.2.6                        File: /etc/pve/cluster.conf

<?xml version="1.0"?>
<cluster config_version="5" name="pmx">
  <cman keyfile="/var/lib/pve-cluster/corosync.authkey"/>
  <clusternodes>
    <clusternode name="pmx1" nodeid="1" votes="1"/>
    <clusternode name="pmx2" nodeid="2" votes="1"/>
    <clusternode name="pmx3" nodeid="3" votes="1"/>
  </clusternodes>
</cluster>
```

The node `add` command has an updated version number and has added the `pmx2` and `pmx3` nodes into the cluster configuration.

Removing nodes from a cluster

At times, it may be necessary to remove a node from a cluster for various reasons. A n can only be removed through the CLI as of Proxmox VE 3.4.

Getting ready

Before removing a node, be sure there are no running VMs in a node. Move any VMs to a different node by following the steps in the *Migrating a virtual machine* recipe, shown later on in this chapter. Log in as the root to a node not being removed through SSH or the Proxmox GUI | **Shell**. Power off the node that needs to be removed.

 Proxmox highly recommends that the removed node does not power up in the same network as it is. Removing a node from cluster is a permanent process. It will delete all cluster information from the node that is being removed.

How to do it...

Use the following steps, to remove nodes from the cluster:

1. Run the following command from a node:

   ```
   #pvecm delnode <hostname_to_be_deleted>
   ```

   In our example cluster, if we want to remove the node pmx3, we will run the following command from either node pmx1 or pmx2:

   ```
   #pvecm delnode pmx3
   ```

2. Verify that the node is removed through the following command:

   ```
   #pvecm nodes
   ```

   The command should display a cluster node list without the deleted node, as shown in the following screenshot:

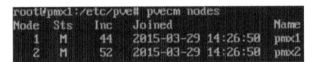

```
root@pmx1:/etc/pve# pvecm nodes
Node  Sts   Inc   Joined                Name
   1   M     44    2015-03-29 14:26:50  pmx1
   2   M     52    2015-03-29 14:26:50  pmx2
```

Rejoining a removed node into a cluster

Sometimes, it may be necessary to rejoin a removed node back into the Proxmox cluster. The node may have been removed by mistake or the node may have become out of order due to hardware failure and needs to be joined back in with same IP address. If the node is going to be rejoined after a clean install of Proxmox on it, then simply follow the steps from the *Adding nodes to a cluster* recipe, shown earlier in this chapter. If the node is rejoined with same Proxmox installation, then it can be joined forcefully or gracefully. To ensure guaranteed operations, clean the installation of Proxmox on the node. Only then is rejoining recommended.

Getting ready

Similar to adding a node, rejoining also must be done from the CLI. Log in as the root into the Proxmox node that is being rejoined.

How to do it...

If reinstalling of Proxmox on the node is not an option, then to rejoin a removed node in the same cluster, graceful joining is highly recommended over forceful. Here are the steps for the graceful rejoining of a removed node:

1. Create a directory to back up existing cluster information:

   ```
   #mkdir /root/pve_backup
   ```

2. Copy the existing cluster information from the /etc/pve to backup directory:

   ```
   #cp -a /etc/pve /root/pve_backup
   ```

3. Stop the cluster service on the node being rejoined:

   ```
   #service pve-cluster stop
   ```

4. Umount the cluster directory:

   ```
   #umount /etc/pve
   ```

5. Remove the cluster configuration file:

   ```
   #rm /etc/cluster/cluster.conf
   ```

6. Remove the cluster files:

   ```
   #rm -rf /var/lib/pve-cluster/*
   ```

7. Restart the cluster service:

   ```
   #service pve-cluster start
   ```

8. Add the nodes to the cluster by pointing to an IP address of an existing node:

```
#pvecm add 172.16.0.71
```

9. To forcefully add a node to the cluster, run the following command:

```
#pvecm add <IP_existing_node> -force
```

10. Run the following command to ensure all the steps were successful:

```
#pvecm nodes
```

There's more...

Although it is possible to rejoin the same node gracefully or forcefully, clean the installation of Proxmox. After this, rejoining is always recommended. It is worth mentioning that graceful rejoining has proven successful in many Proxmox clustered environments without any issue. If you're in doubt, cleaning the installation of Proxmox before rejoining is the safest way to go.

Understanding the Proxmox cluster filesystem

The **Proxmox cluster filesystem** (**pmxcfs**) in short is an integral part of how a Proxmox cluster functions. As the name implies, it is basically a common filesystem shared among all the nodes in a Proxmox cluster. Pmxcfs is a SQLite database-driven filesystem where all the Proxmox configuration files are stored. Any changes to these files are replicated in real time using the **corosync cluster engine**.

 For more information on corosync, visit https://en.wikipedia.org/wiki/Corosync_Cluster_Engine.

Getting ready

To understand pmxcfs, we are going to take a look at how the directory structure is laid out in the filesystem. Pmxcfs can be accessed from any nods in the cluster. Log in as the root into a node through SSH or the Proxmox GUI | **Shell**.

How it works...

Pmxcfs is mounted under `/etc/pve`. The following table shows the directory structure in `/etc/pve` and the type of information it contains:

Directory path	Type of data
`/etc/pve/cluster.conf`	This is the main cluster configuration for corosync.
`/etc/pve/datacenter.cfg`	This contains options, such as admin email, keyboard map, and more.
`/etc/pve/storage.cfg`	This is the configuration for data storage.
`/etc/pve/user.cfg`	This contains user credentials and groups for access control.
`/etc/pve/authkey.pub`	This is the public key for a ticket system.
`/etc/pve/firewall/`	This is the firewall configuration.
`/etc/pve/priv/authkey.key`	This is the private authorization key for a ticket system.
`/etc/pve/priv/shadow.cfg`	This is the shadow password file.
`/etc/pve/nodes/<node>/openvz/`	This is the location for the OpenVZ container configuration files.
`/etc/pve/nodes/<node>/qemu-server/`	This location contains the KVM machine configuration files.
`/etc/pve/nodes/<node>/priv`	This is the private SSL key for a WebGUI.
`/etc/pve/nodes/<node>/pve-ssl.pem`	This is the public SSL key for a WebGUI.

Note that there are three symbolic links in the `/etc/pve` path:

Symbolic links	Destination
`/etc/pve/~local`	`/etc/pve/nodes/<node_name>`
`/etc/pve/~openvz`	`/etc/pve/nodes/<node_name>/openvz`
`/etc/pve/~qemu-server`	`/etc/pve/nodes/<node_name>/qemu-server`

Using the node directory, we can move the VM configuration from one node to another. This is especially useful when a node is down, but needs to access the VMs. Since this filesystem is based on SQLite database as the backend, the function of this filesystem is very limited. It should not be used as a regular file storage.

There's more...

Sometimes, due to a cluster error, pmxcfs may become inaccessible. This will cause errors when trying to access the `/etc/pve` directory. In such scenarios, run the following command to gain access to `/etc/pve`:

```
#pmxcfs -l
```

This command forces the filesystem to start in a local mode. You can then copy data out of it to fix cluster issues. Beware when making any changes to `/etc/pve` while you're in the local mode. All changes will be overwritten when a cluster comes back online in this node.

See also

- ▶ For the official Proxmox Wiki on pmxcfs, visit `https://pve.proxmox.com/wiki/Proxmox_Cluster_file_system_%28pmxcfs%29`

Managing the ISO and OpenVZ templates

Proxmox has features of storing ISO and templates for OpenVZ containers in storage in the cluster that is to be used by virtual machines. In this recipe, we are going to see how to upload ISO and templates into the Proxmox storage.

Getting ready

ISO images for KVM-based VMs and templates for OpenVZ containers can be uploaded and downloaded from the Proxmox GUI. Log in as the root or any other administrative privilege. Then, click on a storage from left navigation window. Each storage has three: tabbed menus: **Summary**, **Content**, and **Permissions**.

How to do it...

Use the following steps to upload ISO and the templates into the Proxmox storage:

1. Click on the **Content** tab to display a list of files stored in the storage. Files are categorized based on the type of content. When there are no files, only the **Templates** and **Upload** menu buttons are enabled, as shown in the following screenshot:

2. Click on **Upload** to the open dialog box, as shown in the following screenshot, to select a file to upload:

3. Select the content type from the **Content:** drop-down menu. Then, click on **Select File...** to select a file to be uploaded from a local computer.

4. Click on **Upload** to start uploading the file to the storage.

 Note that this upload allows three types of files to be uploaded. They are **ISO image**, **OpenVZ template**, and **VZDump backup file**. Proxmox also allows the download of OpenVZ templates from its repository.

5. Click on **Templates** to open the template dialog box, as shown in the following screenshot:

Templates				✕
Type	Package	Version	Description	
⊟ Section: admin (2 Items)				
openvz	request-tracker	3.8.8-2	Extensible trouble-ticket tracking system	
openvz	zenoss	2.5.1-1	Zenoss Core IT monitoring	
⊟ Section: mail (1 Item)				
openvz	proxmox-mailgateway	3.1-2	Proxmox Mail Gateway	
⊟ Section: system (9 Items)				
openvz	debian-5.0-standard	5.0-2	Debian 5.0 (standard)	
openvz	ubuntu-8.04-standard	8.04-3	Ubuntu Hardy (standard)	
openvz	debian-7.0-standard	7.0-2	Debian 7.0 (standard)	
openvz	centos-5-standard	5.8-1	CentOS 5 (standard)	
openvz	debian-4.0-standard	4.0-5	Debian 4.0 (standard)	
openvz	debian-6.0-standard	6.0-6	Debian 6.0 (standard)	
openvz	centos-6-standard	6.3-1	CentOS 6 (standard)	
openvz	ubuntu-12.04-standard	12.04-1	Ubuntu Precise Pangolin (standard)	

Download

6. Select a template, then click on the **Download** button to download the OpenVZ template. These templates are precompiled ready-to-use templates of various distributions and applications. We can also download many more templates for OpenVZ containers from the TurnKey Linux site at `https://www.turnkeylinux.org/`.

 Note that the templates available through this repository are not fully up to date.

7. To remove an ISO image or template, select a file from the list under storage. Then, click on **Remove**.

How it works...

Storages can only contain different file types if the **Content** type is selected from the **Datacenter | Storage** menu. For example, in our demo cluster, all content types are selected for local storage, as shown in the following screenshot:

To change **Content** type, select a storage. Then, click on **Edit** to select the appropriate content type.

There's more...

It is also possible to create your own OpenVZ templates to be used in Proxmox. Complete instructions on creating your own templates or appliances are beyond the scope of this book. However, the following link can give good start on learning to build templates. Visit `https://pve.proxmox.com/wiki/Debian_Appliance_Builder` for this.

ISOs and templates can also be copied through a CLI or a program, such as FileZilla. Connect to a Proxmox node through FileZilla and copy files to the appropriate paths. Note that when using local storage only, these ISO images and templates will need to be uploaded to all nodes in the cluster. With a shared storage in place we can store all the images in one location, thus saving local storage space. We will discuss more on storages in *Chapter 6, Storage Configurations*.

The following table shows the directory paths and template types for a local storage

Directory paths	Template type
`/var/lib/vz/template/iso`	ISO images
`/var/lib/vz/template/cache`	OpenVZ container templates

The following table shows the directory paths and template types for all other storages

Directory paths	Template type
`/mnt/pve/<storage_name>/template/iso`	ISO images
`/mnt/pve/<storage_name>/template/cache`	OpenVZ container templates

Creating a KVM-based virtual machine

Virtual machines are building blocks of a virtual environment. In this recipe, we are going to see how to create a KVM-based virtual machine in a Proxmox cluster.

Getting ready

Upload or download the necessary ISO images or OpenVZ templates, as shown in the preceding recipe. Log in to the Proxmox GUI as the root or any privilege that allows the creation of VMs.

How to do it...

1. Click on **Create VM** to open the VM creation dialog box. The dialog is organized by tabbed menus to configure the VM to be created.

   The following table shows the type of information that needs to be completed for the **General** tab menu:

Menu	Type of values	Description
General	Node	This is the destination node for the VM.
	VM ID	The virtual machine ID is in numerals. The same ID cannot be used for more than one VM.
	Name	This is the alphanumeric string for a VM name.
	Resource pool	Select the pool name this VM is going to belong to. This value is optional. The pool must be precreated to be able to select from this drop-down menu.

   The following screenshot shows the values we have entered under the **General** tab for a VM in our demo cluster:

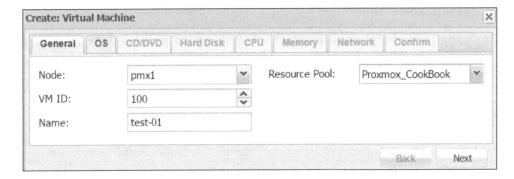

2. Click on **Next** to proceed to the **OS** tabbed menu. The following table shows the type of information that needs to be completed for the **OS** tab menu:

Menu	Type of values
OS	Select an operating system type for the VM.

The OS type optimizes virtual machines based on the type of operating system that is selected.

 It is possible to install Windows on a VM selected as Linux OS type and vice-versa. However, the VM may not function optimally in such cases. With the proper OS type selected, the hypervisor can detect the OS being installed and optimize the VM's performance.

The following screenshot shows the values we have entered for a VM in our demo cluster:

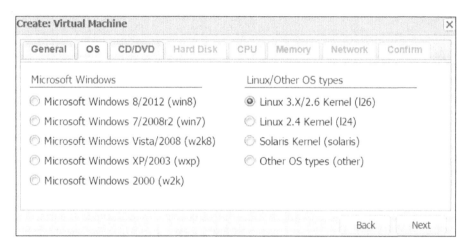

3. Click on **Next** to proceed to the **CD/DVD** tabbed menu. The following table shows the type of information that needs to be completed for the **OS** tab menu:

Menu	Type of values	Description
CD/DVD	**Use CD/DVD disc image file (iso)**	This selects an ISO image already uploaded into the storage.
	Use physical CD/DVD Drive	This selects the physical drive in the Proxmox host instead of an ISO image in storage.
	Do not use any media	Select this not to load any ISO image or physical media at this time.

The following screenshot shows the CentOS ISO image selected for a VM in our demo cluster:

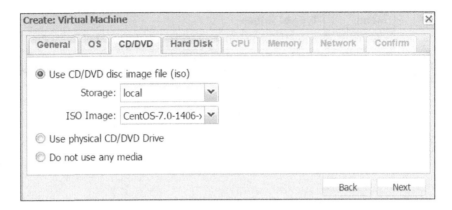

4. Click on **Next** to proceed to the **Hard Disk** tabbed menu. The following table shows the type of information that needs to be completed for the **OS** tab menu:

Menu	Type of values	Description
Hard Disk	Bus/Device	This selects the virtual disk device type. The available options are **IDE**, **SATA**, **VIRTIO**, and **SCSI**. For best performance, select **VIRTIO**. A Windows VM will require additional VirtIO drivers to enable the virtual disk. VirtIO drivers for Windows-based KVM VM can be downloaded at `http://www.linux-kvm.org/page/WindowsGuestDrivers/Download_Drivers`.
	Storage	This selects a storage where the virtual disk will be stored.
	Disk size (GB)	This enters a value for the virtual disk image size in GB.
	Format	This selects the virtual disk image format. The available options are **QEMU**, **RAW**, and **VMDK**. For best performance, select **RAW**. Note that the RAW image format is thick-provisioned, which will allocate the entire disk image size. QEMU and VMDK are thin-provisioned, which will grow as more data is stored in the virtual disk.
	Cache	This selects the caching method for a virtual machine. By default no cache is selected. Available options are: **Default (No cache)**, **Direct sync**, **Writethrough**, **Writeback**, and **Writeback (unsafe)**.
	No backup	This option excludes the VM from all backup schedule.
	Discard	Checking this option enables TRIM, which reclaims unused space of a virtual disk image.

The following screenshot shows the values we have entered for a VM in our demo cluster:

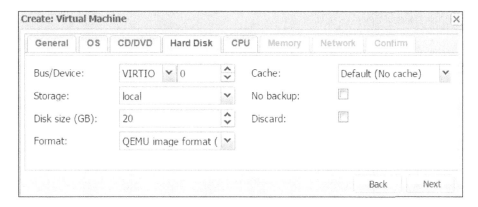

5. Click on **Next** to proceed to the **CPU** tabbed menu. The following table shows the type of information needed to be completed for this menu:

Menu	Type of values	Description
CPU	Sockets	This enters the number of CPU sockets for the VM.
	Cores	This enters number of cores for the VM.
	Enable numa	This option enables the **non-uniform memory access** (**NUMA**) architecture for a VM. Enable this option if the Proxmox host node supports the NUMA architecture. Visit http://en.wikipedia.org/wiki/Non-uniform_memory_access for details on NUMA.
	Type	This selects the appropriate CPU type. By default, KVM64 is selected for maximum compatibility. For maximum performance, select **HOST**. If the VM is going to be migrated to different nodes, be sure the nodes have identical CPUs before selecting **HOST**. It may be difficult to migrate a VM from one host to another with a different CPU type.

The following screenshot shows the values we have entered for a VM in our demo cluster:

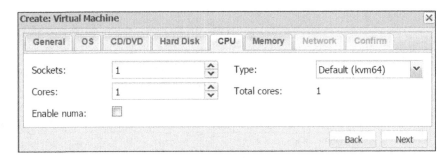

6.   Click on **Next** to proceed to the **Memory** tabbed menu. The following table shows the type of information needed to be completed for this menu:

Menu	Type of values	Description
Memory	**Use fixed size memory**	Select this option and enter the fixed allocated memory size. With this option, all the memory is allocated for the VM.
	Automatically allocate memory within this range	Select this option to allocate a dynamically changing memory range. Depending on the load, memory will be allocated on the fly. For a Windows VM, this option should be avoided. This will increase the CPU load inside the Windows VM.

The following screenshot shows the values we have entered for a VM in our demo cluster:

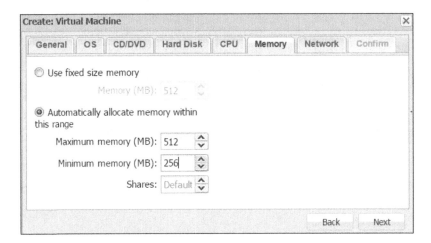

7. Click on **Next** to proceed to the **Network** tabbed menu. The following table shows the type of information needed to be completed for this menu:

Menu	Type of values	Description
Network	**Bridged mode**	Select this option to set up a network interface in the bridge mode. This is the preferred option for a VM network. The bridge mode allows the creation of multiple bridges with VLAN to create an isolated network on the same platform since VMs do not have direct access to the actual local network. Click on the **Firewall** option to enable built-in firewalls for the VM.
	NAT mode	Select this option to give a VM direct access to the network. A VM operates as it was directly connected to the local network similar to other network devices.
	No network device	Select this option to skip configuring network interface at this time.
	Model	Select a network interface driver type. By default, **Intel E1000** is selected. For maximum network performance for a VM, select **VirtIO**. A Windows VM will require an additional VirtIO driver to enable a network interface.
	MAC address	By default, Proxmox creates an automatic unique MAC address for a network interface. Enter a custom MAC address manually, if required
	Rate limit (MB/s)	Enter a numeric value to limit network bandwidth. The value is in MB. Leave blank for no limit.
	Multiqueues	Multiqueues allow the parallel processing of more than one packet, thus increasing network performance. Enter a numeric value to set the number of parallel queues. Note that a value between 4 to 8 multiqueues tend to make network connectivity unstable.
	Disconnect	Click on this option to create a network interface, but do not enable it inside the VM at this time.

The following screenshot shows the values we have entered for a VM in our demo cluster:

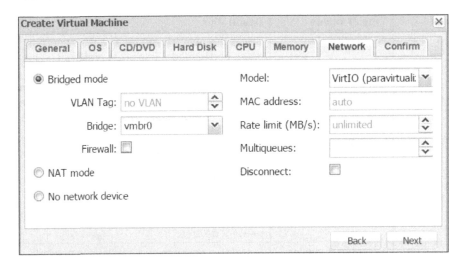

8. Click on **Next** to proceed to the **Confirm** tabbed menu. This menu displays all the values entered or selected for the VM. Check to ensure all the information entered is correct. Then, click on **Finish** to create the VM. If any changes are needed, simply click on a tab or press the **Back** button. The following figure shows the VM with a 100 ID in our demo cluster:

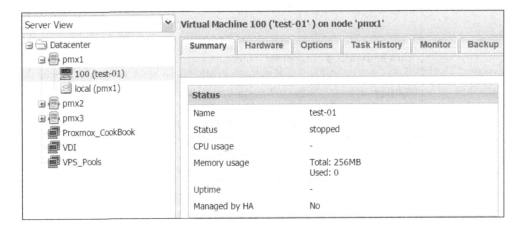

9. It is possible to make further changes to the VM even after it is created. Select the VM, then click on the **Hardware** tab menu to make the necessary changes. However, the changes may not be instant and power cycling the VM may be necessary to initialize these hardware changes. Simply select a hardware and click on **Edit** to make changes.

There's more...

To get the maximum performance possible from a VM, it is important to understand a proper Cache. The Proxmox Wiki has good description of the different caches available at `https://pve.proxmox.com/wiki/Performance_Tweaks#Disk_Cache`.

 Although, by default, Proxmox does not use a cache for overall maximum performance, the writethrough cache is the safest cache to use for a disk image file. If the VM is interrupted abruptly or if the Proxmox host fails, there is no data loss. However, this cache is also the slowest since all the writes are reported only when it is completed or committed to the storage. We can use different virtual disks with different caching on the same VM, thus maximizing performance. For example, the virtual disk with the main operating system can be the writethrough cached. We can create a second virtual disk with a writeback cache to store temporary files, windows page files, and more, which have no consequences if a VM is shutdown abruptly.

In *Chapter 10, Advanced Configurations for VMs*, we will look at some of the advanced features we can change for a VM. Refer back to *Chapter 2, Getting to Know the Proxmox GUI*, to look at both KVM and container-based VM-specific menus and their functions.

Creating an OpenVZ container

In this recipe, we are going to see how to create an OpenVZ container in Proxmox cluster.

Getting ready

Upload or download the necessary ISO images or OpenVZ templates, as shown in the previous section. Log in to the Proxmox GUI as the root or any privilege that allows VM creation.

How to do it...

1. Click on Create CT to open a container creation dialog box. The dialog is also organized by tabbed menus to configure the container that is to be created.

   The following table shows the type of information need to be completed for the **General** tab menu:

Menu	Type of values	Description
General	**Node**	This is the destination node for the container.
	VM ID	This is the container ID in numeric values. The same ID cannot be used for more than one container.
	Hostname	This is the alphanumeric string for a container name.

Menu	Type of values	Description
	Resource Pool	Select the pool name that this VM is going to belong to. This value is optional. A pool must be precreated to be able to select from this drop-down menu.
	Storage	Select a storage where the container will be stored.
	Password	Enter a password for the container.
	Confirm password	Re-enter the password to confirm.

The following screenshot shows the values we have entered under the **General** tab for the container in our demo cluster:

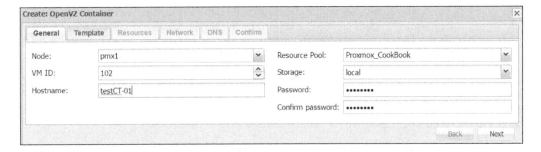

2. Click on **Next** to proceed to the **Template** tabbed menu. The following table shows the type of information needed to be completed for the **Template** menu:

Menu	Type of values	Description
Template	**Storage**	Select the storage where the OpenVZ templates are stored.
	Template	Select a template from the drop-down menu. Templates should be already uploaded or downloaded before creating a container. Refer to the *Managing the ISO and OpenVZ templates* recipe earlier in this chapter for instructions on uploading or downloading of templates.

The following screenshot shows the values we have entered under the **Template** tab for the container in our demo cluster:

3. Click on **Next** to proceed to the **Resources** tabbed menu. The following table shows the type of information needed to be completed for this menu:

Menu	Type of values	Description
Resources	**Memory (MB)**	Enter the amount of memory to be allocated in MB.
	Swap (MB)	Enter the amount of swap space to be allocated in MB.
	Disk size (GB)	Enter the amount of disk image to be allocated in GB.
	CPUs	Enter the number of virtual CPUs for the container.

Following screenshot shows the values we have entered under **Resources** tab for the container in our demo cluster:

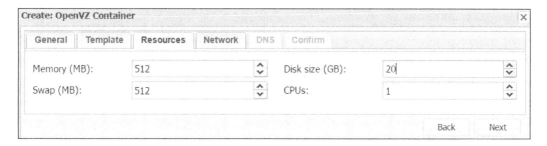

4. Click on **Next** to proceed to the **Network** tabbed menu. The following table shows the type of information need to be completed for this menu:

Menu	Type of values	Description
Network	Routed mode	Select this option to give the container direct access to the local network. It must provide a valid IP address within the local network subnet. This mode gives a VM direct access to the Proxmox host network. Multiple subnetting on the same virtual cluster is not possible with this mode.
	Bridge mode	Select this option to set up networks through bridges. Select **Firewall** to enable the firewall option. The bridge mode allows us to create multiple isolated networks within a virtual environment. Each virtual bridge acts as a separate network switch where VMs are connected.

The following screenshot shows the values we have entered under the **Network** tab for the container in our demo cluster:

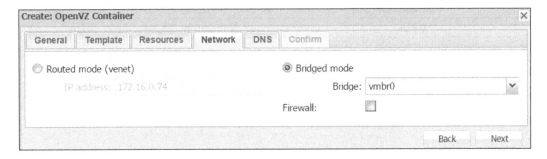

5. Click on **Next** to proceed to the **DNS** tabbed menu. The following table shows the type of information needed to be completed for this menu:

Menu	Type of values	Description
DNS	DNS domain	Enter a domain name or leave it blank.
	DNS server 1	Enter the first DNS server IP address. This is only enabled when a domain name is entered.
	DNS server 2	Enter a second DNS server IP address. This is only enabled when a domain name is entered.

The following screenshot shows the values we have entered under the **DNS** tab for the container in our demo cluster:

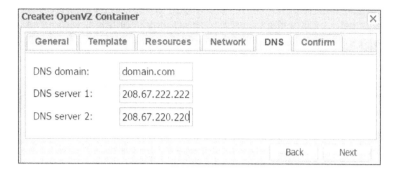

6. Click on **Next** to proceed to the **Confirm** tabbed menu. This menu displays all the values entered or selected for the container. Check to ensure that all the information entered is correct. Then, click on **Finish** to create the container. If any changes are needed, simply click on a tab or press the **Back** button.

The following figure shows the container with a `101` ID in our demo cluster:

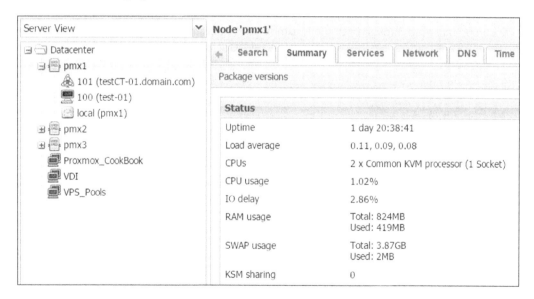

There's more...

As with a KVM-based VM, we can also make changes to the container after it is created. However, changes gets applied immediately to the OpenVZ container without requiring a power cycle. Refer to the *Accessing OpenVZ-specific menus* recipe in *Chapter 2, Getting to Know the Proxmox GUI*, to see all available menu options for OpenVZ containers.

Migrating a virtual machine

Migration is one of the commonly performed tasks in a clustered environment, where a VM may be moved to a different node in the cluster due to various reasons. Here are some of the possible scenarios where VM migration may be necessary:

- ▶ Physical node failure
- ▶ A node requiring reboot after applying updates or hardware maintenance
- ▶ Moving a VM from a low-performing to a high-performing node

Getting ready

A VM can be migrated through both the Proxmox GUI or CLI with or without powering down the VM. First, we are going to see how to migrate using a GUI, and later we will see the CLI steps of VM migration.

How to do it...

This recipe is to show VM migration using the Proxmox GUI. Let's take a look at the following steps:

1. Log in to the Proxmox GUI.
2. Select the VM to be migrated. Then, click on the **Migrate** button, as shown in the following screenshot:

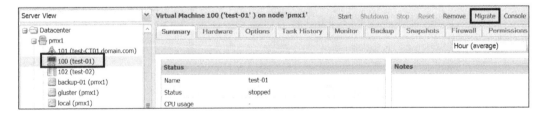

Clicking on the **Migrate** button opens a migration dialog box, as shown in the following screenshot:

3. Select a destination node where the VM will be migrated to. Select the **Online** checkbox if the VM is powered up and needs to do an online migration. Click on **Migrate** to start the migration process. The same GUI option will perform migration for both the KVM VM and OpenVZ containers.

How to do it...

This recipe is to show VM migration using a CLI. There are two different commands available for KVM and OpenVZ-based VMs, shown as follows:

▶   To migrate a KVM VM through a CLI, enter the following command through SSH or Shell:

```
#qm migrate <vm_id> <target_node_name> -online
```

▶   To migrate an OpenVZ container through a CLI, enter the following command through SSH or Shell:

```
#vzmigrate <target_node_name/IP> <ct_id> --live
```

> Use the -online option for KVM and the -live option for containers when commencing live migrations.

How it works...

To migrate a VM live or online, the virtual disk image must be stored on a shared storage. Online migration provides maximum uptime, while it is also slower. The reason is during online migration without powering down, the process has to copy the entire memory content of the VM to the new node. The larger the allocated memory of the VM, the longer it will take to migrate.

When a virtual disk image of a VM is stored on the local storage of a Proxmox node, online migration is not possible. In such cases, a VM must be powered down before migrating. During locally stored VM migration, Proxmox will copy the entire virtual disk using **rsync** to the target node. To be able to commit online migrations, the virtual disk must be stored on a shared storage. We will take a look at the different storage options that can be used with Proxmox in *Chapter 6, Storage Configurations*.

Cloning a virtual machine

Cloning allows mass creation of identically configured VM in Proxmox clusters. This saves lots of time from setting up many VMs individually. Cloning can only be done on a KVM-based VM. We cannot create a clone from an OpenVZ container. In this recipe, we will see how VMs are cloned in Proxmox and how to create a template for cloning.

Getting ready

All VM cloning features are accessible through the Proxmox GUI. Log in to the GUI as the root or any other privilege, which allows for VM creation.

How to do it...

Use the following steps for cloning VMs in Proxmox:

1. Create a VM with the necessary configurations or use an already existing VM to customize. Ensure that the configuration of the VM is as desired because all clones created from this VM will have identical configurations.

2. Right-click on the VM to open the context menu.

3. From the menu, select **Clone** to open a cloning dialog box, as shown in the following screenshot:

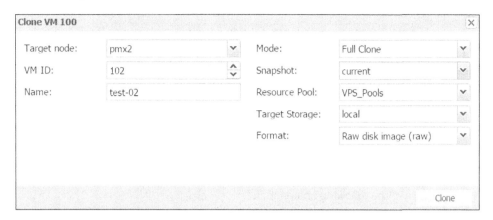

The following table shows the type of information needed to be completed before clicking on the **Clone** button to start cloning:

Type of values	Description
Target node	This selects the target node for the cloned VM.
VM ID	This enters an ID for the VM.
Name	This is an alphanumeric string for VM name.
Mode	This selects a cloning method. The available options are **Full Clone** and **Linked Clone**. A full clone creates a fully independent replica of an original VM, whereas a linked clone creates a VM that needs the original VM to function. Since a linked VM is dependent on an original VM, it requires less storage space than a full cloned VM.
Snapshot	This selects a snapshot to create the clone from. If there are multiple snapshots available for the VM, it can be selected from drop-down menu.
Resource Pool	This selects a pool that the VM will belong to.
Target Storage	This selects a storage for the cloned virtual disk.
Format	This selects a virtual disk image format.

4. Click on Clone to start the cloning process.

We can also create a template of a VM for purely cloning purposes. A VM that is converted to a template cannot be powered on or reverted back to a functioning VM.

 Note that the term "template for cloning" is not the same as "template for OpenVZ container". Here, "template" only refers to a master VM from which cloned VMs are created. Converting a VM ensures that the original configuration of the VM will never change since it can be powered up.

The following steps are used to convert a VM into a template for cloning:

1. Right-click on a VM to open the context menu.

2. Select **Convert to template**. When prompted to confirm the template creation, click on **Yes**. In our demo cluster, we converted a 102 VM named test-02 to a template, as shown in the following screenshot:

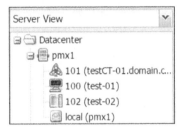

 Note that VMs converted to templates have a unique icon to identify them easily, as we can see from the preceding screenshot where the test-02 VM is now a template.

The steps to create new clones from this templates are the same as laid out in this recipe.

There's more...

Keep in mind that only KVM-based VMs can be converted to templates for cloning purposes. The OpenVZ container has no **Convert to template** option. Templates can be very useful when creating a large number of VMs of similar configurations. Multiple templates can be created with separate configurations and use separate pools to categorize them. For example, a VPS hosting company may create templates based on their different VPS offerings and when a client makes a VPS purchase, their VPS can simply be cloned from a template.

 As of Proxmox VE 3.4, there is no autocloning option available.

Managing a virtual disk image

A virtual disk image is the heart of a virtual machine, where all the VM data is stored. In this recipe, we are going to see how to accomplish tasks, such as adding, resizing, and moving a virtual disk image file. A virtual disk image can be managed through the Proxmox GUI.

How to do it...

Use the following steps to add a virtual disk image to a VM:

1. Log in to the GUI as the root or any other privilege, which allows disk image and storage manipulation.

2. Select a VM from the left navigation menu. Then, click on the **Hardware** tab. After selecting a disk image, all the related menus become available, such as **Add**, **Remove**, **Edit**, **Resize disk**, **Move disk**, and **Disk Throttle**.

3. To add additional disk images to the VM, click on **Add: Hard Disk** to open a dialog box, as shown in the following screenshot:

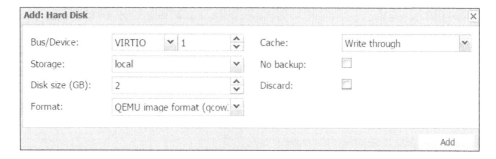

The information that needs to be completed is identical to the **Hard disk** tab menu for the *Creating a KVM-based virtual machine* recipe.

4. After entering the necessary values, click on Add to finish adding the virtual disk. In our example, we add a 2 GB virtual disk image to the 100 VM.

For the disk image to be available inside the VM without power cycling it, the hot plug option needs to configured. We will discuss more on hot plugging in *Chapter 10, Advanced Configurations for VMs*.

Here are the steps to remove a virtual disk:

1. Select a disk image of the VM.

2. Click on **Remove**.

3. Click on **Yes** to confirm when prompted.

When a virtual disk is removed from the VM for the first time, it only detaches itself, but is not completely deleted. It detaches itself from the VM and lists as "Unused Disk", as shown in the following screenshot:

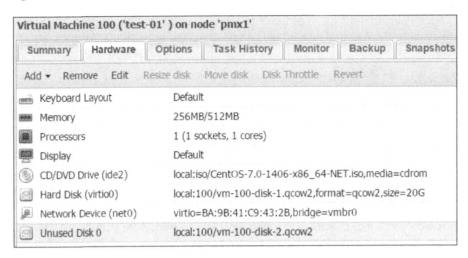

To permanently delete the disk image, select the unused disk, then click on **Remove**. If a disk image has been removed by mistake, simply reattach it to the VM again by following these steps:

1. Select the unused disk.

2. Click on **Edit** open a dialog box.

3. From the dialog box, change **Bus/Device** if needed.

4. Click on Add to reattach the disk image.

As of Proxmox VE 3.4, it is only possible to increase the size of the disk image, but not decrease it.

 Care should be taken when decreasing the size of a virtual disk. If the amount of space that needs to be decreased contains any data, it will be erased permanently.

Here are the steps to resize the disk to the desired size:

1. Select a virtual disk image.

2. Click on **Resize** to open the dialog box.

3. Enter a value to increase the disk size. For example, if the existing disk size is 20 GB, type in 10 GB to resize the disk to 30 GB.

4. Click on **Resize Disk** to finish resizing.

Note that the resize feature only resizes the disk image from outside the VM and a full power cycle of the VM may be needed to see the resized space. Additional tasks, such as resizing partitions or filesystems inside a virtual machine must be performed by following the instructions for operating systems in use.

Virtual disk images can be moved from one storage to another within the same cluster. These steps will perform the task to move a disk image:

1. Select a disk image to be moved.

2. Click on **Move disk** from the menu to open a dialog box, as shown in the following screenshot:

3. Select **Target Storage** from the drop-down menu. The target storage is where the virtual disk image is going to be moved.

4. Select the **Format** disk image from the drop-down menu, if necessary. This is a useful option to convert disk images from one format to another.

5. Select the **Delete source** checkbox to automatically delete a source disk image after it is moved to a new storage.

6. Click on **Move disk** to start moving a disk image.

To limit the disk access bandwidth and operations per second, the **Disk Throttle** option can be used. These steps will perform disk throttling for a disk image:

1. Select a disk image to be throttled.

2. Click on **Disk Throttle** from the menu to open a dialog box.

3. Enter the bandwidth limit in MBs and the number of operations per second as numeric values. The burst limit can also be set from the same dialog box. Values can be entered for all the limits or just read/write limits.

4. Click on **OK** to save the limit or **Reset** to remove all the custom values.

   The following screenshot shows the disk throttling dialog box:

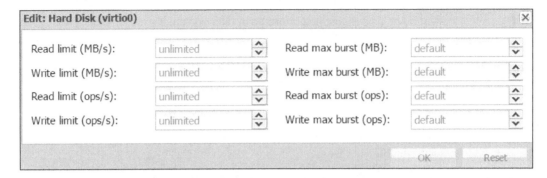

Managing OpenVZ containers

In this recipe, we are going to see how to manage an OpenVZ container to perform tasks, such as resource and network management through the Proxmox GUI.

How to do it...

The following steps show how to change container resources, such as CPU, memory, and disk space:

1. Log in to the GUI as the root or another administrative privileged user.

2. Select a container from the left navigation pane. Then, click on the **Resource** tab, as shown in the following screenshot:

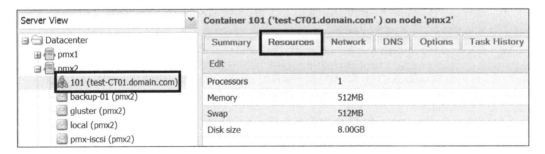

3. Click on any line item to change **Processors**, **Memory**, **Swap**, and **Disk size** and then click on **Edit**.

4. Each item will open a dialog box to change values. After the desired values have been entered, click on **OK** to finalize the changes.

The following steps show how to change the network interface for container:

1.   Click on the **Network** tab while the container is selected from the left navigation pane. The display will list all the virtual network interfaces configured for the container, as shown in the following screenshot:

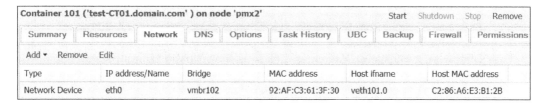

| Container 101 ('test-CT01.domain.com') on node 'pmx2' | | | | Start | Shutdown | Stop | Remove |

| Summary | Resources | Network | DNS | Options | Task History | UBC | Backup | Firewall | Permissions |

Add ▾   Remove   Edit

Type	IP address/Name	Bridge	MAC address	Host ifname	Host MAC address
Network Device	eth0	vmbr102	92:AF:C3:61:3F:30	veth101.0	C2:86:A6:E3:B1:2B

2.   Select the interface, then click on **Edit** to make changes. By clicking on **Add** or **Remove**, we can add a new interface or delete existing one. After clicking on **Edit**, a dialog box will open, as shown in the following screenshot:

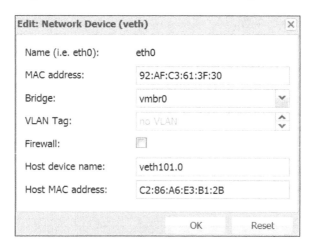

Edit: Network Device (veth)   ✕

Name (i.e. eth0):	eth0
MAC address:	92:AF:C3:61:3F:30
Bridge:	vmbr0
VLAN Tag:	no VLAN
Firewall:	☐
Host device name:	veth101.0
Host MAC address:	C2:86:A6:E3:B1:2B

OK   Reset

3.   After making necessary changes, click on **OK** to accept the values.

Understanding OpenVZ user bean counters

User Bean Counters (**UBC**) is the vital component of OpenVZ containers. These counters are set to a limit, which controls how resources are distributed among containers to guarantee proper container operations. For most containers, these limit values can be left as default. In some cases, changing the values may be necessary depending on the load of the container. The Proxmox GUI can only show the values. Any changes needs to be made through a CLI.

How to do it...

The following steps shows how to view the runtime values of a container through the Proxmox GUI:

1. Log in to the Proxmox GUI.

2. Select a container from the left navigation pane, then click on the **UBC** tabbed menu. If the container is not running, the UBC display will not show any values at all. Otherwise, it will show the counter values, as shown in the following screenshot:

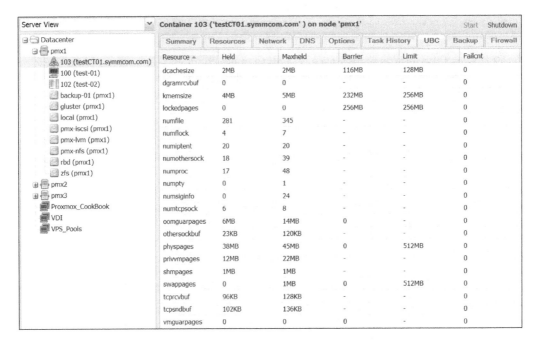

Resource ▲	Held	Maxheld	Barrier	Limit	Failcnt
dcachesize	2MB	2MB	116MB	128MB	0
dgramrcvbuf	0	0	-	-	0
kmemsize	4MB	5MB	232MB	256MB	0
lockedpages	0	0	256MB	256MB	0
numfile	281	345	-	-	0
numflock	4	7	-	-	0
numiptent	20	20	-	-	0
numothersock	18	39	-	-	0
numproc	17	48	-	-	0
numpty	0	1	-	-	0
numsiginfo	0	24	-	-	0
numtcpsock	6	8	-	-	0
oomguarpages	6MB	14MB	0	-	0
othersockbuf	23KB	120KB	-	-	0
physpages	38MB	45MB	0	512MB	0
privvmpages	12MB	22MB	-	-	0
shmpages	1MB	1MB	-	-	0
swappages	0	1MB	0	512MB	0
tcprcvbuf	96KB	128KB	-	-	0
tcpsndbuf	102KB	136KB	-	-	0
vmguarpages	0	0	0	-	0

The following steps show how to change a limit for a UBC container through a CLI:

1. Log in through a console or SSH into the Proxmox node where the OpenVZ container is hosted.

2. From the Proxmox GUI, get the resource name for which the limit needs to be changed.

3. The following command format will change the limit for a resource:

```
#vzctl set <ct_id> --<resource_name> <barrier>:<limit> --save
```

 The `barrier` value cannot be greater than the `limit` value.

For our example, we are going to change the `kmemsize` value for the container #103 to 288 MB as the limit and 260 MB as the barrier. The following command will change the `kmemsize` limit:

```
#vzctl set 103 --kmemsize 260m:288m –save
```

If the command is successful, it will display a message, as shown in following screenshot, after saving the configuration:

```
root@pmx1:~# vzctl set 103 --kmemsize 260m:288m --save
UB limits were set successfully
CT configuration saved to /etc/pve/openvz/103.conf
```

4. Validate the new configuration changes using the following command:

```
#vzcfgvalidate /etc/vz/conf/103.conf
```

How it works...

The UBC displays a table of various resources with the current, maximum, limit, and number of error values. The column to pay attention is **Failcnt**, which shows the number of failures or the number of times that a particular resource has hit a limit. These values are stored in:

▸ `/proc/user_beancounters` for older OpenVZ

▸ `/proc/bc/<ct_id>/resources` for newer OpenVZ

When changing the values of resources using the `vzctl` command, by default, the command will use bytes or pages as default units. If we want to use different units, we must add suffixes as following:

▸ K or k for KBs

▸ M or m for MBs

▸ G or g for GBs

▸ P or p for pages

In our example recipe, to increase value of `kmemsize`, we have used m to increase the value in MBs.

Note that when changing values for any resources, the `barrier` value cannot be greater than the `limit` value.

See also

▸ Although there are various type of resources in OpenVZ container, the full details of each of them is beyond the scope of this book. For further information on user bean counters, refer to `https://openvz.org/UBC`, `https://openvz.org/UBC_parameter_units` and `https://openvz.org/Resource_shortage`.

4

Network Configurations

We will cover the following topics in this chapter:

- ▶ Configuring a basic network
- ▶ Configuring a bridge
- ▶ Configuring VLAN
- ▶ Configuring network bonding
- ▶ Configuring Network Address Translation
- ▶ Configuring Infiniband
- ▶ Configuring a VM network interface
- ▶ Configuring High Availability

Introduction

In this chapter, we are going to see how a network is configured in Proxmox. Networking acts as glue to bind virtual machines to each other and to a cluster. Like many other hypervisors, Proxmox uses the bridged networking model.

Configuring a basic network

In the recipe, we are going to see how to configure a network in Proxmox. Later recipes in the chapter will cover different components of networking.

Getting ready

Before diving into network configuration, it is important to know that network configuration can be done through a GUI and CLI in Proxmox. Configurations done through a GUI will require a reboot to activate, whereas configurations made through a CLI can be applied in real time.

Configurations applied through a GUI get written in a network configuration file, `/etc/network/interfaces.new`. After the node reboot, the new configuration gets transferred permanently to `/etc/network/interfaces`. If a node reboot is not possible right away, the configuration should be done through a CLI by editing `/etc/network/interface` directly.

How to do it...

Here are the steps are to configure networking through the Proxmox GUI:

1. To edit network configurations through a GUI, log in as a root into the Proxmox GUI.

2. Click on a node to see the **Network** tabbed menu, as shown in the following screenshot:

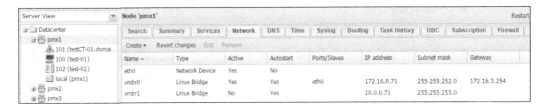

3. To create a new network interface, click on **Create** for a drop-down menu, as shown in the following screenshot:

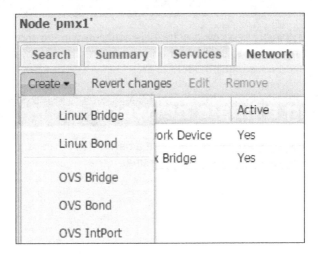

Note that through the Proxmox GUI, we can only create bridge and bond interfaces. Any physical interfaces installed in the host can only be configured and not created.

When a change is made through the Proxmox GUI, **Pending changes** appears, as shown in the following screenshot, before a reboot is commenced:

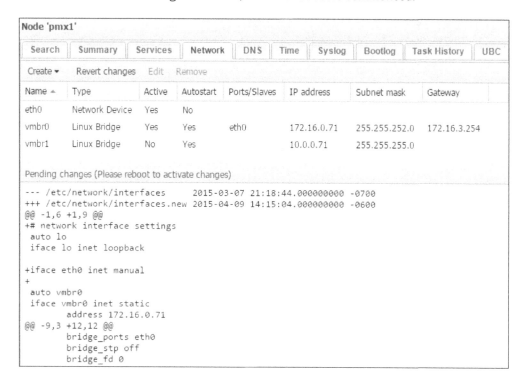

4. To revert the changes before rebooting, simply click on **Revert changes**. This will undo all the changes in /etc/network/interfaces.new.

The following steps are needed in order to configure networking through the Proxmox GUI:

1. Log in to the Proxmox node using an SSH program, such as PuTTY.

2. Open /etc/network/interfaces with an editor.

3. Make the necessary changes to the configuration. For example, if we want to configure a second network interface with a static IP in the node, we will make the following changes:

```
# nano /etc/network/interfaces
auto eth2
iface eth2 inet static
    address 192.168.1.1
    netmask 255.255.255.0
    gateway 192.168.1.254
    bridge_ports eth2
    bridge_stp off
    bridge_fd 0
#ifup eth2
```

4. Save and exit the editor.

5. Bring the new interface online by running the following command:

   #ifup eth2

 If the changes were for any existing interface, it will be necessary to offline the interface using the following command and then bring it online again:

#ifdown eth2

There's more...

As of Proxmox VE 3.4, a physical network interface cannot be configured directly for a particular virtual machine. All VMs must be configured with a bridge or network bond. This applies to both KVM virtual machines and OpenVZ containers.

Configuring a bridge

In this recipe, we are going to see what a bridge is in Proxmox networking, and how to configure it to create a virtual network of VMs.

Getting ready

A bridge is a virtual implementation of a physical network switch. Virtual machines can be connected to a bridge much in the same way that a physical computer can be connected to a network switch to communicate with other network devices. The naming term for a bridge interface is vmbrX, where X can be an integer number from 0 to maximum of 4096. By default, a new Proxmox installation creates a bridge named vmbr0 in each node.

Each bridge can be attached to a physical network interface of a node or without it. A bridge configured without any physical network interface cannot direct traffic outside the node itself. The traffic can only flow in between whichever VMs are connected to this physical interfaceless bridge. The following diagram shows a network diagram of a bridge with and without a physical network interface:

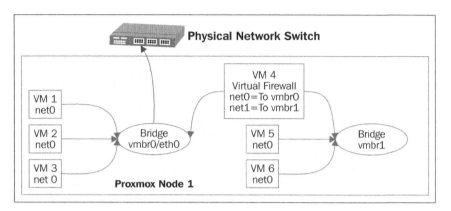

In the preceding diagram, **VM 1**, **VM 2**, and **VM 3** are directly connected to the **vmbr0** bridge. The bridge is configured with a **eth0** physical network interface, which is connected to a physical switch. **VM 4** is configured as a virtual firewall, which has two virtual network interfaces, **net0** and **net1**. The **net0** interface is connected to the **vmbr0** bridge and the **net1** interface is connected to a **vmbr1** bridge along with **VM 5** and **VM 6**. The **vmbr1** bridge is not configured with any physical interfaces, therefore, **VM 5** and **VM 6** can only communicate with each other and **VM 4**.

Only one physical network interface can be configured per bridge. An interface used in a bridge cannot be used in another bridge. By creating multiple bridges for groups of VMs, we can create an isolated virtual network within the same virtual environment. Utilizing a virtual firewall for each group of VMs can be Internet enabled without compromising on isolation.

How to do it...

The following steps are needed to create a virtual bridge through the Proxmox GUI. For our example, we are going to create bridge named vmbr1, without a physical network interface:

1. Select a node from the left navigation view where the bridge will be configured.
2. Click on the **Network** tabbed menu.

3. Click on **Create** to open a drop-down menu, then select **Linux Bridge** to open a bridge creation dialog box, as shown in the following screenshot:

4. For a bridge without any physical interface, we are going to leave all the boxes blank, except the **Name** textbox. To assign a physical interface to a bridge, simply enter the interface name, such as `eth0`, `eth1`, and so on, in the **Bridge Ports** textbox.

5. After entering necessary information, click on **Create** to finish creating the `vmbr1` bridge.

   The following screenshot shows the newly created bridge with a pending reboot since the changes were made through the Proxmox GUI:

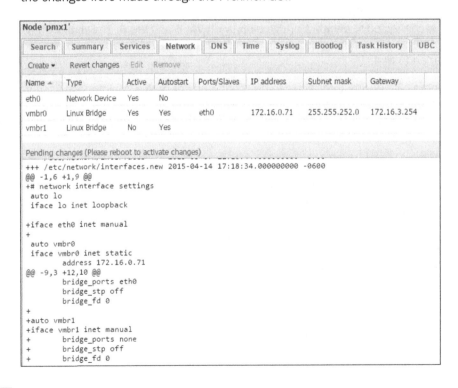

The following steps are needed to create a virtual bridge through a CLI:

1. Log in to the Proxmox node through SSH or directly from a console.

2. Open the network configuration files in `/etc/network/interfaces` with an editor.

3. Add a new bridge with the following configuration format. In our example, we add a new virtual bridge named `vmbr1`:

   ```
   auto vmbr1
   iface vmbr1`inet manual
        bridge_ports none
        bridge_stp off
        bridge_fd 0
   #ifup vmbr1
   ```

4. Save the file and exit.

5. Activate the bridge with the following command:

   ```
   #ifup vmbr1
   ```

How it works...

Bridge configurations are node-specific. For example, if there is a bridge named vmbr1 in node 1 where VM 2 is connected, we have to create another bride vmbr1 in node 2 if we are to migrate VM 2 to this node. If a bridge is connected to a physical interface that is connected to a switch along with other Proxmox nodes in the cluster, then inter communication between VMs on multiple nodes is possible. A bridge without a physical network interface is limited to the node where it exists.

As a general good practice, it is advised to duplicate bridge configurations on all Proxmox nodes so that VM migration can occur with minimal downtime.

There's more...

To create a virtual network of any size, a good understanding of bridges is essential. If you have access to a Proxmox cluster and know how to create bridges, it will be beneficial to spend some time creating multiple bridges on different nodes as a hands-on practice. Here is an example of a network diagram of a fictional cloud service provider company where bridges are used extensively:

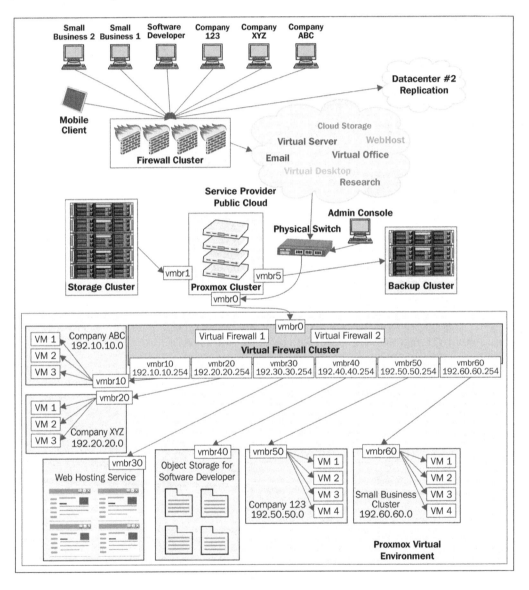

Configuring VLAN

A **Virtual LAN** (**VLAN**) is a network standard based on 802.1q to create a logical partition on the same network interface to isolate traffic for multiple networks. In this recipe, we will see how to configure VLAN in Proxmox networking.

Getting ready

In order for a VLAN to work, the physical switch in a network environment must be VLAN capable. Almost all smart and managed switches have VLAN capability. Check your switch manual before configuring VLAN in Proxmox. The following screenshot shows the management panel of Netgear GS748T, which is a 48 port Gigabit smart switch with VLAN ability:

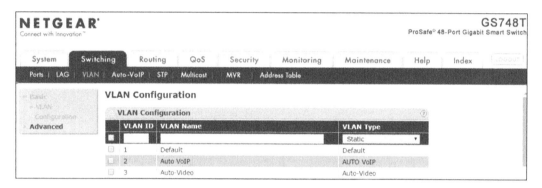

Each VLAN is assigned a unique integer number called **VLAN tag**. There can be a maximum of 4096 tags. A tag is unique for a logical network or for each VLAN in the same network media. Any network device or interface in the network configured with a VLAN tag can only communicate with a device or interface with same VLAN tag, thus keeping network traffic isolated. Network packets get tagged by a switch with a defined VLAN tag.

For details on VLAN, visit `http://en.wikipedia.org/wiki/Virtual_LAN`.

How to do it...

In Proxmox, there are two ways we can assign VLAN to a virtual machine. They are as follows:

► Assign a VLAN tag to each VM network interface. This can be done through a GUI.
► Create a VLAN subinterface and dedicated virtual bridge. This must be done through a CLI.

Both procedures produce a similar VLAN result. However, depending on the use case scenario, one may be preferable over the other. By assigning a VLAN tag to each VM network interface, VM can talk directly to a switch. With a VLAN subinterface and dedicated bridge, each VM is connected to a VLAN tagged bridge and no individual VM tagging is required.

The following steps are used to assign a VLAN tag to each VM network interface separately through the Proxmox GUI:

1. Select a node from left navigation bar.

2. Click on the **Hardware** tabbed menu, then select **Network Device**.

3. Click on **Edit** to open dialog box, as shown in the following screenshot:

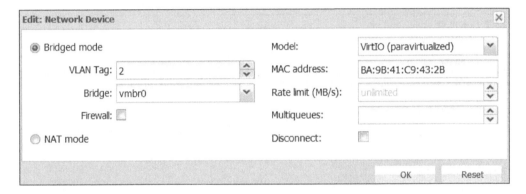

4. Type in the numeric VLAN ID in the **VLAN Tag** textbox. In our example, we have added VLAN ID as 2.

5. Click on **OK** to finish.

6. Power cycle the VM to activate the VLAN tag.

   The following screenshot shows the VM network interface with the VLAN tag added:

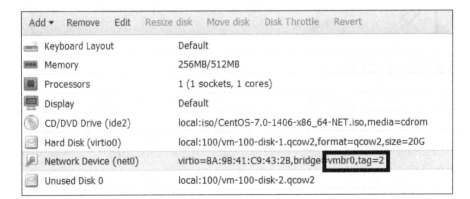

The following steps shows how to create a VLAN subinterface and dedicated bridge for VLAN through a CLI:

1. Log in through SSH or putty as a root or a similar administrative access.

2. Using a text editor, open the Proxmox host network configuration file:

   #nano /etc/network/interfaces

3. Add the following lines to create a VLAN subinterface. Change the interface according to your environment. For our example, we are using the eth2 interface to create a VLAN subinterface for VLAN ID 2:

```
auto vlan2
iface vlan2 inet manual
      vlan_raw_device eth2
auto vmbr2
iface vmbr2 inet manual
      bridge_ports vlan2
      bridge_stp off
      bridge_fd 0
```

4. Save and exit the text editor.

5. Run the following command to activate the VLAN subinterface and bridge without rebooting:

   #ifup vlan2

   #ifup vmbr2

6. Assign the bridge to the VM, as shown in the following screenshot:

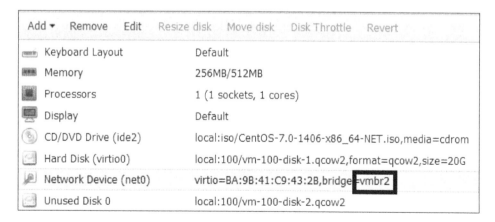

How it works...

In a scenario where VLAN tags are assigned to each VM virtual network interface, all VMs are connected to a single bridge.

By creating VLAN subinterfaces, we can create multiple bridges for multiple VLANs on the same physical network interface. The following are content network configurations in /etc/network/interfaces, where three VLAN subinterfaces are created on one physical network interface along with three dedicated bridges:

```
auto vlan10
iface vlan10 inet manual
    vlan_raw_device eth1
auto vlan20
iface vlan20 inet manual
    vlan_raw_device eth1
auto vlan30
iface vlan30 inet manual
    vlan_raw_device eth1

auto vmbr10
iface vmbr10 inet manual
    bridge_ports vlan10
    bridge_stp off
    bridge_fd 0
auto vmbr20
iface vmbr20 inet manual
    bridge_ports vlan20
    bridge_stp off
    bridge_fd 0
auto vmbr30
iface vmbr30 inet manual
    bridge_ports vlan30
    bridge_stp off
    bridge_fd 0
```

While assigning names to bridges, it is a good idea to assign the same number as the VLAN ID. This way, it is easy to discern which VLAN a bridge belongs to.

Configuring network bonding

Network bonding, trunking, or link aggregation is a process where several network interfaces are combined to create a large bandwidth or implement redundancy for network connectivity. In this recipe, we are going to see the types of bonding and how to create bonding configurations.

Getting ready

Before configuring bondings, it is important to know the types or different modes of bonding that are available and what they have to offer. Only one type of bonding can be configured at a time. The following table shows the bond types and their features. Note that the table is for information purposes only:

Mode	Feature	Fault Tolerance	Special switch
0	**Round-robin**: These are packets sent sequentially on all member network ports.	Yes	No
1	**Active-backup**: Only one member port is active at a time.	Yes	No
2	**Balance XOR**: These are packets sent through member ports based on selectable hashing algorithms.	Yes	No
3	**Broadcast**: These are packets that are sent on all member ports.	Yes	No
4	**802.3ad or LACP**: These are packets that are sent based on a 802.3ad specification through an aggregation group on the same speed and settings.	Yes	Yes
5	**Balance TLB**: These are packets that are sent according to the load through all member ports. Incoming packets are received by a current port. During port failure, the new port gains the MAC address of a failed port.	Yes	No
6	**Balance ALB**: This is similar to mode 5, but also receives packets on all the ports through an ARP negotiation.	Yes	No

Bonding mode 2 and 4 use hashing algorithms to transmit network packets. Here are three hashing policies available in Proxmox bonding:

Hash policy	Description
Layer 2	This policy sends data packets to a network device on the same member port. A hash is generated using an XOR of a MAC address.
Layer 2+3	This policy also sends data packets to a network device on the same member port. A hash is generated using both XORs of MAC addresses and an IP address.
Layer 3+4	This policy sends data packets to a network device spanning all member ports. A hash is generated using higher protocol layer information.

Regardless of different modes of network bonding, the configuration process is the same for all modes. A bonding interface can be created through both a Proxmox GUI and a CLI.

How to do it...

Before bonding can be used in Proxmox, there are some modules that need to be loaded in a kernel. They are as follows:

- The `bonding` module
- The `mii` module

We can load them during a boot by adding them in separate lines in `/etc/modules`. To check if bonding modules are available to load or not, we can run the following command from a CLI:

`#modprobe bonding`

If a module is not found, then we have to install `ifenslave` with the following command:

`#apt-get install ifenslave-2.6`

The following steps show how to create a bonding interface through the Proxmox GUI:

1. Select a node from the left navigation bar.
2. Click on the **Hardware** tabbed menu, then select **Network Device**.

3. Click on Edit to open dialog box, as shown in the following screenshot:

4. Type in the necessary information in the dialog box. All ports that are going to be part of the bond must be entered in the **Slaves** textbox separated by a space. If mode 2 or 4 are selected, then select the desired hashing policy also. In our example, we have named our bond `bond0`, which will include the `eth3` and `eth4` member ports. The **balance-xor** mode has been selected with the **layer2** hashing policy.

5. Click on **Create** to finish.

6. Reboot the Proxmox node to activate the bonding.

The following steps show how to create bonding through a CLI:

1. Log in through SSH or PuTTY as a root or a similar administrative access.

2. Using a text editor, open the Proxmox host network configuration file:

   ```
   #nano /etc/network/interfaces
   ```

3. Add the following lines to create a bonding interface. Change the interface name according to your environment. For our example, we use the `eth3` and `eth4` interfaces to create bonding:

   ```
   auto bond0
   iface bond0 inet manual
           slaves eth3 eth4
           bond_miimon 100
           bond_mode balance-xor
           bond_xmit_hash_policy layer2
   ```

4. Save and exit the text editor.

5. Run the following command to activate the bonding interface:

   ```
   #ifup bond0
   ```

A bonding interface can be used with a bridge in a similar way to a standard interface. Simply replace the bridge port with an appropriate bond interface as follows:

```
auto vmbr0
iface vmbr0 inet manual
bridge_ports bond0
bridge_stp off
bridge_fd 0
```

There's more...

Bonding can be an excellent, economical way to increase the overall network throughput or simply create a redundant network connection to increase uptime. A clear understanding of different bonding modes will aid in the selection of the right mode for different requirements. For example, using multiple switches and network interfaces, we can easily create a round-robin bonding, which provides redundancy not just for network cables but also for network switches. The network may resemble the following diagram:

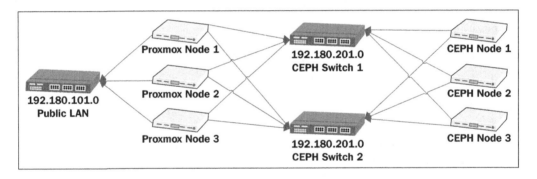

In the preceding diagram, the Proxmox and Ceph storage nodes are connected to two physical switches. Network interfaces on all nodes are configured with a balance-rr bonding. In this scenario, if switch 1 fails, all the nodes will still function with switch 2.

Although this works, it is not a recommended setup for critical production environments. Due to packet loss in this policy, packets are often resent.

Configuring Network Address Translation

In this recipe, we are going to see what **Network Address Translation** (**NAT**) is and how to configure it in Proxmox.

Getting ready

NAT is a networking technique that allows a node with a private IP in a network connect to the Internet through a NAT-enabled interface or router without needing an Internet-based public IP. NAT also provides security since the original IP remains hidden behind NAT.

Without NAT, each device would require a public IP in order to connect to the Internet. With the scarcity of IPv4 IP addresses and the high cost of obtaining them, NAT provides a solution for networks of all sizes.

In Proxmox, a NAT configuration can only be done through a CLI.

How to do it...

IP forwarding must be allowed in order for NAT to work. By default, it is not enabled. The following steps show how to enable IP forwarding, then configure NAT for a network interface:

1. Use a text editor to open the /etc/sysctl.conf file:

   #nano /etc/sysctl.conf

2. Uncomment the following line:

   net.ipv4.ip_forward=1

3. Save the file and reboot to activate the change.

4. Open the network interface configuration with a text editor:

   #nano /etc/network/interfaces

5. Add and remove the configurations from an interface as follows. Changes made to the configuration are shown in bold:

   auto vmbr0

   iface vmbr0 inet static

   address 192.168.10.1

   netmask 255.255.255.0

   bridge_ports none

   bridge_stp off

```
bridge_fd 0

post-up echo 1 > /proc/sys/net/ipv4/ip_forward
post-up iptables -t nat -A POSTROUTING -s '192.168.10.0/24' -o
eth0 -j MASQUERADE
post-down iptables -t nat -D POSTROUTING -s '192.168.10.0/24'
-o eth0 -j MASQUERADE
```

6. Save the configuration file and reboot to activate the changes.

How it works...

Based on the configuration made in the previous section, all traffic on the vmbr0 virtual interface passes through eth0, while all the IP information of VMs remains hidden behind the vmbr0 bridge.

This result can also be achieved by using a virtualized firewall, where the firewall acts as a NAT device for VMs and the Internet. It should be noted that although NAT provides security on networks, a firewall, either physical or virtualized one, should always be in place.

Configuring Infiniband

In this recipe, we are going to see what Infiniband is and how it can be configured to create a high bandwidth network for a Proxmox cluster.

Getting ready

With very low latency, **Infiniband** (**IB**) competes with gigabit, 10 GbE and 100 GbE. Originated in 1999, Infiniband continues to provide the means to create high-performing cluster beating Ethernet both on latency and price. IB is an excellent choice for connecting a storage cluster to a compute cluster in a virtual environment. Linux provides full support for IBs. Some kernel modules must be loaded in order to use IB. Network configuration is similar to any other interface. IB configuration must be done through a CLI. It cannot be edited or configured through the Proxmox GUI.

 For more information on Inifniband, visit http://en.wikipedia.org/wiki/InfiniBand.

The following image is an example of an Infiniband QDR adapter from Mellanox Technlogoies Inc.:

There are different types of IB cards based on different speed and latency. Each category has a unique name identified by three letters. The following table shows the different ratings of IB:

Model	Throughput (Gbit/s)	Latency (microseconds)
Single Data Rate (SDR)	10	5
Double Data Rate (DDR)	20	2.5
Quad Data Rate (QDR)	40	1.3
Fourteen Data Rate (FDR)	56	0.7
Enhanced Data Rate (EDR)	100	0.5

How to do it...

The following steps show how to load IB modules and configure networking for an IB interface:

1. Log in to the Proxmox node through SSH or a console as the root.

2. Add the following lines in /etc/modules so that IB modules are loaded during boot:

```
mlx4_ib
ib_ipoib
```

3. Add the following into /etc/network/interfaces to configure an IB interface. Adjust the IP information based on your environment:

```
auto ib0
iface ib0 inet static
        address 192.168.10.1
```

```
netmask 255.255.255.0
pre-up echo connected > /sys/class/net/ib0/mode
mtu 65520
```

4. Save the network configuration file and reboot.

5. Check the IB interface status by running this:

   `#ibstat`

   The command should display information similar to the following screenshot:

```
CA 'mlx4_0'
        CA type: MT26428
        Number of ports: 1
        Firmware version: 2.8.600
        Hardware version: b0
        Node GUID: 0x0002c903004ae05e
        System image GUID: 0x0002c903004ae061
        Port 1:
                State: Active
                Physical state: LinkUp
                Rate: 40
                Base lid: 12
                LMC: 0
                SM lid: 4
                Capability mask: 0x02510868
                Port GUID: 0x0002c903004ae05f
```

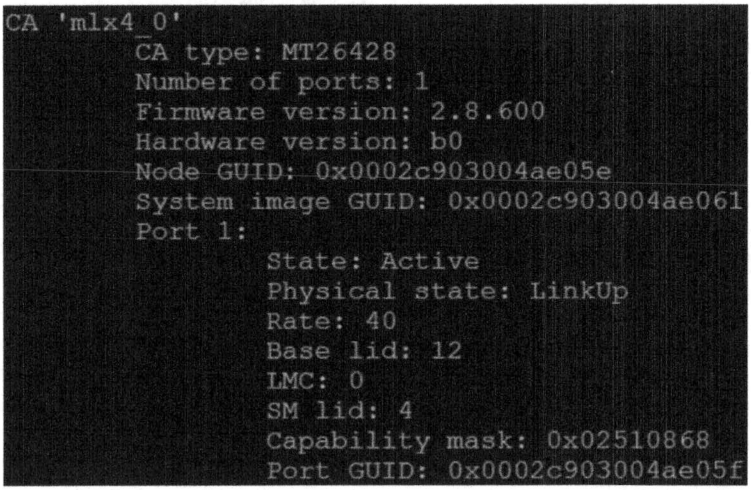

If the `ibstat` command is missing, install the IB tools using following command:

`#apt-get install infiniband-diags`

The following screenshot shows the configured IB interface from the Proxmox GUI:

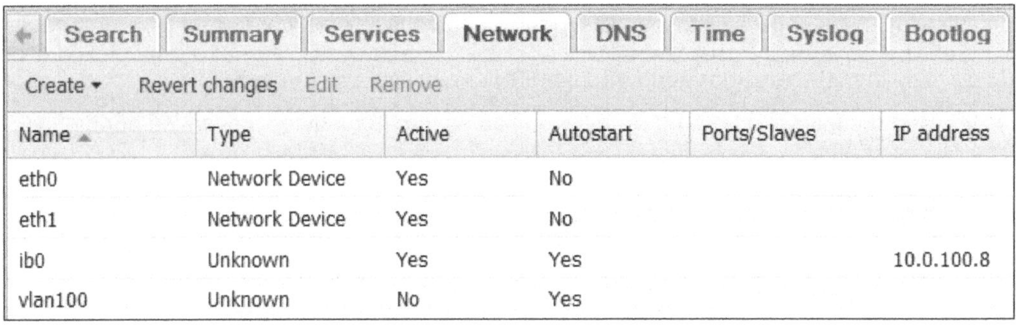

Search	Summary	Services	Network	DNS	Time	Syslog	Bootlog

Create ▾ Revert changes Edit Remove

Name ▲	Type	Active	Autostart	Ports/Slaves	IP address
eth0	Network Device	Yes	No		
eth1	Network Device	Yes	No		
ib0	Unknown	Yes	Yes		10.0.100.8
vlan100	Unknown	No	Yes		

How it works...

IB uses a completely different protocol and set of hardware. Standard Ethernet cables and switches do not apply to IB. Before you start investing in IB, consider the existing network in place and how a drastic change to IB may affect regular operations. IB can also be added on to the existing network by installing additional IB cards in nodes.

IB requires a subnet manager to function properly. The subnet manager can be integrated in an IB switch or it can be configured in one of the nodes with an IB interface card. Installing and running a subnet manager on a node is the easiest and preferred way to have redundancy. **Opensm** is the subnet manager for Linux-based operating systems. Simply install it in any Proxmox node, then run it using the following commands:

```
#apt-get install opensm
#opensm
```

Opensm will start and scan the attached IB switch and all the other interfaces connected to the switch.

As of Proxmox 3.4, it is not possible to configure VLAN on top of IB. It can only have one subnet at a time. Also, IB ports cannot be bonded in active-active state. Only one port can be active at all times. So, the only reason to bond IB ports is to implement redundancy, rather than to increase network bandwidth.

Configuring a VM network interface

In this recipe, we are going to see a different model of a virtual network interface available to be used with a virtual machine and how to properly configure them.

Getting ready

As of Proxmox VE 3.4, there are four virtual network interface models available for a virtual machine:

1. Intel E1000
2. VirtIO (paravirtualized)
3. Realtec RTL8139
4. VMWare vmxnet3

Out of the four, Intel E1000 and VirtIO interfaces are the most widely used in the Proxmox environment. To achieve the maximum network performance possible, using VirtIO is recommended. Almost all Linux-based operating systems can automatically configure either virtual network interfaces. However, the Windows operating system installation media does not come with a VirtIO driver, which needs to be manually loaded. For Intel E1000, built-in drivers in Windows 7 and Windows Server 2008 work fine. However, for earlier versions of Windows or in some case for Windows Server 2012, drivers may be need to be provided manually.

How to do it...

The following steps show how to download the VirtIO and Intel E1000 drivers, then load them in a Windows-based VM:

1. Go to the `http://www.linux-kvm.org/page/WindowsGuestDrivers/Download_Drivers` to download the latest VirtIO driver in an ISO format.

2. Go to the `https://downloadcenter.intel.com/download/22283/Intel-Ethernet-Connections-CD` to download the latest Intel E1000 driver in an ISO format.

3. Upload the ISOs to an ISO image enabled storage. Refer to the *Managing the ISO and OpenVZ templates* recipe in *Chapter 3, Cluster and VM Management*, for details on the ISO upload option. The following screenshot displays the ISO images after they are uploaded in a storage:

Summary	Content	Permissions		
Restore	Remove	Templates	Upload	
Name			Format	Size
⊟ ISO image (9 Items)				
Intel_e1000_20.iso			iso	247MB
Virtio-win-0.1-100.iso			iso	67MB
Windows-7-Professional-W32.iso			iso	2.27GB
Windows-7-Professional-W64.iso			iso	2.96GB

4. Load the ISO image into the VM as shown in the following screenshot:

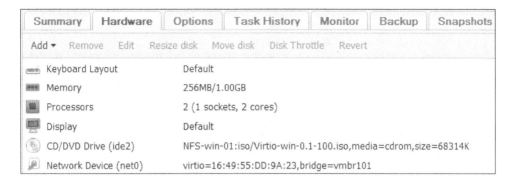

5. Power up the VM if it is not already, then install the necessary driver from the ISO through **Control Panel | Device Manager**.

Configuring High Availability

Proxmox **High Availability** (**HA**) enables a HA configured virtual machine to automatically restart on another node in the cluster if the physical node fails. Proxmox HA is built on long standing proven Linux HA technology. In this recipe, we are going to see how to configure HA in Proxmox to automigrate a virtual machine during a node or network failure.

There are three primary requirements before HA can be configured:

- **Cluster**: Since the main function of HA is to auto restart a VM from a failed node to a different node, it is goes without saying that Proxmox HA can only be configured on a cluster. This is one of the minimum requirements of Proxmox HA.

- **Fencing**: This the second most important requirement for HA. In order to configure HA, there must be a fencing device or hardware in place. Currently, there is no software-based fencing. In simple words, fencing is when a cluster forces or knocks down a faulty node and prevents it from coming back online. This is done to prevent the VM from running on multiple nodes at the same time, which in almost all cases may cause data error.

> For information on configuring fence device, visit
> http://pve.proxmox.com/wiki/Fencing.

- **Shared storage**: The Proxmox cluster also must have shared storage configured. In order for HA to migrate a VM, the virtual disk must be stored on a shared storage.

How to do it...

1. Log in to the Proxmox node through SSH or directly from the console. The fencing device configuration must be done through a CLI. Cluster configuration in `/etc/pve/cluster.conf` should appear in following format before the fencing device is added:

```
<?xml version="1.0"?>
<cluster config_version="9" name="pmx">
  <cman keyfile="/var/lib/pve-cluster/corosync.authkey"/>

  <clusternodes>
      <clusternode name="pmx1" nodeid="1" votes="1"/>
      <clusternode name="pmx2" nodeid="2" votes="1"/>
      <clusternode name="pmx3" nodeid="3" votes="1"/>
  </clusternodes>
  <rm/>
</cluster>
```

2. Add the fencing device based on documentation at `http://pve.proxmox.com/wiki/Fencing`.

   For our example, we have chosen an APC fencing device. After adding the fencing device on our example cluster, the configuration appears as follows:

```
<?xml version="1.0"?>
<cluster config_version="10" name="pmx">
 <cman keyfile="/var/lib/pve-cluster/corosync.authkey"/>

<fencedevices>
    <fencedevice agent="fence_apc" ipaddr="172.16.0.51" login="apcfence" passwd="password"
                 power_wait="10"/>
</febcedevices>

  <clusternodes>
    <clusternode name="pmx1" nodeid="1" votes="1"/>
    <clusternode name="pmx2" nodeid="2" votes="1"/>
    <clusternode name="pmx3" nodeid="3" votes="1"/>
  </clusternodes>
  <rm/>
</cluster>
```

3. Save the configuration and reboot the node.

4. Log in to the Proxmox GUI as the root after rebooting.

5. Ensure the VM to be configured with HA is completely powered off. The HA status should be **No** on the **Summary** page of the VM before the VM is added to HA, as shown in the following screenshot:

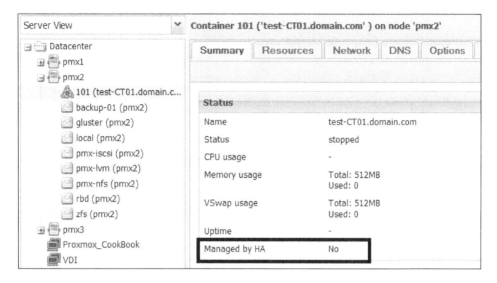

6. Click on **Datacenter** from the left navigation pane, then click on **HA** from the tabbed menu. The following screenshot shows the **HA** page with a current cluster configuration with the fence device added:

7. Click on the **Add** drop-down menu and select **HA managed VM/CT** to open a dialog box, as shown in the following screenshot. In our example, we add a `101` container ID in HA:

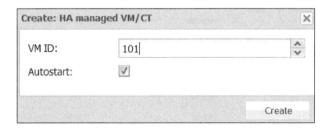

8. Click on the **Create** button to add the VM to HA.

9. Click on **Activate** to finalize the configuration or click on **Revert changes** to redo the configuration.

10. Verify that the VM is now configured with **HA** through the **Summary** page. If all is successful, the HA status of the VM now should show **Yes**, as shown in the following screenshot:

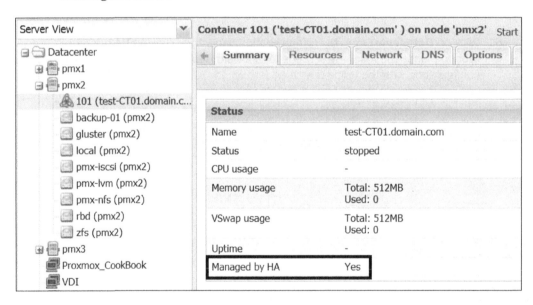

11. To test the HA configuration, unplug the Proxmox node with the VM and observe it being auto restarted in another node in the cluster.

There's more...

Proxmox HA is a great way to increase the maximum uptime when node failure occurs and IT staff cannot address the issue in time. Despite the benefit of HA, there are many virtual environments where this feature is not used. For example, in a large environment, many VMs per node may cause some issue when HA is configured. In such an environment, during node failure, a large number of VMs will be auto started on other nodes. If these nodes do not have enough resources, new VMs will not be able to restart.

In a smaller noncritical environment, a network manager can simply ignore the HA feature and just manually move VMs around, thus eliminating any need to include a fencing device in the budget. The use of HA completely depends on requirements. Test the proper usage of HA ahead of time before diving into it. This will prevent unnecessary complexities of configuring Proxmox HA.

5

Firewall Configurations

In this chapter, we will see a firewall configuration, one of the prominent features of Proxmox. We will cover the following topics in this chapter:

- ▸ Configuring a cluster-specific firewall
- ▸ Configuring a host-specific firewall
- ▸ Configuring a VM-specific firewall
- ▸ Integrating a Suricata IPS
- ▸ Commonly-used firewall CLI commands
- ▸ Logging a firewall

Introduction

The firewall feature in Proxmox VE provides an excellent means to strengthen security within a virtual environment. Proxmox firewall is built on a well-established Linux-based **netfilter** technology. Netfilter is based on a packet filtering framework, where network data packets are allowed or denied based on a set of defined rules. All the rules are defined as table structures in **iptables**.

 To learn more about netfilter, visit http://www.netfilter.org/.

The firewall feature in Proxmox is also a stateful firewall. A stateful firewall is not just a data packet filter, but it also keeps a constant track of the state of active network connections, such as TCP or UDP protocols. It is also known as dynamic packet filtering, which matches firewall rules with the nature of active connections, providing better protection than simply filtering packets.

For information on stateful firewalls, visit `https://en.wikipedia.org/wiki/Stateful_firewall`.

The Proxmox firewall operates in a distributed manner where the main configuration resides in a Proxmox cluster filesystem, but the rules in iptables are stored in individual Proxmox nodes. This provides isolation between virtual machines, thus providing higher bandwidth than a centralized firewall option.

The Proxmox firewall can be configured through both a GUI and a CLI. The Proxmox GUI provides a very easy user-friendly environment to manage firewall configurations.

 Note that, although Proxmox firewall provides excellent protection, you must have a physical firewall for the entire network. This firewall is also known as an **edge firewall**, since it sits at the main entry point of the Internet. An Internet connection should not be directly connected into the Proxmox nodes. A virtualized firewall should not be used as a substitute for a physical firewall.

In Proxmox, we can set up a firewall for an entire cluster level, specific node levels, and also for each VM. A firewall menu is available for a datacenter, node, and virtual machine-specific menu tabs. Log in to the Proxmox GUI, then select an entity, such as **Datacenter**, Proxmox node, or a virtual machine, through the left navigation bar to display the menu tabs. The following screenshot shows the **Firewall** menu for the **Datacenter**:

To configure a firewall through a CLI, there are some configuration files that need to be edited. Here are the locations for the firewall configuration files for the datacenter, node, and VM-wide firewall settings:

Configuration files	Location
Datacenter or cluster-specific	`/etc/pve/firewall/cluster.fw`
Node-specific	`/etc/pve/nodes/<node_name>/host.fw`
VM-specific	`/etc/pve/firewall/<vmid>.fw`

Here are the components that the Proxmox firewall consists of:

- ▸ Zones
- ▸ Security groups
- ▸ IPSets
- ▸ Rules
    - ❑ Directions
    - ❑ Actions
- ▸ Macros
- ▸ Protocols

Zones

There are two logical zones in Proxmox firewall that groups all the firewall rules for all incoming and outgoing traffic. Here are the two zones:

- ▸ **Host**: Rules in this zone define traffic to and from a physical node in a Proxmox cluster
- ▸ **VM**: Rules in this zone define traffic to and from a KVM or OpenVZ virtual machine in the cluster

Security groups

A security group allows the grouping of a few firewall rules together with single rules and makes them applicable to any node or VM. For example, we can create a security group named `webserver` and create some rules to open all standard web server TCP ports, such as `80, 443, 21, 22`, and more. Then, we can apply a single `webserver` group to any node or VM instead of creating individual rules. The following screenshot shows a security group created for `webserver` to open ports for the **HTTP**, **HTTPS**, **SSH**, and **FTP** protocols:

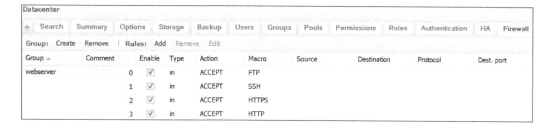

Similarly, another security group can be created with ports, such as IMAP/SMTP, for mail servers. A security group makes identical rule-creation for multiple nodes or virtual machines much easier.

IPSets

In Proxmox firewall, it is possible to apply firewall rules to specific IP addresses. If the same rule is applied to multiple IP addresses, IPSet allows the grouping of IP addresses so that one rule can be created for all IP addresses. Much like **Security Group**, IPSet allows the grouping of multiple IP addresses to create a single firewall rule. With IPSet, we can create sets of blacklists and whitelists of IP address to allow or deny network traffic.

Rules

Rules are the heart of a firewall configuration. Through rules, we can define the flow of traffic and the type of traffic that will be allowed or dropped. There are only two directions in which traffic can flow:

- **in**: This refers to incoming traffic from an outside source
- **out**: This refers to outgoing traffic from a Proxmox node, cluster, or VM

There are three types of actions that a firewall rule can take. They are:

- **ACCEPT**: This allows traffic packets
- **REJECT**: This refers to traffic packets that are received, and then sent back to the sender
- **DROP**: This refers to traffic packets that are received, and then dropped silently without any acknowledgement being sent to the sender

A typical firewall rule looks like the following, in a firewall configuration file as taken from `/etc/pve/firewall/100.fw` for the `100` VM:

```
[RULES]
IN ACCEPT -p tcp -dport 80
```

This rule allows port `80` and TCP protocol based network traffic. The following screenshot shows the rule from the Proxmox GUI:

Sometimes, firewall rules can conflict with each other due to misconfiguration. Keep in mind that, in such cases, any rules stated first will always take precedence over later rules. For example, there is a rule to accept packets on port 21, but there is another rule to drop all packets for port 21. In such a scenario, the firewall will always accept data on port 21 since this is the first rule. Take extra care in such scenarios.

Macros

Proxmox firewall provides various precreated port configurations for most known services, such as **BGP**, **SSH**, **Telnet**, **MySQL**, **NTP**, **OpenVPN**, **SMTP**, **Squid**, and more, to name just a few. The following screenshot shows the **Macro** menu in the **Firewall** rule configuration dialog box:

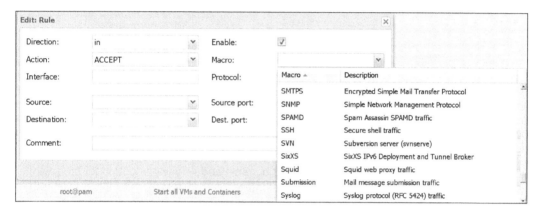

Macro provides a quick way to create firewall rules only when using a default service port. For example, if you're using custom port number 2202 for an SSH service, then the default macro will not work, since it will create the rule with the default SSH port 22. The selected macro will not allow the entering of custom port numbers. As of Proxmox VE 3.4, we cannot create custom macros to be used with the Proxmox firewall.

Protocols

A Proxmox firewall allows rules based on various network protocols, such as TCP, UDP, ICMP, EGP, and more. Depending on application requirements, different protocol selections are necessary. For example, if we want to allow a ping for a server, then the **icmp** protocol needs to be selected instead of **tcp**. The following screenshot shows the **Firewall** rule dialog box with the **Protocol** drop-down menu:

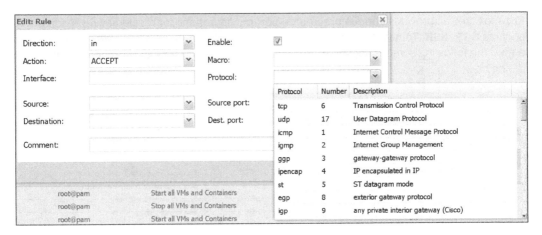

Although the addition of the Proxmox firewall is a stable and very viable option for firewalling, it should not be used as the sole firewall for an entire network. There are simply no substitutes for a physical firewall node separated from the rest of the network, which sits at the main entry point of incoming public Internet connectivity. It is also a matter of debate whether or not a virtualized firewall can take the place of a separate physical firewall. A virtualized firewall residing in the same cluster gives a wider attack footprint than a single physical firewall. The cost of an expensive firewall can be mitigated by using an open source firewall, such as **pfSense**, which can also be configured as a firewall cluster at no cost.

Configuring a cluster-specific firewall

Cluster-specific firewall options affect all the nodes and virtual machines in a cluster. There are a few tasks that should be accomplished from the **Datacenter | Firewall** menu:

- ▸ Enabling a cluster firewall
- ▸ Managing a security group
- ▸ Managing IPSets

Other firewall options, such as **Rules** and **Alias**, can be configured from a host or VM **Firewall** option, as they have no effect on the overall operation of the cluster firewall.

Enabling a cluster firewall

In order to have the Proxmox firewall operational, it needs to be turned on at a cluster-level first.

Getting ready

Log in to the Proxmox GUI as a root or with any another administrative privilege, and then select **Datacenter** from the left navigation bar.

How to do it...

The following steps are used to enable a cluster-wide firewall through a GUI:

1. Click on **Firewall** from the **Datacenter** tabbed menu to open firewall options. The following screenshot displays the firewall status for a new Proxmox installation:

The firewall is currently disabled. The **Input Policy** is set to **DROP** for all incoming traffic, and the **Output Policy** is set to **ACCEPT** for all outgoing traffic. To have a complete lockdown cluster, the **Input Policy** can be left to the **DROP** policy before turning on a firewall.

Keep in mind that if no firewall rule is created to allow the Proxmox GUI traffic on port `8006` prior to enabling a cluster firewall, the GUI will become inaccessible after the firewall is turned on. In such cases, a rule can be created through a CLI to allow access to the Proxmox GUI.

2. To change the policy or enable/disable a firewall, select the line item, and then click on **Edit** to open a dialog box. After making changes, click on **OK** on the dialog box, as shown in the following screenshot:

The following steps are for enabling a cluster-wide firewall through a GUI. This is also useful when a firewall is enabled with the **DROP** input policy without creating rules to accept management traffic for HTTPS or SSH:

1. Log in through SSH or directly at one of the Proxmox node consoles if the SSH port is blocked.

2. Open the cluster firewall configuration file in `/etc/pve/firewall/cluster.fw` with an editor.

3. Change the policy to **ACCEPT** all traffic as follows:

```
[OPTIONS]
enable: 1
policy_in: ACCEPT
```

4. To keep the input policy to drop all the traffic except required ones, make the changes as follows. In this example, we drop all traffic but SSH and the Proxmox GUI:

```
[OPTIONS]
enable: 1
policy_in: DROP

[RULES]
IN ACCEPT -p tcp -dport 22
IN ACCEPT -p tcp -dport 8006
```

5. Save the configuration file and exit the editor. No reboot is required.

How it works...

Any rules or policies configured under a datacenter-specific firewall are applied to all the nodes in the cluster. Rules that apply to all nodes, such as GUI access on port 8006 or SSH access on port 22, can be configured once in a cluster-wide firewall configuration. This saves time from creating rules on each node.

Managing a security group

A security group allows the grouping of multiple firewall rules in to a single rule.

Getting ready

Log in to the Proxmox GUI as a root or with any other administrative privilege, then select the **Datacenter | Firewall** tabbed menu. Security groups can be only created and managed through the datacenter **Firewall** menu. Groups can be applied to hosts or virtual machines through their own **Firewall** menu. The following screenshot shows the **Security Group** menu with no groups created:

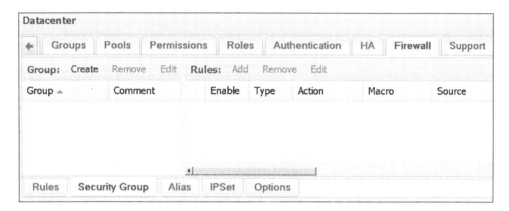

How to do it...

1. Click on **Create** to open the **Security Group** dialog box.

2. Enter a group name and description, as shown in the following screenshot, and then click on **Create**:

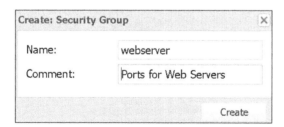

3. Select the newly created group name, and then click on **Add** from the **Rules:** menu on the right-hand side of the screen. This will open a dialog box to create firewall rules.

   The following screenshot shows the dialog box with information entered to allow the incoming HTTP traffic on port 80:

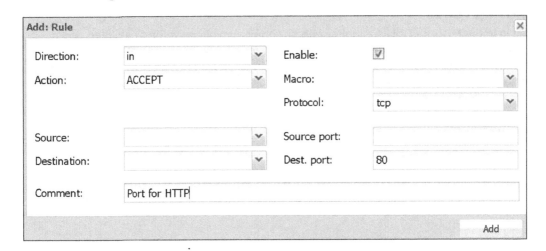

Since this rule will be applied to different servers with different IP addresses, we will not enter any source or destination IP addresses.

4. Click on **Add** after all the necessary information has been entered to create the rule.

5. Follow the same procedure to create other rules in the same group.

   The following screenshot shows rules created to allow HTTP, HTTPS, SSH, and Ping, for a webserver security group:

Managing IPSets

IPSets allow the grouping of multiple IP addresses or IP ranges. This useful when firewall rules need to be applied to specific IP addresses.

Getting ready

Log in to the Proxmox GUI as a root or with any other administrative privilege, and then select the **Datacenter** | **Firewall** tabbed menu. Click on **IPSet** from the bottom tabbed menu in the firewall window.

Any IPSet created under the datacenter firewall menu is available to all the nodes and virtual machines in the cluster. An IPSet created under a VM is only available to the VM in which the set is created. If you want to create an IPSet that will be selectable by any host or VM in the cluster, create it by navigating to the **Datacenter** | **Firewall** | **IPSet** menu.

How to do it...

1. Navigate to **IPSet** | **Create** to open a dialog box. This dialog box only creates the name and description of the IPSet. For our example, we create an IPSet to blacklist specific IPs, as shown in the following screenshot:

2. Select the newly created IPSet, and then click on **IP/CIDR**. Click on the **IP/CIDR** drop-down menu to add an IP address or range. For our example, we have blacklisted a fictitious IP range, 24.123.123.0/24, as shown in the following screenshot:

3. To edit the IPSet name or the IP addresses in the set, select the line item and click on **Edit**.

4. Click on **Remove** while the item is selected to remove a set.

Configuring a host-specific firewall

This firewall configuration only affects the Proxmox node or a host in which the configuration is made.

Getting ready

From the Proxmox GUI, select a node and click on **Firewall** from the tabbed menu. The host-specific firewall menu only has three additional menus named **Rules**, **Options**, and **Log**.

How to do it...

1. To enable a firewall for a specific host, navigate to Node | **Firewall** | **Options**. The options for a newly installed Proxmox will appear as shown in this screenshot:

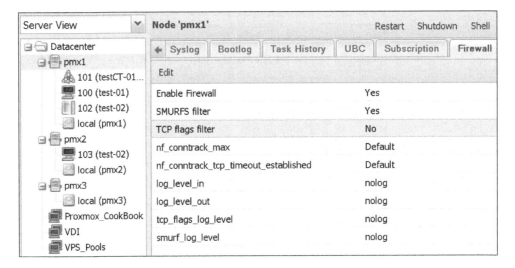

2. To enable or disable a firewall, select **Enable Firewall**, and then click on **Edit**.
3. Similarly, to change any line item options, select the item and click on **Edit**.
4. To create a host-specific firewall rule, click on the **Rule** tab, and then click on **Add** to open a dialog box.

> Keep in mind that these rules will apply to the particular node in which the rule is created.
>
> Refer to the *Managing a security group* section in the *Configuring a cluster-specific firewall* recipe earlier in this chapter to see the rule creation dialog box.

5. To apply a group rule already created through **Security Group**, click on **Insert: Security Group** to open a dialog box, as shown in the following screenshot:

In our example, we have selected **Security Group** named `webserver`, which we created earlier in this chapter.

6. Leave **Interface** blank to apply this rule to all the interfaces of the node.

7. Click on the **Enable** checkbox to activate the rule, or leave it unchecked to activate it later.

8. Finally, click on **Add** to create the rule. A firewall service does not to be restarted to activate the rule change.

> We can make the same changes through a CLI by adding the following line in `/etc/pve/nodes/pmx1/host.fw`:
>
>   [RULES]
>   GROUP webserver # Default Web Server Ports

How it works...

There are no I/O policy configurations for a host-specific firewall. It follows the policies from a datacenter-specific firewall configuration in `/etc/pve/firewall/cluster.fw`. The host-specific firewall configuration, however, is useful to overwrite rules in the datacenter firewall rules. There are no limits to how many firewall rules a host can have.

There are **Source** and **Destination** option boxes in the rule creation dialog box that need further clarification, as they are vital to a proper firewall configuration. The **Source** and **Destination** drop-down menus apply to an IP address or range, whereas **Source port** and **Dest. port** apply to only port numbers. For example, if we want to allow HTTP traffic on port 80 from only a 192.168.1.10 static IP address, then the configuration will look like the following screenshot:

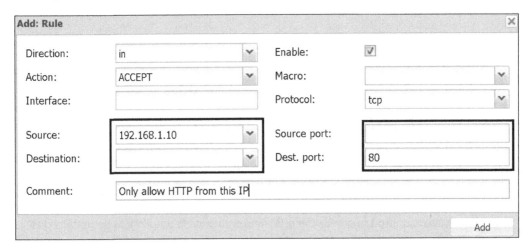

When the **Direction** is set as **in**, the destination is the Proxmox node and the source is external traffic. When the **Direction** set as **out**, the source becomes the Proxmox node and the destination is the external network. To clarify, we can look at another example. In this scenario, we want the Proxmox node with a 172.16.0.71 IP address to allow no other network traffic other than HTTP traffic to go out. The following screenshot shows the configuration for this scenario:

Configuring a VM-specific firewall

This configuration is done at virtual machine level, which only affects the virtual machine itself and not the other VMs in the cluster.

Getting ready

VM-specific firewall configuration options are similar to clusters and host-specific firewalls. Log in to the Proxmox GUI and select a VM to configure a firewall. From the tabbed menu, click on **Firewall** to display the configuration.

How to do it...

A VM-specific firewall menu is similar to a host and cluster:

1. To enable a firewall, navigate to **Firewall | Options**.
2. To create firewall rules, navigate to **Firewall | Rules**.
3. To create or select an already defined IPSet, navigate to **Firewall | IPSet**.
4. To create an IP alias, navigate to **Firewall | Alias**.

Refer to the *Configuring a cluster-specific firewall* recipe and the *Configuring a host-specific firewall* recipe earlier in this chapter to find out more details about the dialog boxes. To change rules through the CLI, the VM firewall configuration in `/etc/pve/firewall/<vm_id>.fw` needs to be edited.

How it works...

As mentioned earlier, rules created through VM firewall options only affect the VM itself. Rules can be created from scratch or selected from a security group and created through a datacenter firewall configuration.

Any IPSet or alias created under the VM firewall configuration is selectable by the same VM. As a rule of thumb, I/O policies for a VM firewall should be set to **DROP** so that the VM operates with all ports closed. Then, add firewall rules as needed. This will ensure that only required ports or traffic are allowed.

Integrating a Suricata IPS

It is possible to integrate Suricata **Intrusion Prevention System** (**IPS**) into the Proxmox firewall. Suricata is an excellent high-performing IPS and Network Security Monitoring engine. Suricata is a multithreaded IPS which allows load balancing on all the available processors of a system that Suricata is operating on.

 For more details, please visit the official Suricata site at `http://suricata-ids.org`.

Getting ready

Suricata needs to be installed and configured through a CLI only. Log in to the Proxmox node through SSH or a console. This needs to be done individually on all Proxmox nodes that require this feature.

How to do it...

1. Before installing Suricata, ensure that the Proxmox node is up to date using the following commands:

   ```
   # apt-get update
   ```

   ```
   # apt-get dist-upgrade
   ```

2. Install Suricata using the following command:

   ```
   # apt-get install suricata
   ```

3. Enable Suricata for a VM by opening the firewall configuration of the VM in `/etc/pve/firewall/<vm_id>.fw` and add the following entries:

   ```
   [OPTIONS]
   ips: 1
   ips_queues: 0
   ```

How it works...

When Suricata is enabled, all the packets get forwarded to it only after the Proxmox firewall accepts the packets. Any data packets that are dropped or rejected do not get forwarded to the Suricata intrusion prevention system. Since Suricata is multithreaded, it can achieve tremendous performance without sacrificing extensive rulesets in a large environment with lots of traffic.

Commonly-used firewall CLI commands

Although almost all firewall configurations can be performed through the Proxmox GUI, sometimes it may be necessary to perform certain tasks through a CLI. In this section, we are going to see some commands that can be used to manage the Proxmox firewall.

Getting ready

Log in to the Proxmox node using SSH, or directly from a console, as a root or with any other administrative privilege.

How to do it...

Here are some of the CLI commands to manage the Proxmox VE firewall:

1. To start a firewall service:

   ```
   # pve-firewall start
   ```

2. To stop a firewall service:

   ```
   # pve-firewall stop
   ```

3. To check the status of a firewall service:

   ```
   # pve-firewall status
   ```

4. To view the generated iptables rules:

   ```
   # iptables-save
   ```

5. To edit a cluster-specific firewall:

   ```
   # nano /etc/pve/firewall/cluster.fw
   ```

6. To edit a host-specific firewall:

   ```
   # nano /etc/pve/nodes/<node_name>/host.fw
   ```

7. To edit a VM-specific firewall:

   ```
   # nano /etc/pve/firewall/<vm_id>.fw
   ```

There's more...

For the official Proxmox Wiki on firewalls, visit https://pve.proxmox.com/wiki/Proxmox_VE_Firewall.

Logging a firewall

In this recipe, we will see how to enable logging for the Proxmox firewall and display log entries.

Getting ready

Logging into the Proxmox firewall allows us to view the activities of data transmission in and out of clusters, nodes, and VMs. It is a very useful tool, not only for the Proxmox firewall, but also for any firewall to pinpoint the source and destination of traffic, and to verify that rules are working as expected. In Proxmox, we can set various levels of logging, depending on the requirements. The log option is only available for host and VM-specific firewall. There are no logging options for a datacenter or cluster-wide firewalls. Host-level logging will display all activities from all the VMs in a host. Logging for a VM only displays activities for a particular VM. Logging helps us to see not just what was denied, but also what traffic was allowed to pinpoint an intruder.

How to do it...

The following steps are used to enable logging for a node or host and a VM-specific firewall configuration. Logging can be enabled through a GUI:

1. Log in to the Proxmox GUI and select a node or VM.
2. Click on the **Options** tabbed menu under the **Firewall** feature. Logging is disabled by default for both the host and VM firewall features. The following screenshot shows the **Options** page under **Firewall** for container 103 in our example cluster:

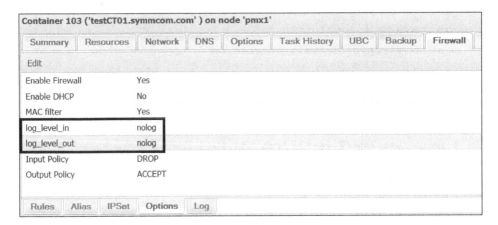

3. Select the `log_level_in` item for incoming, and `log_level_out` for outgoing traffic logging, and then click on **Edit**. This will open a dialog box, as shown in the following screenshot, to change various logging levels:

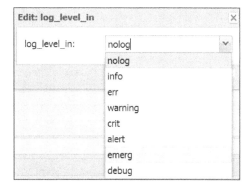

4. Select a level and click on **OK** to accept the change. In our example, we have selected an info level for both in and out traffic.

5. Click on the **Log** tabbed menu under **Firewall** to view the logs for the node or VM. The following screenshot shows the firewall log for container `103` in our example cluster:

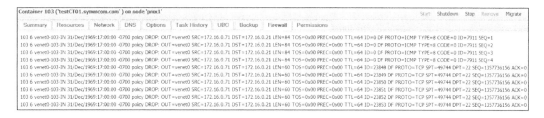

How it works...

The logging levels are simply different verbosity of logs. This means that, depending of the level selected, it will display more or fewer firewall activities. In our example, we have selected the **info** log level. This will show all the activities of a firewall. However, if we select **err**, it will only show error logs and nothing else.

Keep in mind, when selecting log level info for both incoming and outgoing connections, that everything will be logged. This will create many hundreds of log entries in a very short period of time, depending on how many active connections to and from a VM or node the firewall has to deal with. Apart from the **nolog** level, all other log levels will log dropped activities.

See also

▶ For further detailed information on logging for iptables-based firewalls, visit `http://gr8idea.info/os/tutorials/security/iptables5.html`

6

Storage Configurations

In this chapter, we are going to see how storages are configured in the Proxmox VE. We will cover the following topics in this chapter:

- ▶ Basic storage configurations
- ▶ Installing the FreeNAS storage
- ▶ Connecting the iSCSI storage
- ▶ Connecting the LVM storage
- ▶ Connecting the NFS storage
- ▶ Connecting the Ceph RBD storage
- ▶ Connecting the ZFS storage
- ▶ Connecting the GlusterFS storage

Introduction

A storage is where virtual disk images of virtual machines reside. There are many different types of storage systems with many different features, performances, and use case scenarios. Whether it is a local storage configured with direct attached disks or a shared storage with hundreds of disks, the main responsibility of a storage is to hold virtual disk images, templates, backups, and so on. Proxmox supports different types of storages, such as NFS, Ceph, GlusterFS, and ZFS. Different storage types can hold different types of data.

For example, a local storage can hold any type of data, such as disk images, ISO/container templates, backup files and so on. A Ceph storage, on the other hand, can only hold a `.raw` format disk image. In order to provide the right type of storage for the right scenario, it is vital to have a proper understanding of different types of storages. The full details of each storage is beyond the scope of this book, but we will look at how to connect them to Proxmox and maintain a storage system for VMs.

Storages can be configured into two main categories:

- ▸ Local storage
- ▸ Shared storage

Local storage

Any storage that resides in the node itself by using directly attached disks is known as a local storage. This type of storage has no redundancy other than a RAID controller that manages an array. If the node itself fails, the storage becomes completely inaccessible. The live migration of a VM is impossible when VMs are stored on a local storage because during migration, the virtual disk of the VM has to be copied entirely to another node.

 A VM can only be live-migrated when there are several Proxmox nodes in a cluster and the virtual disk is stored on a shared storage accessed by all the nodes in the cluster.

Shared storage

A shared storage is one that is available to all the nodes in a cluster through some form of network media. In a virtual environment with shared storage, the actual virtual disk of the VM may be stored on a shared storage, while the VM actually runs on another Proxmox host node. With shared storage, the live migration of a VM becomes possible without powering down the VM. Multiple Proxmox nodes can share one shared storage, and VMs can be moved around since the virtual disk is stored on different shared storages. Usually, a few dedicated nodes are used to configure a shared storage with their own resources apart from sharing the resources of a Proxmox node, which could be used to host VMs.

In recent releases, Proxmox has added some new storage plugins that allow users to take advantage of some great storage systems and integrating them with the Proxmox environment. Most of the storage configurations can be performed through the Proxmox GUI.

Ceph storage

Ceph is a powerful distributed storage system, which provides **RADOS Block Device** (**RBD**) object storage, **Ceph filesystem** (**CephFS**), and Ceph Object Storage. Ceph is built with a very high-level of reliability, scalability, and performance in mind. A Ceph cluster can be expanded to several petabytes without compromising data integrity, and can be configured using commodity hardware. Any data written to the storage gets replicated across a Ceph cluster. Ceph was originally designed with big data in mind. Unlike other types of storages, the bigger a Ceph cluster becomes, the higher the performance. However, it can also be used in small environments just as easily for data redundancy. A lower performance can be mitigated using SSD to store Ceph journals. Refer to the OSD Journal subsection in this section for information on journals.

The built-in self-healing features of Ceph provide unprecedented resilience without a single point of failure. In a multinode Ceph cluster, the storage can tolerate not just hard drive failure, but also an entire node failure without losing data. Currently, only an RBD block device is supported in Proxmox.

Ceph comprises a few components that are crucial for you to understand in order to configure and operate the storage. The following components are what Ceph is made of:

- Monitor daemon (MON)
- Object Storage Daemon (OSD)
- OSD Journal
- Metadata Server (MSD)
- Controlled Replication Under Scalable Hashing map (CRUSH map)
- Placement Group (PG)
- Pool

MON

Monitor daemons form quorums for a Ceph distributed cluster. There must be a minimum of three monitor daemons configured on separate nodes for each cluster. Monitor daemons can also be configured as virtual machines instead of using physical nodes. Monitors require a very small amount of resources to function, so allocated resources can be very small. A monitor can be set up through the Proxmox GUI after the initial cluster creation.

OSD

Object Storage Daemons (**OSDs**) are responsible for the storage and retrieval of actual cluster data. Usually, each physical storage device, such as HDD or SSD, is configured as a single OSD. Although several OSDs can be configured on a single physical disk, it is not recommended for any production environment at all. Each OSD requires a journal device where data first gets written and later gets transferred to an actual OSD. By storing journals on fast-performing SSDs, we can increase the Ceph I/O performance significantly.

Thanks to the Ceph architecture, as more and more OSDs are added into the cluster, the I/O performance also increases. An SSD journal works very well on small clusters with about eight OSDs per node. OSDs can be set up through the Proxmox GUI after the initial MON creation.

OSD Journal

Every single piece of data that is destined to be a Ceph OSD first gets written in a journal. A journal allows OSD daemons to write smaller chunks to allow the actual drives to commit writes that give more time. In simpler terms, all data gets written to journals first, then the journal filesystem sends data to an actual drive for permanent writes. So, if the journal is kept on a fast-performing drive, such as SSD, incoming data will be written at a much higher speed, while behind the scenes, slower performing SATA drives can commit the writes at a slower speed. Journals on SSD can really improve the performance of a Ceph cluster, especially if the cluster is small, with only a few terabytes of data.

It should also be noted that if there is a journal failure, it will take down all the OSDs that the journal is kept on the journal drive. In some environments, it may be necessary to put two SSDs to mirror RAIDs and use them as journaling. In a large environment with more than 12 OSDs per node, performance can actually be gained by collocating a journal on the same OSD drive instead of using SSD for a journal.

MDS

The **Metadata Server** (**MDS**) daemon is responsible for providing the Ceph filesystem (CephFS) in a Ceph distributed storage system. MDS can be configured on separate nodes or coexist with already configured monitor nodes or virtual machines. Although CephFS has come a long way, it is still not fully recommended to use in a production environment. It is worth mentioning here that there are many virtual environments actively running MDS and CephFS without any issues. Currently, it is not recommended to configure more than two MDSs in a Ceph cluster. CephFS is not currently supported by a Proxmox storage plugin. However, it can be configured as a local mount and then connected to a Proxmox cluster through the **Directory** storage. MDS cannot be set up through the Proxmox GUI as of version 3.4.

CRUSH map

A CRUSH map is the heart of the Ceph distributed storage. The algorithm for storing and retrieving user data in Ceph clusters is laid out in the CRUSH map. CRUSH allows a Ceph client to directly access an OSD. This eliminates a single point of failure and any physical limitations of scalability since there are no centralized servers or controllers to manage read and write operations of stored data. Throughout Ceph clusters, CRUSH maintains a map of all MONs and OSDs. CRUSH determines how data should be chunked and replicated among OSDs spread across several local nodes or even nodes located remotely.

A default CRUSH map is created on a freshly installed Ceph cluster. This can be further customized based on user requirements. For smaller Ceph clusters, this map should work just fine. However, when Ceph is deployed with very big data in mind, this map should be customized. A customized map will allow better control of a massive Ceph cluster.

To operate Ceph clusters of any size successfully, a clear understanding of the CRUSH map is mandatory.

 For more details on the Ceph CRUSH map, visit `http://ceph.com/docs/master/rados/operations/crush-map/` and `http://cephnotes.ksperis.com/blog/2015/02/02/crushmap-example-of-a-hierarchical-cluster-map`.

As of Proxmox VE 3.4, we cannot customize the CRUSH map throughout the Proxmox GUI. It can only be viewed through a GUI and edited through a CLI.

PG

In a Ceph storage, data objects are aggregated in groups determined by CRUSH algorithms. This is known as a **Placement Group** (**PG**) since CRUSH places this group in various OSDs depending on the replication level set in the CRUSH map and the number of OSDs and nodes. By tracking a group of objects instead of the object itself, a massive amount of hardware resources can be saved. It would be impossible to track millions of individual objects in a cluster. The following diagram shows how objects are aggregated in groups and how PG relates to OSD:

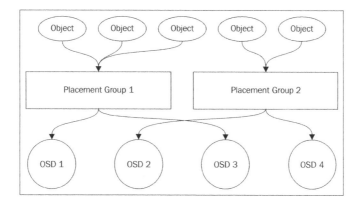

To balance available hardware resources, it is necessary to assign the right number of PGs. The number of PGs should vary depending on the number of OSDs in a cluster. The following is a table of PG suggestions made by Ceph developers:

Number of OSDs	Number of PGs
Less than 5 OSDs	128
Between 5-10 OSDs	512
Between 10-50 OSDs	4096

Selecting the proper number of PGs is crucial since each PG will consume node resources. Too many PGs for the wrong number of OSDs will actually penalize the resource usage of an OSD node, while very few assigned PGs in a large cluster will put data at risk. A rule of thumb is to start with the lowest number of PGs possible, then increase them as the number of OSDs increases.

 For details on Placement Groups, visit `http://ceph.com/docs/master/rados/operations/placement-groups/`.

There's a great PG calculator created by Ceph developers to calculate the recommended number of PGs for various sizes of Ceph clusters at `http://ceph.com/pgcalc/`.

Pools

Pools in Ceph are like partitions on a hard drive. We can create multiple pools on a Ceph cluster to separate stored data. For example, a pool named `accounting` can hold all the accounting department data, while another pool can store the human resources data of a company. When creating a pool, assigning the number of PGs is necessary. During the initial Ceph configuration, three default pools are created. They are `data`, `metadata`, and `rbd`. Deleting a pool will delete all stored objects permanently.

 For details on Ceph and its components, visit `http://ceph.com/docs/master/`.

The following diagram shows a basic *Proxmox+Ceph* cluster:

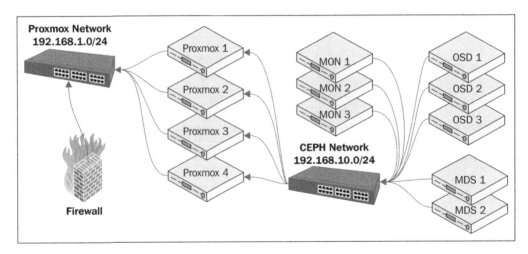

The preceding diagram shows four Proxmox nodes, three Monitor nodes, three OSD nodes, and two MDS nodes comprising a *Proxmox+Ceph* cluster. Note that Ceph is on a different network than the Proxmox public network. Depending on the set replication number, each incoming data object needs to be written more than once. This causes high bandwidth usage. By separating Ceph on a dedicated network, we can ensure that a Ceph network can fully utilize the bandwidth.

On advanced clusters, a third network is created only between Ceph nodes for cluster replication, thus improving network performance even further. As of Proxmox VE 3.4, the same node can be used for both Proxmox and Ceph. This provides a great way to manage all the nodes from the same Proxmox GUI. It is not advisable to put Proxmox VMs on a node that is also configured as Ceph. During day-to-day operations, Ceph nodes do not consume large amounts of resources, such as CPU or memory. However, when Ceph goes into rebalancing mode due to OSD or node failure, a large amount of data replication occurs, which takes up lots of resources. Performance will degrade significantly if resources are shared by both VMs and Ceph.

 Ceph RBD storage can only store `.raw` virtual disk image files.

Ceph itself does not come with a GUI to manage, so having the option to manage Ceph nodes through the Proxmox GUI makes administrative tasks mush easier. Refer to the *Monitoring the Ceph storage* subsection under the *How to do it...* section of the *Connecting the Ceph RBD storage* recipe later in this chapter to learn how to install a great read-only GUI to monitor Ceph clusters.

Basic storage configurations

You can configure a storage in a Proxmox cluster through both a GUI and CLI. Refer to the *Accessing datacenter-specific menus* recipe in *Chapter 2, Getting to Know the Proxmox GUI* for storage GUI options. The storage configuration is stored in the `/etc/pve/storage.cfg` directory path.

How to do it...

You can edit this file directly to add storages, through the Proxmox GUI, and the configurations get saved automatically. The following screenshot is of a storage configuration file as it appears after a clean install of Proxmox:

```
GNU nano 2.2.6                    File: /etc/pve/storage.cfg

dir: local
        path /var/lib/vz
        shared
        content images,iso,vztmpl,backup,rootdir
        maxfiles 3
```

The storage configuration usually has the following multiline format:

```
<type of storage> : <storage_id>
        <path_to_storage>
        <enable/disable share>
        content types
        maxfiles <numeric value of maximum backups to keep>
```

Based on the configuration, there is a local storage attached to a Proxmox cluster where all the files are going to be stored in the /var/lib/vz local directory path. The storage can store content types including disk images, ISOs, container templates, and backup files. The storage will keep a maximum of three recent backup files. The following screenshot shows the storage from the Proxmox GUI:

Changing the storage configuration does not require any reboot and takes effect immediately.

Installing the FreeNAS storage

FreeNAS is one of the most popular freely available storage systems that is easy to set up and maintain. It provides common storage protocols, such as iSCSI, NFS, CIFS, AFP, and more. Using an off-the-shelf commodity hardware, one can set up a fully functional shared storage within minutes. There is a paid version of FreeNAS that comes with a preinstalled storage system sold by iXsystems called TrueNAS. For more details on TrueNAS, visit http://www.ixsystems.com/truenas/.

Note that for the purpose of this book, we have used FreeNAS since it is very easy to set up for a beginner, and it has lots of storage features that don't involve too much investment. One single FreeNAS node can provide a variety of storage options for you to try. You can use any other storage of your choice to try different storage plugins available in Proxmox.

There are a few other viable choices besides FreeNAS, which also provide very good shared storage without the added cost:

Storage system	Link
Nexenta	`http://www.nexenta.com/`
NAS4Free	`http://www.nas4free.org/`
napp-it	`http://www.napp-it.org/`

The following screenshot shows the GUI of FreeNAS after a clean installation:

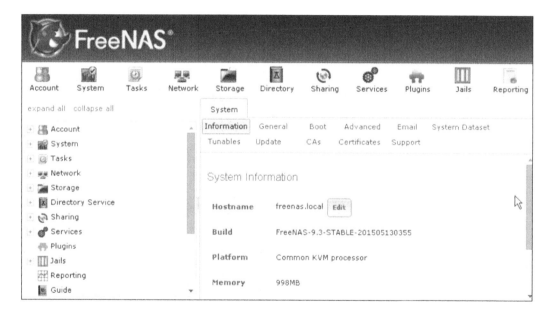

Getting ready

For the purpose of this chapter, you will need to set up a storage system in order to create iSCSI, LVM, and NFS-based storages, so that they can be connected to Proxmox clusters. If you already have such a storage setup, please skip this section. For the purpose of learning, FreeNAS can be set up as a virtual machine on a Proxmox cluster. Download the latest FreeNAS ISO file from `http://www.freenas.org/download-freenas-release.html`.

How to do it...

If you're installing FreeNAS on a physical node, use the following steps:

1. Prepare a CD with a FreeNAS ISO image.
2. Insert at least an 8 GB USB flash drive in to a USB port.
3. Boot a node from an ISO disk.
4. Select the USB drive as the installation drive when prompted.
5. Follow the installer through the GUI and reboot when done.
6. Configure the network with the proper IP information after rebooting.
7. Access the FreeNAS GUI from a browser using the IP.

If you're installing FreeNAS on a virtual machine, use the following steps:

1. Upload a FreeNAS ISO image on to the Proxmox storage.
2. Create a VM with one 8 GB virtual disk and one or more virtual disks with the desired size.
3. Power up the VM from the ISO image.
4. Select the 8 GB virtual disk as the installation drive when prompted.
5. Follow the installer through the GUI and reboot when done.
6. Configure the network with the proper IP information after reboot.
7. Access the FreeNAS GUI from a browser using the IP.

There's more...

Full details of how to configure different storage types in FreeNAS are beyond the scope of this book. The FreeNAS official documentation at `http://doc.freenas.org/9.3/freenas.html` helps to create iSCSI and NFS shares, which we will use later in this chapter.

If you have a different storage system that provides iSCSI and NFS, you can use them for the hands-on parts of this chapter. If you are not familiar with any storage systems and are just starting out in the world of shared storage and virtualization, then FreeNAS could be a good starting point.

 Spending some time with FreeNAS prior to diving into Proxmox would be a good idea.

Connecting the iSCSI storage

Internet Small Computer System Interface (**iSCSI**) is based on an Internet protocol which allows the transmission of SCSI commands over a standard IP-based network. iSCSI devices can be set up locally or over vast distances to provide storage options. To a client, an attached iSCSI device appears as if it is a physically connected disk drive.

 For some details on iSCSI, visit `http://en.wikipedia.org/wiki/ISCSI`.

In this section, we are going to look at how to connect an iSCSI storage to a Proxmox cluster.

Getting ready

We are going to configure the storage through the Proxmox GUI. Log in to the GUI as a root or any other root-privileged user. In Proxmox, iSCSI is primarily used to set up network backing **Logical Volume Manager** (**LVM**) storage. So, before we are able to configure an LVM storage, there must be some iSCSI targets configured on which LVM will sit. If you have not done so, create an iSCSI target named `pmx-iscsi` or any other name in a shared storage system, such as FreeNAS.

How to do it...

1. From the Proxmox GUI, click on **Datacenter** from the left navigation window.
2. Click on **Storage** from the tabbed menu.
3. Click on **Add** to open a storage plugin drop-down menu, as shown in the following screenshot:

4. Click on **iSCSI** to open a storage dialog box.

5. Fill in the necessary information as shown in the following table. The entered value may be different depending on your environment:

Item	Type of information	Entered value
ID	The name of the storage.	`pmx-iscsi.`
Portal	The IP of the shared storage node.	`172.16.0.74.`
Target	The iSCSI target configured on the shared storage node.	**iqn.2015-05.com.domain.ctl:iscsi-tgt**.
Use LUNs directly	Enabling/disabling the direct LUN usage. The option should be disabled. Enabling it may cause data loss.	Uncheck to disable.

The following screenshot shows the iSCSI storage dialog box with information already entered:

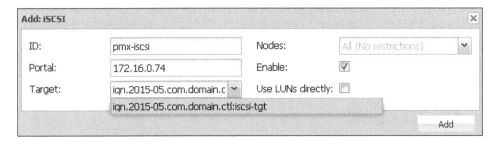

6. Click on **Add** to attach the storage.

The following screenshot shows the iSCSI storage as it appears from the Proxmox GUI:

How it works...

The following screenshot shows the storage configuration file with the iSCSI storage configurations added. We can also make changes by directly editing this configuration file:

```
GNU nano 2.2.6                      File: /etc/pve/storage.cfg

dir: local
        path /var/lib/vz
        shared
        content images,iso,vztmpl,backup,rootdir
        maxfiles 3

iscsi: pmx-iscsi
        target iqn.2015-05.com.domain.ctl:iscsi-tgt
        portal 172.16.0.74
        content none
```

There's more...

Note that the iSCSI storage is not usable on its own. It is merely presented as a block device or a virtual empty hard drive. No files can be stored on an attached iSCSI storage. It can only be used to create an LVM storage using iSCSI targets as underlying devices.

Connecting the LVM storage

An LVM storage provides a very high level of flexibility because logical volumes can be easily created or moved around between physical storages attached to a node. We can only store a .raw virtual disk image on an LVM storage. It is not possible to store any OpenVZ templates or containers on an LVM storage.

Getting ready

LVM can be configured using both locally attached disk storage or iSCSI attached devices from a different node. A locally attached LVM must be configured using a CLI. As of Proxmox VE 3.4, it is not possible to configure a locally attached LVM through the GUI.

 Note that, by default, the Proxmox installation creates an LVM storage on a local operating system disk to store Proxmox itself.

How to do it...

The following sections show how to add the LVM storage with local devices and create LVM with shared storage as a backend.

Adding the LVM storage with local devices

The following steps show how to add an LVM storage with local devices:

 Be sure that the device does not have any partition or filesystem on it, as these will be erased permanently.

1. Log in to the Proxmox node console through SSH.
2. Create a physical volume on a locally attached device:

    ```
    # pvcreate /dev/sda(id)
    ```

3. Create a volume group named pmx-lvmvg or any other desired name:

    ```
    # vgcreate pmx-lvmvg /dev/sda(id)
    ```

4. Log in to the Proxmox GUI and go to the **Storage** tabbed menu.
5. Click on **Add** and select **LVM** from the drop-down menu.
6. Enter pmx-lvm as the storage name.
7. Select **Existing volume groups** from the **Base Storage** drop-down menu.
8. Enter pmx-lvmvg in the **Volume group** textbox.
9. Click on the **Enable** and **Shared** checkboxes.
10. Click on **Add** to create the LVM storage.

Creating LVM with a shared storage as the backend

Now, we are going to see how to create LVM with shared storage as the backend. The following steps show how to add the LVM storage in networked iSCSI devices through a GUI:

1. Log in to the Proxmox GUI and go to the **Storage** tabbed menu.
2. Click on **Add** and select **LVM** from the drop-down menu.
3. Enter pmx-lvm as the storage name.
4. Select pmx-iscsi from the **Base Storage** drop-down menu. This is the same iSCSI target we have attached in the *Connecting the iSCSI storage* recipe.
5. Enter pmx-lvmvg in the **Volume group** text box.
6. Click on the **Enable** and **Shared** checkboxes.
7. Click on **Add** to create the LVM storage.

The following screenshot shows the LVM storage dialog box for the iSCSI-backed LVM storage:

How it works...

Here is the content of the storage configuration file in `/etc/pve/storage.cfg` after adding the LVM storage:

```
lvm: pmx-lvm
    vgname pmx-lvmvg
    shared
    content images
```

There's more...

LVM is widely used in all sorts of network environments and is the main operating system storage locally due to its manageability and functionality. If you are new to LVMs, it is worth learning how to manage it as it can also be used in a Linux-based VM. Almost all major Linux distributions, including Proxmox, use LVMs during installation as the main OS drive partitions. For a good how-to for LVM storage, visit `https://www.howtoforge.com/linux_lvm`.

Connecting the NFS storage

Originally developed by Sun Microsystems, **Network File System** (**NFS**) is probably one of the most popular file sharing protocols to this day. Currently at version 4, an NFS share allows storage of all Proxmox file types, such as disk images, ISO templates, OpenVZ containers, and more. Almost all virtual or physical network environments around the globe implement some form NFS storage.

In this section, we are going to see how to connect an NFS share with a Proxmox cluster.

Getting ready

In order to connect an NFS share, the share must first be created on the shared storage system. Follow the documentation of the storage you are using to create a NFS share. For our example, we created a share named `pmx-nfs` on the FreeNAS shared storage.

There are four versions of NFS to date. Version mismatches between NFS servers and client nodes can cause connectivity issues. By default, Proxmox uses a version 3 NFS client. If you're unsure of which version is being used for a NFS share, we can run the following command on a Proxmox node to view the version of NFS:

```
#mount -v | grep <mounted_nfs_share_path>
```

In our example node, we can see the following result after running the command that shows Proxmox using version 3 as in `vers=3` and the NFS server also uses version 3 as in `mountvers=3`:

```
root@pmx1:~# mount -v | grep /mnt/pve/pmx-nfs
172.16.0.74:/mnt/pmx-nfs on /mnt/pve/pmx-nfs type nfs (rw,realatime,
vers=3,proto=tcp,sec=sys,mountaddr=172.16.0.74,mountvers=3,mountproto
=udp,local_lock=none_
```

If the NFS server is behind a firewall, we will have to open some ports in order to access the NFS server share. There are two ports that are usually used by an NFS server:

- Port `110` TCP/UDP
- Port `2049` TCP/UDP

The NFS storage can be attached to a Proxmox cluster through the GUI or by directly editing the Proxmox storage configuration file in `/etc/pve/storage.cfg`. If we need to change the NFS version number used by Proxmox, we will have to edit this configuration file.

How to do it...

1. Log in to the GUI with a root or any other administrative privilege.
2. Select NFS from the storage plugin. Add a drop-down menu to open the NFS storage creation dialog box.
3. Enter the required information, as shown in the following table:

Item	Type of information	Example value
ID	The name of the storage.	`pmx-nfs`
Server	The IP address of the shared storage node.	`172.16.0.74`
Export	Select available NFS shares from the drop down menu.	`pmx-nfs`

Item	Type of information	Example value
Content	Select type of content to be stored.	**Disk Image, ISO image**
Nodes	Select Proxmox nodes that can use this storage.	All
Enable	The checkbox for enabling/disabling the storage.	Checked
Max Backups	The numeric value of the maximum backup files to keep. Older backup files will be automatically deleted.	2

4. Click on **Add** to attach the NFS storage.

The following screenshot shows the NFS storage dialog box with the necessary values entered:

There's more...

If we need to change the NFS version number in Proxmox, we will need to edit the NFS share segment in the storage configuration file. Simply change the option parameter value as shown in the following code:

```
nfs: pmx-nfs
    path/mnt/pve/pmx-nfs
    server 172.16.0.74
    export /mnt/pmx-nfs
    options vers=3     //change to 4 for version 4
    content images, iso
    maxfiles 2
```

Connecting the Ceph RBD storage

In this section, we are going to see how to configure a Ceph block storage with a Proxmox cluster.

Getting ready

The initial Ceph configuration on a Proxmox cluster must be accomplished through a CLI. After the Ceph installation, initial configurations and one monitor creation for all other tasks can be accomplished through the Proxmox GUI.

How to do it...

We will now see how to configure the Ceph block storage with Proxmox.

Installing Ceph on Proxmox

Ceph is not installed by default. Prior to configuring a Proxmox node for the Ceph role, Ceph needs to be installed and the initial configuration must be created through a CLI.

The following steps need to be performed on all Proxmox nodes that will be part of the Ceph cluster:

1. Log in to each node through SSH or a console.
2. Configure a second network interface to create a separate Ceph network with a different subnet.
3. Reboot the nodes to initialize the network configuration.
4. Using the following command, install the Ceph package on each node:

   ```
   # pveceph install -version giant
   ```

Initializing the Ceph configuration

Before Ceph is usable, we have to create the initial Ceph configuration file on one *Proxmox+Ceph* node.

The following steps need to be performed only on one Proxmox node that will be part of the Ceph cluster:

1. Log in to the node using SSH or a console.
2. Run the following command create the initial Ceph configuration:

   ```
   # pveceph init -network <ceph_subnet>/CIDR
   ```

3. Run the following command to create the first monitor:

   ```
   # pveceph createmon
   ```

Configuring Ceph through the Proxmox GUI

After the initial Ceph configuration and the creation of the first monitor, we can continue with further Ceph configurations through the Proxmox GUI or simply run the Ceph Monitor creation command on other nodes.

The following steps show how to create Ceph Monitors and OSDs from the Proxmox GUI:

1. Log in to the Proxmox GUI as a root or with any other administrative privilege.

2. Select a node where the initial monitor was created in previous steps, and then click on **Ceph** from the tabbed menu. The following screenshot shows a Ceph cluster as it appears after the initial Ceph configuration:

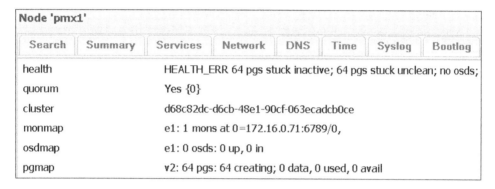

Since no OSDs have been created yet, it is normal for a new Ceph cluster to show PGs stuck and unclean error

3. Click on **Disks** on the bottom tabbed menu under **Ceph** to display the disks attached to the node, as shown in the following screenshot:

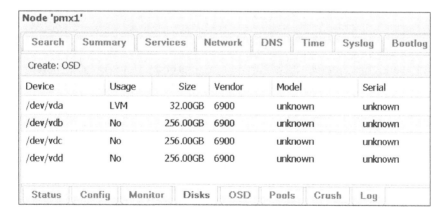

4. Select an available attached disk, then click on the **Create: OSD** button to open the OSD dialog box, as shown in the following screenshot:

5. Click on the **Journal Disk** drop-down menu to select a different device or collocate the journal on the same OSD by keeping it as the default.

6. Click on **Create** to finish the OSD creation.

7. Create additional OSDs on Ceph nodes as needed.

The following screenshot shows a Proxmox node with three OSDs configured:

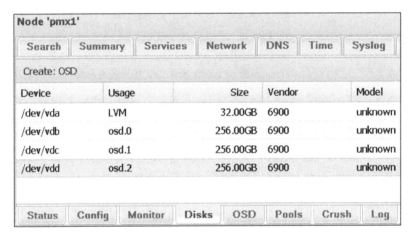

By default, Proxmox has created OSDs with an ext3 partition. However, sometimes, it may be necessary to create OSDs with different partition types due to a requirement or for performance improvement. Enter the following command format through the CLI to create an OSD with a different partition type:

```
# pveceph createosd -fstype ext4 /dev/sdX
```

The following steps show how to create Monitors through the Proxmox GUI:

1. Click on **Monitor** from the tabbed menu under the **Ceph** feature. The following screenshot shows the **Monitor** status with the initial Ceph Monitor we created earlier in this chapter:

2. Click on **Create** to open the **Monitor** dialog box.
3. Select a Proxmox node from the drop-down menu.
4. Click on the **Create** button to start the monitor creation process.
5. Create a total of three Ceph monitors to establish a Ceph quorum.

The following screenshot shows the Ceph status with three monitors and OSDs added:

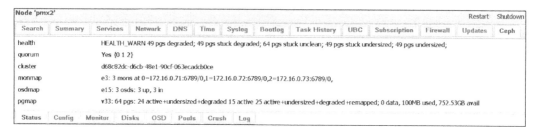

Note that even with three OSDs added, the PGs are still stuck with errors. This is because by default, the Ceph CRUSH is set up for two replicas. So far, we've only created OSDs on one node. For a successful replication, we need to add some OSDs on the second node so that data objects can be replicated twice. Follow the steps described earlier to create three additional OSDs on the second node. After creating three more OSDs, the Ceph status should look like the following screenshot:

Node 'pmx2'								
Search	Summary	Services	Network	DNS	Time	Syslog	Bootlog	Task History

health	HEALTH_OK
quorum	Yes {0 1 2}
cluster	d68c82dc-d6cb-48e1-90cf-063ecadcb0ce
monmap	e3: 3 mons at 0=172.16.0.71:6789/0,1=172.16.0.72:6789/0,2=172.16.0.73:6789/0,
osdmap	e68: 6 osds: 6 up, 6 in
pgmap	v149: 256 pgs: 256 active+clean; 0 data, 221MB used, 1.47TB avail

Status	Config	Monitor	Disks	OSD	Pools	Crush	Log

Managing Ceph pools

It is possible to perform basic tasks, such as creating and removing Ceph pools through the Proxmox GUI. Besides these, we can see check the list, status, number of PGs, and usage of the Ceph pools.

The following steps show how to check, create, and remove Ceph pools through the Proxmox GUI:

1. Click on the **Pools** tabbed menu under **Ceph** in the Proxmox GUI. The following screenshot shows the status of the default rbd pool, which has replica 1, 256 PG, and 0% usage:

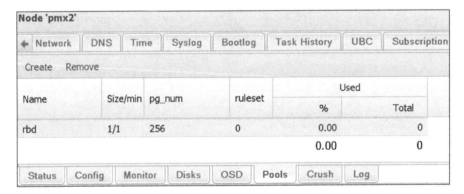

2. Click on **Create** to open the pool creation dialog box.

3. Fill in the required information, such as the name of the pool, replica size, and number of PGs. Unless the CRUSH map has been fully customized, the ruleset should be left at the default value 0.

4. Click on **OK** to create the pool.

5. To remove a pool, select the pool and click on **Remove**. Remember that once a Ceph pool is removed, all the data stored in this pool is deleted permanently.

To increase the number of PGs, run the following command through the CLI:

```
#ceph osd pool set <pool_name> pg_num <value>
#ceph osd pool set <pool_name> pgp_num <value>
```

 It is only possible to increase the PG value. Once increased, the PG value can never be decreased.

Connecting RBD to Proxmox

Once a Ceph cluster is fully configured, we can proceed to attach it to the Proxmox cluster.

During the initial configuration file creation, Ceph also creates an authentication keyring in the /etc/ceph/ceph.client.admin.keyring directory path.

This keyring needs to be copied and renamed to match the name of the storage ID to be created in Proxmox. Run the following commands to create a directory and copy the keyring:

```
# mkdir /etc/pve/priv/ceph
# cd /etc/ceph/
# cp ceph.client.admin.keyring /etc/pve/priv/ceph/<storage>.keyring
```

For our storage, we are naming it rbd.keyring. After the keyring is copied, we can attach the Ceph RBD storage with Proxmox using the GUI:

1. Click on **Datacenter**, then click on **Storage** from the tabbed menu.

2. Click on the **Add** drop-down menu and select the **RBD** storage plugin.

3. Enter the information as described in the following table:

Item	Type of value	Entered value
ID	The name of the storage.	rbd
Pool	The name of the Ceph pool.	rbd
Monitor Host	The IP address and port number of the Ceph MONs. We can enter multiple MON hosts for redundancy.	172.16.0.71:6789; 172.16.0.72:6789; 172.16.0.73:6789
User name	The default Ceph administrator.	Admin

Item	Type of value	Entered value
Nodes	The Proxmox nodes that will be able to use the storage.	All
Enable	The checkbox for enabling/disabling the storage.	Enabled

4. Click on **Add** to attach the RBD storage. The following screenshot shows the RBD storage under **Summary**:

Storage 'rbd' on node 'pmx1'

| Summary | Content | Permissions |

Status

Enabled	Yes
Active	Yes
Content	Disk image
Type	RBD
Shared	Yes
Size	1.47TB
Used	226MB
Avail	1.47TB

Monitoring the Ceph storage

Ceph itself does not come with any GUI to manage or monitor the cluster. We can view the cluster status and perform various Ceph-related tasks through the Proxmox GUI. There are several third-party software that allow GUI for Ceph to manage and monitor the cluster. Some software provide management features, while others provide read-only features for Ceph monitoring. Ceph Dash is such a software that provides an appealing read-only GUI to monitor the entire Ceph cluster without logging on to the Proxmox GUI. Ceph Dash is freely available through GitHub. There are other heavyweight Ceph GUI dashboards, such as Kraken, Calamari, and others. In this section, we are only going to see how to set up the Ceph Dash cluster monitoring GUI.

The following steps can be used to download and start Ceph Dash to monitor a Ceph cluster using any browser:

1. Log in to any Proxmox node, which is also a Ceph MON.

2. Run the following commands to download and start the dashboard:

```
# mkdir /home/tools
# apt-get install git
# git clone https://github.com/Crapworks/ceph-dash
# cd /home/tools/ceph-dash
# ./ceph_dash.py
```

3. Ceph Dash will now start listening on port 5000 of the node. If the node is behind a firewall, open port 5000 or any other ports with port forwarding in the firewall.

4. Open any browser and enter <node_ip>:5000 to open the dashboard. The following screenshot shows the dashboard of the Ceph cluster we have created:

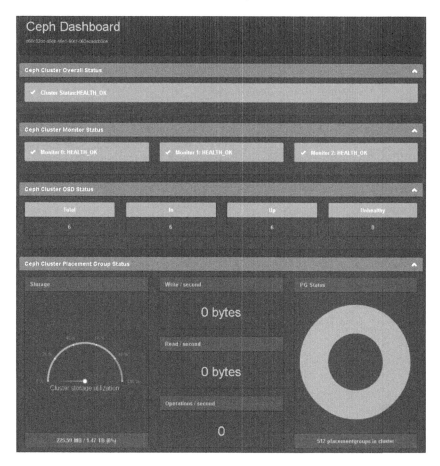

We can also monitor the status of the Ceph cluster through a CLI using the following commands:

1. To check the Ceph status:

   ```
   # ceph -s
   ```

2. To view OSDs in different nodes:

   ```
   # ceph osd tree
   ```

3. To display real-time Ceph logs:

   ```
   # ceph -w
   ```

4. To display a list of Ceph pools:

   ```
   # rados lspools
   ```

5. To change the number of replicas of a pool:

   ```
   # ceph osd pool set size <value>
   ```

Besides the preceding commands, there are many more CLI commands to manage Ceph and perform advanced tasks. The Ceph official documentation has a wealth of information and how-to guides along with the CLI commands to perform them. The documentation can be found at http://ceph.com/docs/master/.

How it works...

At this point, we have successfully integrated a Ceph cluster with a Proxmox cluster, which comprises six OSDs, three MONs, and three nodes. By viewing the Ceph **Status** page, we can get lot of information about a Ceph cluster at a quick glance. From the previous figure, we can see that there are 256 PGs in the cluster and the total cluster storage space is 1.47 TB. A healthy cluster will have the PG status as *active+clean*. Based on the nature of issue, the PGs can have various states, such as *active+unclean*, *inactive+degraded*, *active+stale*, and so on.

 To learn details about all the states, visit http://ceph.com/docs/master/rados/operations/pg-states/.

By configuring a second network interface, we can separate a Ceph network from the main network.

The #`pveceph init` command creates a Ceph configuration file in the `/etc/pve/ceph.conf` directory path. A newly configured Ceph configuration file looks similar to the following screenshot:

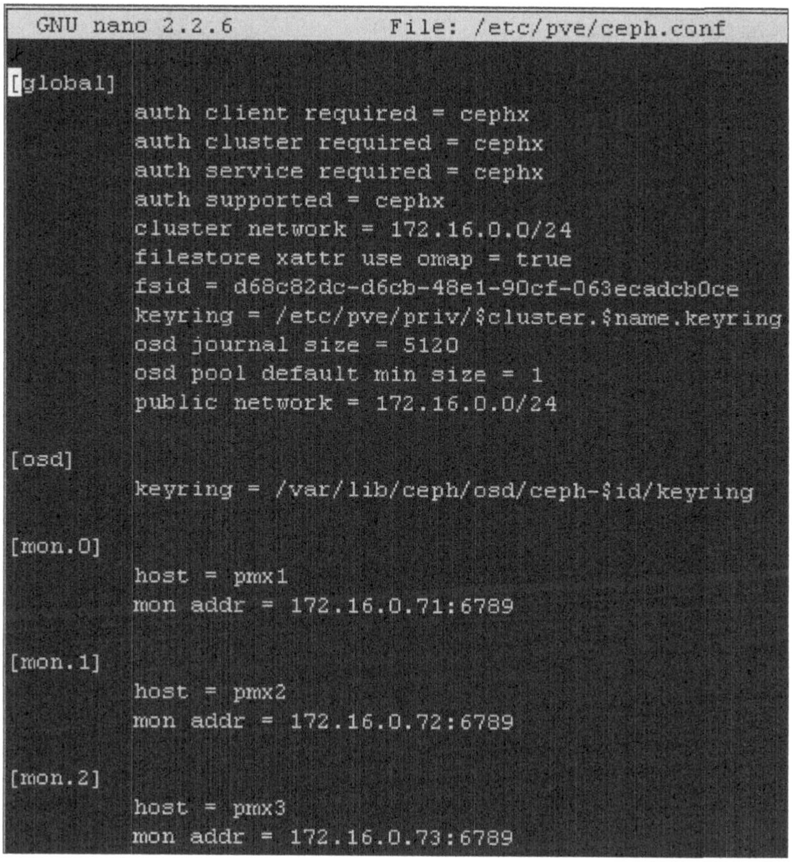

```
  GNU nano 2.2.6              File: /etc/pve/ceph.conf

[global]
        auth client required = cephx
        auth cluster required = cephx
        auth service required = cephx
        auth supported = cephx
        cluster network = 172.16.0.0/24
        filestore xattr use omap = true
        fsid = d68c82dc-d6cb-48e1-90cf-063ecadcb0ce
        keyring = /etc/pve/priv/$cluster.$name.keyring
        osd journal size = 5120
        osd pool default min size = 1
        public network = 172.16.0.0/24

[osd]
        keyring = /var/lib/ceph/osd/ceph-$id/keyring

[mon.0]
        host = pmx1
        mon addr = 172.16.0.71:6789

[mon.1]
        host = pmx2
        mon addr = 172.16.0.72:6789

[mon.2]
        host = pmx3
        mon addr = 172.16.0.73:6789
```

Since the `ceph.conf` configuration file is stored in `pmxcfs`, any changes made to it are immediately replicated in all the Proxmox nodes in the cluster.

As of Proxmox VE 3.4, Ceph RBD can only store a `.raw` image format. No templates, containers, or backup files can be stored on the RBD block storage.

Here is the content of a storage configuration file after adding the Ceph RBD storage:

```
rbd: rbd
    monhost 172.16.0.71:6789;172.16.0.72:6789;172.16.0.73:6789
    pool rbd
    content images
    username admin
```

If a situation dictates the IP address change of any node, we can simply edit this content in the configuration file to manually change the IP address of the Ceph MON nodes.

See also

▸ To learn about Ceph in greater detail, visit `http://ceph.com/docs/master/` for the official Ceph documentation

▸ Also, visit `https://indico.cern.ch/event/214784/session/6/ contribution/68/material/slides/0.pdf` to find out why Ceph is being used at CERN to store the massive data generated by the **Large Hadron Collider (LHC)**

Connecting the ZFS storage

Originally developed by Sun Microsystems, ZFS storage is a combination filesystem and LVM, providing high-capacity storage with important features, such as data protection, data compression, self healing, and snapshots. ZFS has a built-in software defined RAID, which makes the use of a hardware-based RAID unnecessary. A disk array with ZFS RAID can be migrated to a completely different node without rebuilding the entire array.

For more details on ZFS, visit `http://en.wikipedia.org/ wiki/ZFS`.

As of Proxmox VE 3.4, a ZFS storage plugin is included, which leverages the use of ZFS natively in Proxmox cluster nodes. A ZFS pool supports the following RAID types:

RAID type	Minimum requirement
RAID-0 pool	1 disks
RAID-1 pool	2 disks
RAID-10 pool	4 disks
RAIDZ-1 pool	3 disks
RAIDZ-2 pool	4 disks

We can store only the `.raw` format virtual disk images on ZFS storage.

Getting ready

ZFS uses pools to define storage. Pools can only be created through a CLI as of Proxmox VE 3.4. Once pools are created, they can be attached with Proxmox through the Proxmox GUI. The following table shows which string to use for different level of ZFS RAID:

RAID type	String to use
RAID-0	No string
RAID-1	mirror
RAID-10	mirror
RAIDZ-1	raidz1
RAIDZ-2	raidz2

How to do it...

For our example, we are going to create a RAID1 mirrored pool named `zfspool1` and connect it to Proxmox. The command used to create the ZFS pool is as follows:

```
# zpool create -f <pool_name> <raid_type> <dev1_name> <dev2_name> ...
```

In the following two sections, we will discuss two things:

▸ Creating a ZFS pool and attaching it to a Proxmox cluster

▸ Sharing a ZFS storage between Proxmox nodes

Creating a ZFS pool and attaching it to a Proxmox cluster

1. Log in to a Proxmox node console with enough attached disks.

2. Create a ZFS pool using the following command format:

   ```
   # zpool create -f zfspool1 mirror /dev/<id> /dev/<id>
   ```

3. Verify the pool creation using the following command:

   ```
   # zpool list
   ```

4. A successful ZFS pool creation will display the pool list as follows:

```
root@pmx1:~# zpool list
NAME       SIZE   ALLOC   FREE    CAP  DEDUP  HEALTH   ALTROOT
zfspool1  29.8G   116K   29.7G    0%   1.00x  ONLINE   -
root@pmx1:~#
```

The following command format will attach the ZFS pool to a Proxmox cluster through a CLI:

```
# pvesm add <storage_ID>  -type <storage_type> -pool <pool_name>
```

For our example, we are going to attach the ZFS pool, named `zfspool1`, using the following command:

```
# pvesm add zfs -type zfspool -pool zfspool1
```

The command to attach the ZFS pool to the Proxmox cluster must be run from the node where the ZFS pool is created.

Sharing the ZFS storage between Proxmox nodes

The ZFS pool will only function locally from the node where the pool is created. Other nodes in the Proxmox cluster will not be able to share the storage. By mounting a ZFS pool locally and creating an NFS share, it is possible to share ZFS pools between all the Proxmox nodes.

The process of mounting and sharing needs to be done through a CLI only. From the Proxmox GUI, we can only attach the NFS share with an underlying ZFS pool:

1. By default, the ZFS pool is automatically mounted in the `/<pool_name>` root directory path. We need to create the following directory where we will remount the pool:

    ```
    # mkdir /mnt/zfs
    ```

2. We can remount the ZFS pool in a newly created directory using the following command:

    ```
    # zfs set mountpoint=/mnt/zfs zfspool1
    ```

3. Install the NFS server using the following command on the Proxmox node if it is not installed yet:

    ```
    # apt-get install nfs-kernel-server
    ```

4. Enter the following line in `/etc/exports`:

    ```
    /mnt/zfs/ 172.16.0.71/24(rw,nohide,async,no_root_squash)
    ```

5. Start an NFS service using the following command:

    ```
    # service nfs-kernel-server start
    ```

6. Log in to the Proxmox GUI and follow the steps from the *Connecting the NFS storage* recipe earlier in this chapter to connect the new share with Proxmox.

How it works...

By combining the ZFS pool with the NFS share, we can create a shared storage with full ZFS features, thus creating a flexible shared storage to use with all the Proxmox nodes in the cluster. By using this technique, we can create a backup storage node, which is also manageable through the Proxmox GUI. This way, during a node crisis, we can also migrate VMs to the backup nodes temporarily.

Here is the content of a storage configuration file after adding the ZFS storage:

```
zfspool: zfs
    pool zfspool1
    content images
```

Connecting the GlusterFS storage

Unlike other storage systems, GlusterFS is a distributed filesystem that is capable of scaling to several petabytes and serving many thousands of clients. The filesystem requires no metadata server, thus there is no single point of failure. GlusterFS allows the creation of highly available storage clusters using commodity hardware, thus reducing costs and eliminating vendor lock-ins. As of Proxmox VE 3.4, there is a native storage plugin to attach GlusterFS to Proxmox clusters.

> To learn more about GlusterFS, view the official documentation at http://gluster.readthedocs.org/en/latest/ Administrator%20Guide/GlusterFS%20Introduction/.

Getting ready...

Unlike ZFS, Proxmox does not have GlusterFS packages preinstalled. It is possible to install Gluster packages on the same Proxmox node or set up a different node only for GlusterFS purposes. Unlike Ceph, Gluster installation is not fully built into Proxmox with custom commands. The full details of GlusterFS installation are beyond the scope of this book.

> For instructions on how to set up a GlusterFS cluster, visit http://gluster.readthedocs.org/en/latest/ Quick-Start-Guide/Quickstart/.

Following the official guide, create two Gluster nodes in a replicated mode. At the end of the GlusterFS installation, create a Gluster volume named gfsvol1or or any other desired name so that you can use it to connect to a Proxmox cluster in the next section.

How to do it...

The following steps will connect a GlusterFS pool to Proxmox through a GUI:

1. Log in to the Proxmox GUI.

2. Go to the **Storage** tabbed menu and click on the **Add** drop-down menu to select the **GlusterFS** plugin.

3. The following table shows the type of information needed and the values used for our example to attach GlusterFS:

Item	Description	Entered values
ID	The new name of the storage.	gluster
Server	The IP address of the first Gluster node.	172.16.0.72
Second Server	The IP address of the second Gluster node.	172.16.0.73
Volume name	The drop-down menu for selecting available volumes on a Gluster node.	gfsvol11
Content	Select the type of files to be stored.	**Disk image, ISO image**
Nodes	Select the nodes that can access the storage.	All
Enable	Enabling or disabling the storage.	Enabled
Max Backups	The maximum number of recent backup files that can be stored. Older backups will be deleted automatically during the backup process.	2

4. Click on the **Add** button to attach the storage.

How it works...

Here is the content of a storage configuration file after adding the Gluster storage:

```
glusterfs: gluster
    volume gfsvol1
    path /mnt/pve/gluster
    content images
    server 172.16.0.72
    server 172.16.0.73
    maxfiles 2
```

7

Backup and Restore

Backup and restore are crucial components of any computer network environment. In this chapter, we are going to look at how to configure backup and restore in a Proxmox cluster. We will cover the following topics in this chapter:

- ▸ Configuring a backup storage
- ▸ Scheduling backups
- ▸ Performing a manual backup
- ▸ Managing snapshots
- ▸ Restoring a backup
- ▸ Configuring a backup with vzdump.conf
- ▸ Backing up through the command line
- ▸ Restoring through the command line

Introduction

The Proxmox VE comes equipped with a robust backup and restore system to ensure data safety of virtual machines in a cluster. A good backup and restore system is mandatory for any sound disaster planning strategy. It is not matter of if, but when a disaster strikes, we must have the ability to restore virtual machines from as much of a latest backup as possible. A disaster can include a wide variety of situations, such as hardware failure, environmental damage, accidental deletions, misconfigurations, or anything else of this nature.

In a virtual environment, the importance of a sound backup/restore strategy is even higher. Since VMs are created and discarded frequently, without a proper strategy, a backup can quickly go out of control. A restore plan is also equally important since a backup is useless if we cannot restore in a timely and proper manner after a disaster. Although the Proxmox VE does not have the ability to do any granular file-level backups, it does offer great features for full backups and snapshots of virtual machines. If a file-level backup is a requirement, then a third-party solution must be implemented along with the Proxmox VE backup system. Options such as BackupPC, BareOS, Zamanda, and others, can be great additions to a disaster recovery plan.

Types of backup

There are two types of backup available in the Proxmox VE:

- Full backup
- Snapshots

Full backup

This type is a full backup of each virtual machine. Each backup holds a virtual machine's configuration files and all the virtual disk images for the VM. A full backup is equivalent to a bare metal backup, and a virtual machine can be restored even when the original VM no longer exists. There are three backup modes available for this backup option:

- Snapshot
- Suspend
- Stop

Snapshot

This is not the same as snapshots of a VM where it freezes the state of the VM at a moment in time. A snapshot backup is just a mode where a full backup occurs without powering off or temporarily suspending the VM. It is also known as a **live backup**. There is no downtime for this backup, although some backups may cause a minor slowdown of VM functions. Since a backup occurs in parallel with the regular operation of the VM, it also has the longest backup time.

Suspend

This mode commits a full backup by temporarily suspending or freezing the VM. There is no need to completely power off the VM, thus downtime is moderate during the backup. After the backup is completed, the VM resumes its operations.

Stop

This backup mode completely powers off a VM before committing a backup. After the backup is finished, the VM is powered up again. This mode has the longest downtime since the VM must be fully powered off. This mode also guarantees 100% accurate backups of all data and takes the lowest amount of time to commit the backup.

Backup compression

The Proxmox VE supports two types of compression method for full backups:

- LZO
- GZIP

LZO

This provides a shorter backup time than GZIP, and at a lower compression. It also has a very fast decompression rate, making restore of a VM faster.

GZIP

This method not only provides high compression, but also has a longer backup time. Due to an increased compression rate, this method consumes much more CPU and memory resources. Ensure that the backup nodes have sufficient processing abilities before enabling this compression method.

Snapshots

Snapshots are the frozen state of a VM at a point in time. They do not create any full backups and should not be used as the primary backup method of a virtual machine. Snapshots are only available for a KVM-based VM. There is no snapshotting option for OpenVZ containers. The advantage of snapshots over full backups is that they take significantly less time than a full backup. A VM can be reverted to previous snapshots in a fraction of the time it takes to restore a VM from a full backup. Snapshots are a great option when applying a new patch or update, and also to preserve the running state of a VM by saving the content of its memory. If something goes wrong during these patches or updates, it is very easy to rollback to the previous state. Also, snapshots can be used in between full backups. All snapshots are dependent on the original VM, thus if the VM gets destroyed completely, it is not possible to roll back from the snapshots. During a full backup, all the snapshots of a VM are ignored to reduce the backup storage consumption.

 A full backup should never be substituted with snapshots. Always include a full backup in a primary data safety strategy.

As of Proxmox VE 3.4, there is no option to schedule automated snapshots. All snapshots must be created manually.

Configuring a backup storage

All backups must be stored on a separate node configured for backup purposes only. If backups are stored on the same Proxmox node, during hardware failure, it will not be possible to restore VMs for a damaged node. There are different options to set up a backup node. The most popular option is to set up a node with an NFS share to store backups. In enterprise or a mission-critical environment, a backup node cluster is common with redundancy. In smaller environments, good redundancy can still be achieved by using options, such as Gluster or DRBD. With the addition of ZFS and Gluster in the Proxmox VE, it is also a viable option to turn a Proxmox node into a backup node by using Gluster with ZFS.

Refer to *Chapter 6, Storage Configurations*, for different storage options available and steps on how to set up these storages. The advantage of using a Proxmox node as a backup node is the ability to monitor the node along with rest of the nodes in the cluster.

Getting ready

For a single backup storage node, FreeNAS is a great option without the redundancy out of the box. Before setting up a backup node, be sure that the storage will support the storage of backup files. For example, a Ceph storage does not support the storage of any backup files; thus it cannot be used as a backup node for Proxmox.

How to do it...

The following screenshot shows the storage configuration dialog box for a NFS share used as a backup storage node:

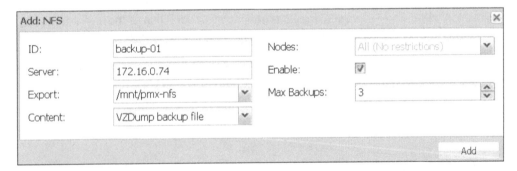

Be sure to set an appropriate value for **Max Backups**. This value defines the maximum number of backup files of a VM that are going to be kept. When a full backup reaches this value, any older backup files of the VM are automatically deleted. If the value is high without enough backup storage space, the backup will not be able to proceed. In such cases, some files must be manually deleted before a backup can resume.

Scheduling backups

In this section, we are going to see how to configure or schedule a full backup of a VM.

Getting ready

In Proxmox VE, full backup can be scheduled to commit automatically, or you can perform manual backups of VMs. All backup tasks can be performed through the Proxmox GUI. The backup is accessible through **Datacenter** or a VM tabbed menu. The datacenter **Backup** menu allows the scheduling of backup tasks for all VMs cluster-wide. The VM **Backup** menu allows performing a backup for an individual VM. The VM **Backup** menu does not allow any backup scheduling. It must be performed through the datacenter **Backup** menu.

When scheduling automated backups, care needs to be taken over how many backup jobs are going to performed simultaneously. For example, if there are six Proxmox nodes with VMs, and a schedule has been created to back up six VMs at the same time onto the same backup nodes, failure may occur if the backup node does not have sufficient processing power. In large environments with many hundreds of VMs, backup scheduling may become a tedious job to balance resources. Attention to the backup node hardware must be given when selecting proper components. For example, a multisocket configuration will always outperform a single socket one due to increased threads, provided that there is enough network bandwidth available for an I/O operation.

In some cases, this issue can be mitigated by using more than one backup node. Also, using a separate network for backup purposes only will increase the backup performance instead of using the same client network. By default, only one backup job is allowed in Proxmox per node.

How to do it...

The following steps show how to schedule a backup task through the datacenter **Backup** menu:

1. Log in to the Proxmox GUI.

2. Select **Datacenter** and then click on the **Backup** menu.

3. Click on **Add** to open the backup dialog box.

4. Select a node from the Node drop-down menu to display a VM only on that node or leave it at -- **All** -- to display all the VMs. A backup job is created with -- **All** -- that will follow the VM no matter which Proxmox node the VM is moved to. If a job is created based on a particular node when the VM is moved to a different node, then the backup task will not be performed for that node.

5. Select a backup storage node from the **Storage** drop-down menu.

6. Select the days when the backup job should be performed through the **Day of week** drop-down menu.

7. Select the **Start Time** to start the backup job.

8. Select how the VM should be selected from the **Selection mode** drop-down menu.

9. Enter an e-mail address in the **Send mail to** box. This is the e-mail address that backup logs will be sent to.

10. Select the **Email notification** type to choose when to send the e-mail. If **On failure only** is selected, then the e-mail will only be sent if there is an error in backup. This option will also avoid you getting too many e-mails a day and running into the issue of skipping over an error e-mail.

11. Select the **Compression** method from the drop-down menu.

 When selecting a method, keep in mind the trade-offs between the backup duration and CPU impact due to increased compression and backup storage space.

12. Select a backup **Mode** from the drop-down menu.

13. Select the VMs from the VM list.

14. Click on **Create** to finish creating the backup task.

The following screenshot shows the backup dialog box with the appropriate information selected and entered:

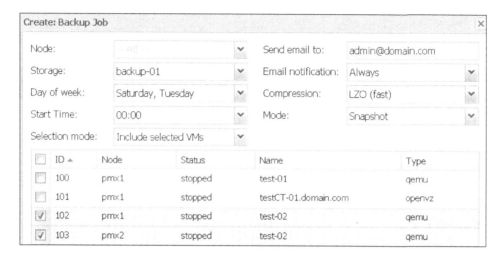

This screenshot shows the **Backup** menu with the example backup job scheduled:

How it works...

As of Proxmox VE 3.4, we can only perform automatic backups on a weekly basis. To store backup files for more than one week, it is necessary to move backup files to different backup nodes for a longer storage cycle. By adjusting the **Max Backups** value and the days of the week, we can also increase the backup length. For example, if we set the **Max Backups** value to 8 and create a backup job for a VM to perform once a week only, we can keep two months of backup files in hand at all times because every month, there will be four backup files. In between weekly backups, we can use snapshots daily.

Backup files are named in the following format and do not contain the virtual machine name or any comment related to the VM:

```
vzdump-qemu-<vm_id>-YYYY_MM_DD_HH_MM_SS.vma.<lzo|gz>
```

Performing a manual backup

In this section, we are going to see how to commit manual backup for VMs.

Getting ready

A manual backup can be performed on a particular VM at any point in time. Similar to a backup that is scheduled, a manual backup can also be performed fully through the Proxmox GUI.

How to do it...

The following steps show how to commit manual backups for a VM:

1. Log in to the Proxmox GUI.
2. Select a VM from the left navigation bar for which a manual backup needs to be performed, and then click on the **Backup** tabbed menu.
3. Click on **Backup now** to open the backup dialog box.
4. Select the backup storage from the **Storage** drop-down menu.
5. Select the backup mode.
6. Select the backup compression type.
7. Click on **Backup** to start the backup task.

The following screenshot shows the backup dialog box with the appropriate options selected:

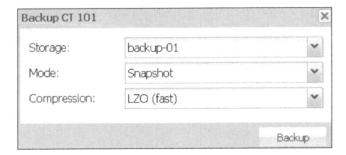

This screenshot shows the list of backup files after the manual backup is completed:

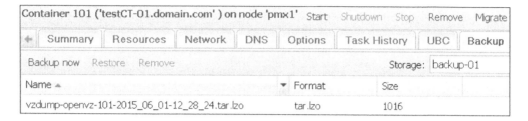

Managing snapshots

In this section, we are going to see how to create snapshots of a KVM-based VM and roll back to the previous state.

Getting ready

Snapshots can be created and rolled back through the Proxmox GUI. The **Snapshots** menu is only available through a VM-specific tabbed menu.

How to do it...

The following steps show how to create a snapshot of a VM:

1. Select a VM for which snapshots need to be created and click on the **Snapshots** tabbed menu.

2. Click on **Take Snapshot** to open a dialog box.

3. Enter the name of the snapshot. The string must start with at least one alphabetic letter.

4. If the snapshot is being created for a powered up VM, then select the **Include RAM** checkbox or else uncheck it.

> This option will save the state of a running VM, saving the content of the memory. If it is not selected, then the snapshot is created only for the disk image. This can lead to filesystem inconsistency when reverting back.

5. Enter a description for the snapshot.

6. Click on the **Take Snapshot** button to create the snapshot.

The following screenshot shows the **Snapshots** feature with the snapshot created:

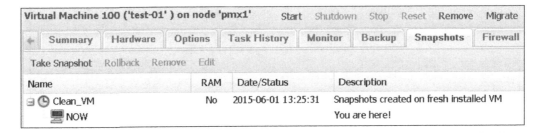

To roll back to a previous snapshot, simply select **Snapshots** and click on the **Rollback** button. This will revert the VM to the previous state.

To delete a snapshot, select the snapshot and click on **Remove**.

The **Edit** button only allows you to change the description of the snapshot. The current VM will always be at the bottom of the snapshots list, **NOW**, with the description, **You are here!**.

Restoring a backup

The restore feature of Proxmox allows the restoration of a VM from backups. In this section, we are going to see how to restore a VM through the Proxmox GUI.

Getting ready

Like backup, a VM can also be restored through the Proxmox GUI. A VM can be restored by selecting the VM if it's available or by selecting the backup storage. If **Restore** is selected through the VM **Backup** option, **VM ID** cannot be changed. However, we can select a backup from a different VM and restore it on a different VM ID, thus effectively changing the ID of the restored VM. If the same VM is restored on the same ID, it will erase the existing VM before restoring. A prompt will require the user to confirm that the removal of the existing VM is okay. The following screenshot shows the restore dialog box when selected through a VM-specific tabbed menu:

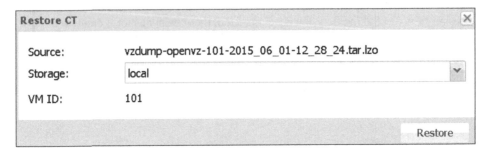

If **Restore** is selected through the backup storage, then **VM ID** can be changed to something else. The destination storage where the VM will be stored can be changed for both restoring options. The following screenshot shows the dialog box when **Restore** is selected through the backup storage:

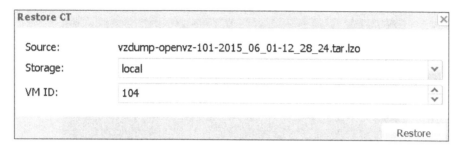

Beware of restoring the same VM on multiple VM IDs. If all of them are up and running at the same time, it will cause networking issues for all of them, as their network configurations will be identical. This can be a common issue when restoring the same VM on multiple IDs for cloning purposes. In such scenarios, only bring one VM online at a time and make network configurations, such as IP changes.

How to do it...

The following steps show how to restore a VM from a full backup:

1. Select the backup storage, then click on **Content** to display the files stored in the storage.
2. Select a backup file of a VM and click on **Restore**.
3. Select the destination storage where the VM will be stored.
4. Click on **Restore**.
5. Click **Yes** to confirm the deletion of the existing VM.

Configuring a backup with vzdump.conf

The `vzdump.conf` file holds backup configurations for both manual and automated backup schedules. It is located in `/etc/vzdump.conf` of each Proxmox node. The configuration is different for each node. Any changes made to the file will not be replicated across the cluster. All the default backup configurations are encoded in the operating system. Any changes made to this file will override any default backup settings.

How to do it...

The following screenshot shows `vzdump.conf` as it appears on a Proxmox node:

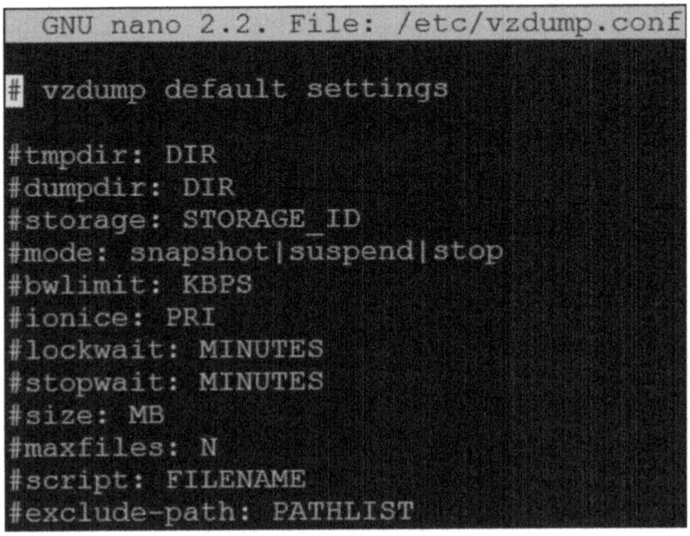

```
  GNU nano 2.2.  File: /etc/vzdump.conf

# vzdump default settings

#tmpdir: DIR
#dumpdir: DIR
#storage: STORAGE_ID
#mode: snapshot|suspend|stop
#bwlimit: KBPS
#ionice: PRI
#lockwait: MINUTES
#stopwait: MINUTES
#size: MB
#maxfiles: N
#script: FILENAME
#exclude-path: PATHLIST
```

By default, all the options are commented. To change an option, simply uncomment and set a value for each option. Here are some of the most commonly used options and their functions.

#bwlimit

This option sets the network bandwidth consumption during backup jobs. The limit must be defined in KBPS. For example, if we want to restrict the backup to 500 Mbps, we will change the limit as follows in the `vzdump.conf` file:

```
bwlimit 500000
```

#lockwait

To prevent multiple backup instances from using the same resource, a running Proxmox backup uses a global lockwait time, which is 180 minutes. Depending on the various sizes of clusters, this lockwait time may need to be increased. The value must be defined in MINUTES. For example, if we want to increase the lockwait to 400 minutes, we will need to change it as follows:

```
lockwait 400
```

#stopwait

This value defines the amount of time the backup job will wait till a VM is stopped. Some VMs take much longer to shut down than others, for example, an exchange or database server. If a VM is not stopped automatically within a set period of time, then the backup task for this VM is skipped. This value also must be defined in MINUTES.

#script

In Proxmox, it is possible to create a script and hook with a backup job. The script is a set of instructions that can be called during a backup job to perform various tasks, such as starting or stopping a VM. A script can be added by adding the following path in vzdump.conf:

```
script: /etc/pve/script/backup.pl
```

An example of this script can be found by visiting https://github.com/proxmox/pve-manager/blob/master/vzdump-hook-script.pl, courtesy of Dietmar Maurer from the Proxmox development team.

#exclude-path

This options allows you to set directories that should be ignored during a backup job. All paths must be entered in one line without breaks. This option only affects OpenVZ containers. The following example ignores a log and cache directory during a backup job:

```
exclude-path: "/log/.+""/var/cache/.+"
```

Backing up through the command line

VZdump is used to backup both KVM-based virtual machines and OpenVZ containers. In Proxmox, a backup can also be performed through the command line.

How to do it...

Data can be backed up in Proxmox using the following command:

```
# vzdump <vmid> [options] [options] ..
```

VZdump has a wide range of options that can be used to perform a backup task. Here are just some of the most commonly used options:

Option	Function
-all	This option will backup all VMs in a Proxmox node. The default is set as 0.
-bwlimit	This is to adjust the backup bandwidth in KBPS.
-mailto	This is the e-mail address to send backup logs to.

Option	Function
-maxfiles	This value is to set the maximum number of backup files to keep.
-mode	This is set as the backup mode. Available options are snapshot, stop, and suspend. The default is stop.
-compress	This is a set compression method. Available options are LZO and Gzip.
-remove	This is to remove older backups if more than the value used in maxfiles.
-lockwait	This is the maximum time taken in minutes to wait for a global lock. The default is 180.
-storage	This is the storage ID of a destination backup storage.
-tmpdir	This specifies a temporary directory to store files in during a backup.

Restoring through the command line

Although the same `vzdump` command can be used to back up both KVM and OpenVZ VMs, there are separate commands to restore each of them:

- ▶ `qmrestore`: This is to restore a KVM-based VM
- ▶ `vzrestore`: This is to restore OpenVZ containers

How to do it...

The following command will restore KVM VMs through a command line:

```
# qmrestore <backup_file> <vmid> [options]
```

These options can be used with the `qmrestore` command:

Option	Function
-force	This has a boolean value of 0 or 1 to allow the overwriting of an existing VM.
-unique	This has a boolean value of 0 or 1 to assign a unique random Ethernet address.
-pool	This is the name of the pool to add the VM to.
-storage	This is the storage ID of the destination storage where a VM's disk image will be restored.

This command will restore OpenVZ containers through a command line:

```
# vzrestore <backup_file> <vmid> [options]
```

The following options can be used with the `vzrestore` command:

Option	Function
-force	This has a boolean value of 0 or 1 to allow the overwriting of an existing VM.
-storage	This is the storage ID of the destination storage where a VM's disk image will be restored.

8

Updating and Upgrading Proxmox

In this chapter, we will look at how to update and upgrade a Proxmox node to keep it up to date. We will cover the following topics:

- Updating Proxmox through the GUI
- Updating Proxmox through the CLI
- Updating after a change in subscription
- Rebooting dilemmas after an update

Introduction

A Proxmox update keeps a node up to date with the latest stable packages, patches, security vulnerabilities, and the introduction of new features. Each node checks for the latest updates and alerts administrators through e-mail if there are any available updates. It is vital to keep all the Proxmox nodes up to date, especially when security patches are released. Proxmox developers are very quick to close known vulnerabilities through updates.

The number and nature of updates varies depending on the subscription level. For example, a free version of Proxmox without subscription receives the most up-to-date stable updates, while a node with a subscription level receives updates that are not so cutting edge and goes through additional layers of testing.

This is not to say that a node without a subscription is not as stable as a paid version. Both offer a very high level of stability and performance. The only difference is the delay that allows subscribed updates to receive bug fixes, which may not have been noticed during the initial release of the update in a subscription-free version of Proxmox.

A Proxmox node can be updated through both a GUI and CLI. There is no strict recommendation on which one to use. However, in recent a release, an incident occurred when upgrading through the Proxmox GUI Shell and caused grub issues, making the node unbootable. The issue would not have occurred if the upgrading had been done through a CLI by accessing the node through SSH or by logging in directly into the node console.

There are two ways to update or upgrade a Proxmox node:

 ▸ **Packages upgrade only**: The following command only upgrades already installed packages to their latest version:

```
#apt-get upgrade
```

This does not solve any dependencies for newer packages, nor does it remove any packages. This upgrade can only be done through the CLI. This upgrade process does not guarantee a fully-upgraded, stable system.

 ▸ **Distribution upgrade**: The following command upgrades the entire operating system, including updating kernels, installing new packages, removing obsolete packages, and also installing any dependencies for packages:

```
#apt-get dist-upgrade
```

An update through the Proxmox GUI initiates this upgrade. It can also be done through the CLI. To ensure a fully-upgraded system, this is the recommended upgrade process.

Refer to http://forum.proxmox.com/threads/21045-grub2-update-problems-for-3-4-(GUI-only)-leading-to-not-correctly-installed-packages to learn more about updating issues when using the Proxmox GUI instead of CLI.

This chapter mainly concerns updating nodes where Proxmox has been installed as the bare metal operating system. In some cases, a user may have chosen to install Proxmox on top of the Debian operating system. Steps laid out in this chapter can be applied to Debian-based Proxmox nodes also.

Updating Proxmox through the GUI

In this section, we will see how to update a Proxmox node through a GUI.

Getting ready

Proxmox checks for daily updates and displays relevant packages for which updates are available based on the subscription level. The **Updates** menu in the Proxmox GUI can be accessed by selecting the node and clicking on the **Updates** tabbed menu. The following screenshot shows the available update packages for our pmx1 example node:

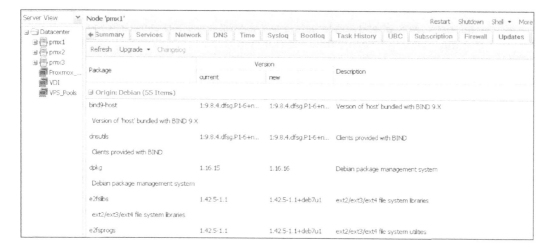

From the preceding screenshot, we can see that node pmx1 has 55 updates available.

How to do it...

The following steps will update a Proxmox node through the GUI:

1. Log in to the Proxmox GUI.
2. Select a node from the left navigation bar.
3. Click on the **Updates** tabbed menu.
4. Click on **Upgrade** to open a shell to start the update process. If the package list is out of date, it will show the message as follows:

```
Your package database is out of date. Please update that first.

starting shell
root@pmx1:/#
```

5. If the package list is out of date, at the console prompt, type the following command to start updating the list:

```
# apt-get update
```

6. After the package list is updated, run the following command to start the upgrading process:

```
# apt-get dist-upgrade
```

7. If the package is already up to date, the shell will open and start upgrading after the **Upgrade** button is selected from the GUI menu.

8. Exit the console after the update is completed.

9. Reboot the node if necessary. Usually, when there is a kernel update or an update for important dependencies that are related to other major components of an operating system, it becomes necessary to reboot the node.

Due to the latest grub2 update, there are some instances when updating the Proxmox node through the GUI can cause issue-breaking packages. To prevent this issue from arising, it is best to upgrade the node through SSH or a console by logging in directly at the node and not through the GUI. If the upgrade has already been applied through the GUI and there are unconfigured packages due to the issue, the following steps laid down by the Proxmox staff will fix the issue:

1. Check the package status with the following command:

```
# pveversion -v
```

2. Before configuring grub, you have to know the device on which Proxmox is installed. You can find the device by running the following command:

```
# parted -l
```

3. If there are incorrect packages, run the following commands to kill the background dpkg process and configure all the packages, including the new grub2:

```
# killall dpkg
```

```
# dpkg --configure -a
```

4. Select the Proxmox device name when prompted during the grub2 installation.

5. Reboot the node.

It is also possible to manually install grub2 into MBR. Run the following command to install grub2 in the device:

```
# grub-install /dev/sdX
```

How it works...

Proxmox downloads an updated package list daily and sends an e-mail to a root e-mail address. The Proxmox GUI update menu visually displays the list. If there are no updates available, the list will be empty with the **No updates available** message, as shown in the following screenshot:

You can also see the latest and previous changes to the packages through the **Changelog** button under the **Updates** tabbed menu. Select a package from the updates list and click on **Changelog**. The following screenshot shows the changelog of a package named bind9-host:

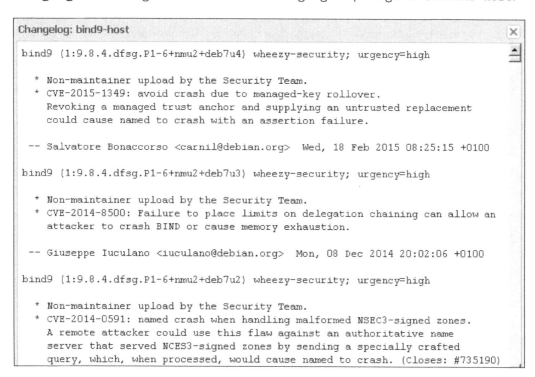

During the upgrade process, additional user prompts may be needed to accept the changes or to read additional information regarding certain changes in the package. The following screenshot shows a prompt requiring user interaction during the node upgrade:

```
curl (7.28.1-1) experimental; urgency=low

  From this version the CURLOPT_SSL_VERIFYHOST option will stop accepting "1"
  as a valid value. From the documentation:

  > When the value is 1, libcurl will return a failure. It was previously (in
  > 7.28.0 and earlier) a debug option of some sorts, but it is no longer
  > supported due to frequently leading to programmer mistakes.

  -- Alessandro Ghedini <ghedo@debian.org>  Mon, 26 Nov 2012 17:46:27 +0100

(q to quit)
```

Updating Proxmox through the CLI

In this section, we will see how to update a Proxmox node through the command line.

How to do it...

The following steps are used to upgrade only installed packages through the command line:

1. Log in to the Proxmox node through SSH or directly from the console.
2. Run the following command to update packages:

   ```
   # apt-get update && apt-get upgrade
   ```

No reboot is necessary for this upgrade.

The following steps will update a node entirely by using the command line:

1. Log in to the Proxmox node through SSH or directly from the console.
2. Run the following command to update packages and upgrade the node:

   ```
   # apt-get update && apt-get dist-upgrade
   ```

3. Reboot the node if necessary. Usually, when there is a kernel update or an update for important dependencies that are related to other major components of an operating system, it becomes necessary to reboot the node.

Updating after a change in subscription

In this section, we will see how to update a node if the subscription level of the node changes at any time.

Getting ready

The Proxmox subscription level for a node can be changed at any time by simply applying a subscription key through a GUI. Different subscription levels have different natures of package updates. If a node starts with no subscription, it can always be changed to any paid subscription at any given time. After the subscription level changes, it is important to update the node accordingly so that the updates related to the subscription level can be applied.

How to do it...

The following steps show you how to update if there is a subscription level change for a node:

1. Log in to the Proxmox GUI and apply a subscription key through the **Subscription** tabbed menu.

2. Log in to the console through SSH or an open shell in the node through the GUI.

3. Edit the repository file in `/etc/apt/sources.list` and `/etc/apt/sources.list.d/pve-enterprise.list` based on the subscription level. Enter the correct repository based on the official Proxmox documentation at `https://pve.proxmox.com/wiki/Package_repositories`.

4. If you're updating through the Proxmox GUI, follow the steps in the *Updating Proxmox through the GUI* recipe in this chapter.

5. If you're updating through a command line, follow the steps in the *Updating Proxmox through the CLI* recipe in this chapter.

How it works...

As mentioned earlier, the updated packages available will vary depending on different subscription levels. On a nonsubscribed node, the subscription repository must be disabled. This can be done by commenting out the repository in the `/etc/apt/sources.list/pve-enterprise.list` file. The same enterprise repository works for all paid subscription levels, such as **COMMUNITY**, **BASIC**, **STANDARD**, and **PREMIUM**. All paid subscriptions receive the same type of updates.

Rebooting dilemmas after an update

After any update or upgrade, all administrators face the question of whether or not the node should be rebooted and whether or not virtual machines need to be power-cycled. A Proxmox upgrade process is usually very informative, letting us know whether the node really needs a reboot. Most updates do not require any reboot. They are simply package updates. However, some upgrades, such as kernel releases, newer grubs, and others, will require a node reboot to apply the new changes. The exact method of rebooting depends on each environment and the number and nature of the VMs that are stored per node. In this section, we are going to look at the most widely used method, which is by no means the only method.

How to do it...

For a minimal virtual machine downtime, we can live-migrate all the VMs from one node to another, then migrate them back to the original node. As of Proxmox VE 3.4, there is a nice GUI feature addition to instruct all VM migrations with a menu instead of selecting and migrating VMs one at a time. The following steps will migrate VMs through the Proxmox GUI:

1. Log in to the Proxmox GUI.

2. Select the node to be rebooted from the left navigation bar.

3. Click on the **More** drop-down menu, as shown in the following screenshot, and then click on **Migrate All VMs**:

4. Restart the node and migrate all the VMs back to the node.

If the Proxmox cluster environment is not very mission-critical and some downtime is allowed, then you can shutdown all the VMs in the node and then restart them. Simply click on **Stop All VMs** from the **More** drop-down menu to shut down all VMs in the node, and then restart the node. After the node restarts, start all the VMs by clicking on **Start All VMs** under the **More** drop-down menu.

There's more...

Always check and read up on all major or minor Proxmox update releases before applying them to a node. The Proxmox Roadmap link (`http://pve.proxmox.com/wiki/Roadmap#Roadmap`) is a good place to explore new feature additions and bug fixes, or simply find information on changes.

The official Proxmox forum is also a great place to hang out to get information on issues that have resulted due to updates. This is also a great place to learn about fixes posted by Proxmox developers in response to any issues with released updates. For the official Proxmox forum, visit `https://forum.proxmox.com`.

9

Monitoring Proxmox

In this chapter, we will see how to monitor and configure notifications so that when something goes wrong in a cluster, we can know about it right away and take the necessary action. We will cover the following topics in this chapter:

- Monitoring with Zabbix
- Proxmox built-in monitoring
- Configuring the disk health notifications
- Configuring SNMP in Proxmox
- Monitoring a Ceph cluster with the Ceph dashboard

Introduction

In a network of any size, it is only a matter of time before something stops working due to intentional or unintentional circumstances. Situations can vary widely depending on various faults, such as hardware failure, software bugs, human errors, or just about any incident that causes a disruption of a network service. Network monitoring is a practice where network management staff can keep a pulse check of the network they are responsible for.

There isn't one system to monitor everything. A good monitoring system is usually put together with various tools and some type of notification option to send alerts automatically. A Proxmox cluster is the sum of switches, network cables, and physical nodes acting as hosts and virtual machines. A monitoring system should be able to monitor all of these components. There are wide ranges of network monitoring tools available today, such as Icinga, Zabbix, Nagios, OpenNMS, Pandora FMS, Zenoss, and more. There are many more options that are both paid and open source.

In this chapter, we are going to see how to use Zabbix to monitor a Proxmox cluster. Zabbix has a user-friendly GUI, graphing abilities, and many more features that are out of the box. It is very easy to learn for a novice or network professional. Once Zabbix is installed, almost all configurations and monitoring can be done through the GUI.

A monitoring node should be a standalone reliable machine. For learning and testing purposes, it can be set up as a virtual machine. However, to monitor a production-level cluster, a separate node outside the main cluster is the ideal solution.

Monitoring with Zabbix

Zabbix was originally conceived in 1998, and the first stable release was in 2004. Zabbix is a robust web-based network monitoring tool capable of monitoring 25,000 hosts and running hundreds of metrics per host every minute. Zabbix is a true open source tool without any enterprise paid versions. It takes just a few minutes to install even by a beginner, and can be fully configured and managed through a web-based interface. The following screenshot shows the Zabbix dashboard after logging in through the WebGUI:

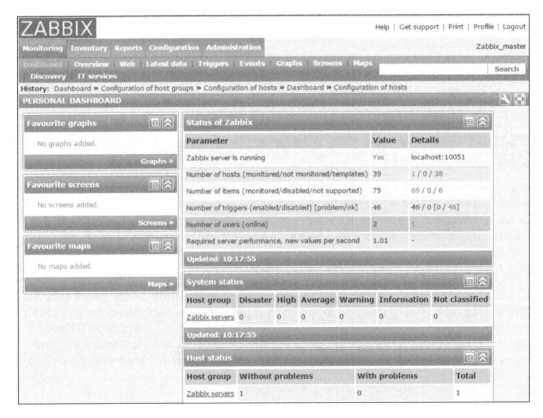

Zabbix has a very active community and many downloadable templates to monitor a variety of devices or equipment. It is also comparatively easier to create your own custom Zabbix template for nonstandard devices. More details on Zabbix can be found on the official Zabbix site at http://www.zabbix.com/. In this section, we are going to see how to install Zabbix and configure it to monitor Proxmox hosts and virtual machines.

Getting ready

Zabbix can be installed on all major Linux distributions. Set up a separate node or a virtual machine with the Linux OS of your choice, then follow the following official installation guide to install Zabbix by visiting https://www.zabbix.com/documentation/2.2/manual/installation.

Zabbix also provides preinstalled and preconfigured downloadable appliances for evaluation purposes. It is great for learning and testing but it is not recommended for production use. Zabbix appliances can be downloaded from http://www.zabbix.com/download.php.

Zabbix will still work without Zabbix Agent installed on a host to be monitored, but an agent can gather much more data from the host. There are agents available for all major operating systems, including Linux, Windows, FreeBSD, AIX, Solaris, and HP-UX. For devices where an agent installation is not possible, such as switch or other network equipment, Zabbix is fully capable of monitoring them through SNMP. After the Zabbix server installation is completed, install Zabbix Agent on some hosts.

> Zabbix Agent can capture much more data than SNMP. Use the agent whenever possible over SNMP. This reduces the complexity of configuring SNMP, while creating a lot more custom checks. Agents are a great option for Proxmox host nodes.

The Zabbix server can be accessed by visiting http://<ip_address>/zabbix.

By default, the **username:password** to log in to the Zabbix WebGUI is **admin:zabbix**. It is recommended to change the password right away after logging in. Navigate to **Administration | Users** then click on the **Admin (Zabbix Administrator)** member to change the administrative password, as shown in the following screenshot:

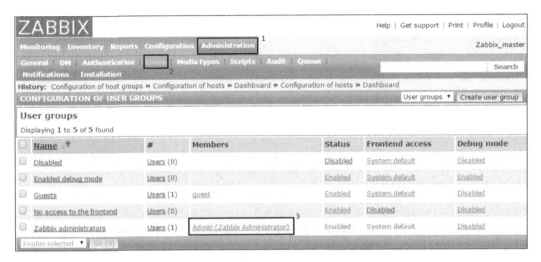

Adding a host to the Zabbix server

In this section, we are going to see how to add a host in the form of a Proxmox node or a virtual machine to the Zabbix monitoring server. This is the same procedure that is used to add any host with Zabbix Agent installed.

How to do it...

The following steps show how to add a host to Zabbix. For our example, we are going to add a `pmx1` Proxmox node with Zabbix Agent installed:

1. Navigate to **Configuration | Hosts**, and click on **Create Host**.

2. Type in **Host name** and **Visible name**. The hostname must match with the hostname entered in the host Zabbix Agent configuration file. We will configure the agent after we have added the host in the Zabbix server. The visible name can be anything.

3. Select an appropriate group. Since we are adding a Proxmox host node, we can select **Hypervisors** as group.

4. When you're adding a host with an agent installed, type in the IP address of the host in **Agent interfaces**. By default, agents listen on port `10050`. If you're using a different port, type in the **Port** number. Be sure to open the port in a firewall if the host is behind any firewall. The following screenshot shows the host configuration page after adding the necessary information:

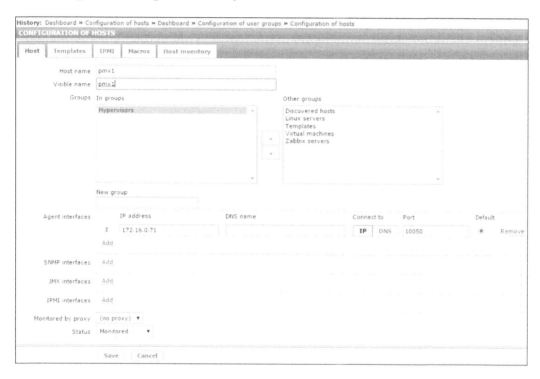

5. Click on the **Templates** tab to add a template to the host. Templates in Zabbix are preconfigured groups of checks. By assigning a template to a host, we can apply multiple checks at once instead of manually adding each check.

6. Type in a template name in the **Link new templates** textbox or select one by clicking on the **Select** button. The textbox is a self search box, so the value does not need to be the exact name of the template. For our example, we have typed in `Linux`, which pulled two possible templates. We are going to select **Template OS Linux** as shown in the following screenshot:

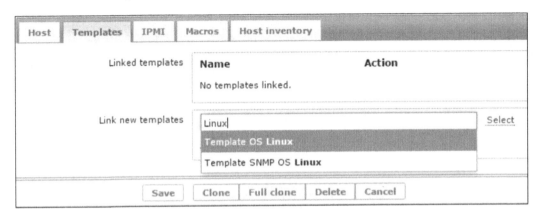

We can also assign an SNMP device using the same template page. Refer to the *Configuring SNMP in Proxmox* recipe later in this chapter for how to install and configure SNMP in Proxmox nodes, then use these steps to add a host using SNMP templates.

7. Click on **Add** to assign the template to the host. The following screenshot shows the **Templates** page after the template is assigned:

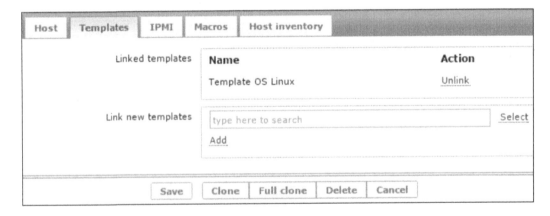

8. Click on **Save** to finish adding the host.

The following steps are to configure Zabbix Agent in the host:

1. Open the Zabbix Agent configuration file in `/etc/zabbix/zabbix_agentd.conf` with an editor.

2. Make the changes for the following option lines:

   ```
   Server=172.16.0.77 //IP of Zabbix Server
   ServerActive=172.16.0.77:10051 //IP_Server:Server_Port
   Hostname=pmx1  //must be same as Hostname typed in Zabbix
   Server for the host
   ```

3. Uncomment the line for `Listenport=10050`. Enter a different IP address if needed. This is the port that the agent will listen on.

4. Save and exit editor.

5. Run the following command to restart Zabbix Agent in the host:

   ```
   # service zabbix-agent restart
   ```

How it works...

Within a minute or so after adding the host, the Zabbix server will run auto checks and discover that the host now has a live agent in the host. The following screenshot shows a host list in the Zabbix server after adding the host and configuring the agent:

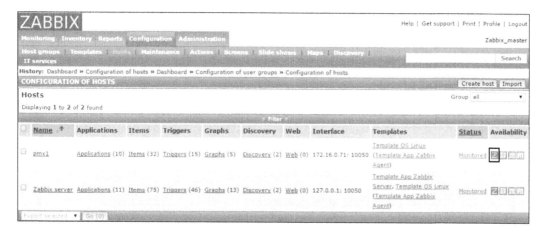

From the list, we can also see that the template has added 32 items, 15 triggers, and 5 graphs to the host. Items are checked by Zabbix and triggers initiate certain actions, such as sending auto notifications for any event. The following screenshot shows the trigger page for the `pmx1` host:

The expression column in the trigger page shows when an event is triggered. For example, the **{pmx1:proc.num[].avg(5m)}>300** expression for **Too many process on {HOST.NAME}** will trigger a warning when processes exceed 300 in the host. Modern servers can run many more processes at once. So, for a host that hosts many virtual machines, this 300 process limit may not be enough and will trigger a warning frequently. We can change the trigger, for example to 1000, to increase the limit.

> To learn more about triggers, visit `https://www.zabbix.com/documentation/2.2/manual/config/triggers/expression`.

There's more...

There are no viable third-party templates available for KVM-based virtual machine monitoring. The best way to monitor them is to add them as individual hosts in Zabbix and configure Zabbix Agent in each virtual machine. If the agent install is not possible in a virtual machine, Zabbix can still retrieve data through the **Template OS Linux** template shipped out of the box in Zabbix.

Adding the OpenVZ Zabbix template

In this section, we are going to see how to add a Zabbix monitoring template to an OpenVZ virtual machine's CPU and memory consumption.

How to do it...

The following steps are to import a Zabbix template and configure a host to monitor OpenVZ-based virtual machines:

1. Download the zipped packaged template from `https://github.com/swarnat/Zabbix-Proxmox` where the Zabbix GUI is accessed.

2. Extract the `template.xml` template file from the zipped package.

3. Navigate to Zabbix **Dashboard** | **Configuration** | **Templates** and click on **Import**, as shown in the following screenshot:

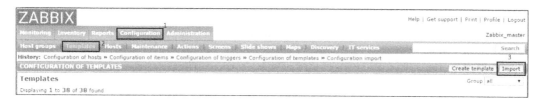

4. Choose the extracted template file in an XML format from the Import page and click on **Import**. Any other third-party downloaded template can also be imported into Zabbix through this menu.

5. The imported template is identified as **Template Proxmox Resources**. By following the steps in the previous section, add the template to a host.

6. Extract the `vzdiscover.sh` file from the zipped package and copy it into the `/var/lib/zabbix/scripts` directory of the Proxmox node where OpenVZ containers are hosted.

7. Make the bash script file executable using the following command:

```
#chmod +x /var/lib/zabbix/scripts/vzdiscover.sh
```

8. The script file needs to be executed as a root. Add the following line in the sudoers file to allow Zabbix to run the scripts without a root password:

```
zabbix ALL=NOPASSWD:/var/lib/zabbix/scripts/vzdiscover.sh,
/usr/sbin/vzlist
```

Open the sudoers file using the `visudo` command. If you get a command not found error, you may have to install `sudo` using this command:

```
#apt-get install sudo
```

9. Add the following content at the end of the Zabbix Agent configuration file in the Proxmox node using a text editor. By default, the location of the configuration file is in `/etc/zabbix/zabbix_agentd.conf`:

```
UserParameter=custom.pve.vzlist,/var/lib/zabbix/scripts/vzd
iscover.sh
UserParameter=custom.vz.cpu[*],sudo /usr/sbin/vzlist -a -o
laverage -H $1        | awk -F/ '{print $$1}'
UserParameter=custom.vz.cpu5[*],sudo /usr/sbin/vzlist -a -o
laverage -H $1        | awk -F/ '{print $$2}'
UserParameter=custom.vz.cpu10[*],sudo /usr/sbin/vzlist -a -
o laverage -H $1        | awk -F/ '{print $$3}'
UserParameter=custom.vz.usedmem[*],sudo /usr/sbin/vzlist -a
-o physpages -H $1 | awk '{print $$1*4/1024}'
```

10. Save and exit the editor, then restart Zabbix Agent in the Proxmox node using the following command:

```
# service zabbix-agent restart
```

11. Go to the Zabbix dashboard and navigate to **Monitoring | Graphs**, then select a host. After Zabbix has committed checks, we will now see some new items in a graph that shows one of the OpenVZ container's CPU and memory usage. The following screenshot shows our example container named `testCT01.symmcom.com` and the CPU usage graph showing 12 hours of data:

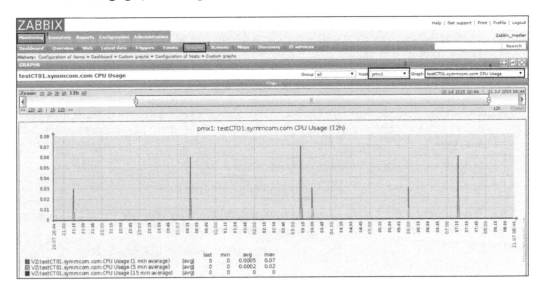

How it works...

The user parameters used in the Zabbix Agent configuration file runs the `vzdiscover.sh` script, which retrieves a list of available OpenVZ containers in the Proxmox node. It then uses the OpenVZ `vzlist` built-in command to retrieve CPU and memory usage data in a JSON format, which is then pushed to the Zabbix server to create graphs.

Note that Proxmox has a built-in RRD graphing tool to display some graphical data. However, by configuring Zabbix to do the same, we can monitor the entire network from a single Zabbix dashboard.

See also

▸   Refer to the *Proxmox built-in monitoring* recipe later on in the chapter to see how we can monitor the Proxmox cluster itself without requiring any third-party tools

Extending the OpenVZ Zabbix template

The third-party template imported in the previous section is only limited to display CPU and memory usage of a container. We can extend it to display just about any data that the `vzlist` command can pull. To see a list of data types that the `vzlist` command can retrieve, run the following command from Proxmox node:

```
# vzlist -L
```

Currently, only the used memory of containers is shown. In this section, we are going to add another check to retrieve the total memory allocated for containers and add it to show both used and total memory usage on the same graph in the Zabbix server.

How to do it...

The following steps are to add checks in the Zabbix Agent configuration file and display new data in the Zabbix graphing tool:

1.   Add the following line in the Zabbix Agent `/etc/zabbix/zabbix_agentd.conf` configuration file:

```
UserParameter=custom.vz.totalmem[*],sudo /usr/sbin/vzlist -
a -o physpages.l -H $1 | awk '{print $$1*4/1024}'
```

2.   Save and exit editor, then restart Zabbix Agent using the following command:

```
#service zabbix-agent restart
```

3.   Go to the Zabbix dashboard and select **Template Proxmox Resources** by navigating to **Configuration | Templates**.

4. Once inside the template, click on **Discovery rules**, as shown in the following screenshot:

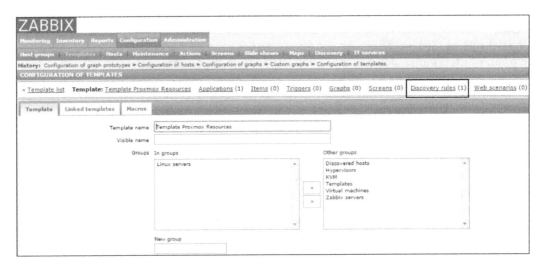

5. Click on **Item prototypes** under the **Items** column. This will display all the currently configured checked items.

6. Since our new item is almost identical to the memory used to show the total memory, we are going to clone the existing memory item. Click on the **VZ:{#VZHOST}:Memory Used** line item, as shown in the following screenshot:

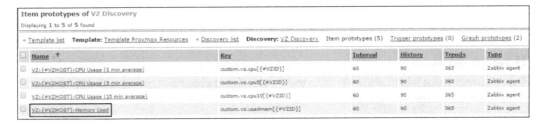

7. Click on `Clone` at the bottom of the page to create a duplicate of this item. Then, only make the following changes:

Set **Name** as `VZ:{#VZHOST}:Total Memory` and **Key** as `custom.vz.totalmem[{#VZID}]`

8. Click on **Save**. The item list should now appear as follows with the item on the fifth line indicating the total memory:

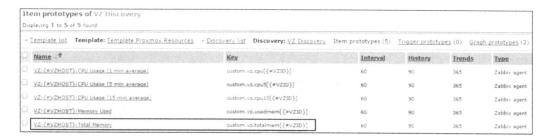

9. While you're still on the same page, click on **Graph prototypes** to see the list of graph items.

10. Since we want to show both the total and used memory on the same graph, we are not going to create a new graph item, but instead edit the existing graph for memory in order to add additional data for graphing. Click on the **{#VZHOST} Memory Usage** line item.

11. Click on **Add Prototype** and select the item we created in the earlier step named **VZ:{#VZHOST}:Total Memory**. After adding the item, it should appear as follows:

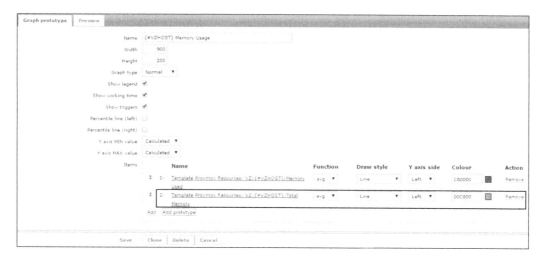

12. To check the new addition to the graphing data, navigate to **Dashboard | Monitoring | Graphs**, then select a host and the `<container_id>` `Memory Usage` graph item. It now displays an additional graph for the total memory allocated for the container, as shown in the following screenshot. For our example container, there is 352 MB of total memory allocated and 35 MB of memory currently in use:

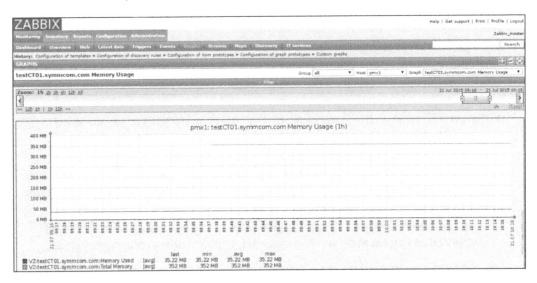

How it works...

By leveraging the vzlist command for OpenVZ containers, we can customize the Zabbix template to display a variety of data. All user bean counter resources can be added as `UserParameter` in the Zabbix Agent configuration files to retrieve container data. In this section, we have added a new data item to retrieve the total allocated memory for containers. The resource field we used for this was `physpages.l`. Other possible formats are `physpages.m`, `physpages.b`, and `physpages.f`. Each suffix displays the specific resource type, where `.m` stands for maxheld, `.b` stands for barrier, `.l` stands for limit, and `.f` stands for fail counter.

When no suffix is used, then only the held or current value is shown. All user bean counter resources can be passed to Zabbix to create graphical data.

See also

▶ For more information on `vzlist`, visit the following official OpenVZ man page at https://openvz.org/Man/vzlist.8

Proxmox built-in monitoring

Although limited to many advanced features, Proxmox can still be monitored through the Proxmox GUI. Proxmox comes with built-in RRD-based graphs to show the historical consumption and performance data up to one year. Using this tool, we can analyze the performance trend of a resource over a period of time.

How to do it...

All consumption and performance data is under the Summary tabbed menu for both Proxmox nodes and virtual machines. The following steps show how to browse Proxmox nodes and virtual machines for statistical data:

1. Log in to the Proxmox GUI.

2. Select a Proxmox node or a virtual machine for both KVM or OpenVZ.

3. Click on the **Summary** tabbed menu. Under **Status**, block all the information regarding the entity shown.

4. To change the period for historical data for graphing, click on the drop-down menu to select the hourly, daily, monthly, or yearly period. The following screenshot shows the monthly **CPU usage** and **Server load** for our example pmx1 node:

There are also ways to display a list of all the nodes and virtual machines in the cluster and sort them by consumption to get a quick glance of the highest or lowest resource-consuming entity. The following steps show how to display the list and sort through the Proxmox GUI:

1. Log in to the Proxmox GUI.

2. Click on **Datacenter** from the left navigation bar.

3. Click on the **Search** tabbed menu to display a list of all the resources in the cluster, including nodes, virtual machines, and storages.

4. Click on the **CPU usage** column to sort by the highest or lowest CPU usage. The following screenshot shows a list with the highest CPU consuming resource. In our example, we can see that the KVM virtual machine 100 is consuming the most CPU resources:

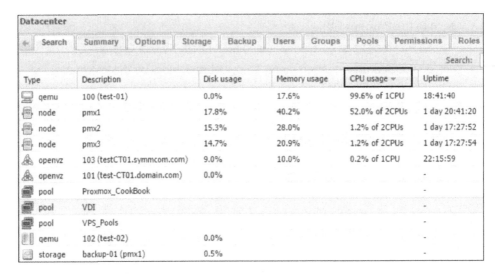

Type	Description	Disk usage	Memory usage	CPU usage ▾	Uptime
qemu	100 (test-01)	0.0%	17.6%	99.6% of 1CPU	18:41:40
node	pmx1	17.8%	40.2%	52.0% of 2CPUs	1 day 20:41:20
node	pmx2	15.3%	28.0%	1.2% of 2CPUs	1 day 17:27:52
node	pmx3	14.7%	20.9%	1.2% of 2CPUs	1 day 17:27:54
openvz	103 (testCT01.symmcom.com)	9.0%	10.0%	0.2% of 1CPU	22:15:59
openvz	101 (test-CT01.domain.com)	0.0%			-
pool	Proxmox_CookBook				-
pool	VDI				-
pool	VPS_Pools				-
qemu	102 (test-02)	0.0%			-
storage	backup-01 (pmx1)	0.5%			-

Configuring the disk health notifications

Almost all HDD or SSD nowadays have a **Self-Monitoring, Analysis and Reporting Technology (S.M.A.R.T.)** ability, which can gather valuable data on disk drive health. By using the S.M.A.R.T. monitoring tool, we can avoid premature drive failures by detecting potential problems early on. We can configure each Proxmox node to send e-mail alerts when any problem is detected in any attached drive.

> Note that if drives are connected to RAID controllers and configured as some form of an array, then the S.M.A.R.T. tool will not be able to retrieve a drive's health data.

How to do it...

The following steps show how to install S.M.A.R.T monitoring tools in a Proxmox node and configure it to send e-mail nominations:

1. Log in to a Proxmox node through an SSH Shell or directly from the console.

2. Run the following command to install the S.M.A.R.T. tool as it is not installed by default in Proxmox:

   ```
   #apt-get update
   ```

   ```
   #apt-get install smartmontools
   ```

3. Retrieve a list of all attached drives using the following command:

   ```
   #fdisk -l
   ```

4. Verify through the following command that each attached drive has a S.M.A.R.T. feature and it is turned on:

   ```
   #smartctl -a /dev/sdX
   ```

   If the drive has a S.M.A.R.T. feature and it is enabled, it will appear as the following screenshot:

   If the feature is available but disabled for any reason, we can enable it using the following command:

   ```
   #smartctl -s on -a /dev/sdX
   ```

5. Open the `/etc/default/smartmontools` file using an editor and uncomment the following lines:

   ```
   enable_smart="/dev/hda /dev/hdb"
   start_smartd=yes
   smartd_opts="-interval=1800"
   ```

6. Enter the drives to be monitored in `enable_smart` line, as follows:

   ```
   enable_smart="/dev/sdX /dev/sdX"
   ```

7. Open the S.M.A.R.T. daemon configuration file in `/etc/smartd.conf` and comment out the following line:

```
DEVICESCAN -d removable -n standby -m root -M exec
/usr/share/smartmontools/smartd-runner
```

8. Add the following line to add the drives, schedule checks, and a mail option. For our example we have added drives `sda` and `sdb`, to run checks every seventh day or Saturday of the week at 8 A.M.:

```
/dev/sda -d sat -s L/../../7/08 -m root
/dev/sdb -d sat -s L/../../7/08 -m root
```

When there is an issue, this will send an e-mail to the root e-mail address. To send an e-mail to any other e-mail, we have to enter the e-mail address in place of `root` as follows:

```
/dev/sda -d sat -s L/../../7/08 -m email@domain.com
/dev/sdb -d sat -s L/../../7/08 -m email@domain.com
```

9. Save the configuration file and exit the editor.

10. Start the S.M.A.R.T. daemon using the following command:

```
#service smartmontools start
```

Configuring SNMP in Proxmox

Simple Network Management Protocol (**SNMP**) is a network management protocol used to monitor a wide variety of network devices. It is especially useful when a full network monitoring agent installation is not possible, such as switches, routers, printers, IP-based devices, and more. Almost all network monitoring programs support some level of SNMP.

If the choice of monitoring package does not have any agents, SNMP is the best option to monitor those devices. SNMP is fully configurable in Linux distribution, and since Proxmox is based on Debian, it inherits all the benefits of SNMP.

 To learn more about SNMP, visit `https://en.wikipedia.org/wiki/Simple_Network_Management_Protocol`.

There are a few components of SNMP worth mentioning here since we will be using them to configure SNMP. They are as follows:

▶ **Object Identifier (OID)**: OID refers to objects that SNMP queries to gather information from a device. An object could be a network interface status, disk storage usage, device name, and so on. These object identifiers are extremely structured in a hierarchical tree manner. Each OID is specifically numbered. For example, the OID of the object that gathers a device name is `1.3.6.1.2.1.1.5.0`. OIDs are always a numerical value. OIDs can be compared with IP addresses where numeric values are used to identify a device in a network.

Each dot in an OID represents the segmentation of a network element. We can think of an OID like the address of a location. Let's take the following address:

```
Wasim Ahmed
111 Server Street, 4th Floor
Calgary, AB 111-222
Canada
```

If we put this address in an OID format, it would look like this:

```
Canada.AB.Calgary.111-222.Server Street.111.4th Floor.Wasim
Ahmed
```

Putting this in a formula would like the this:

Country.Province.City.Postal code.Street name.Street number.Unit number.Contact name

Just like the the address example, OIDs also follow a strict hierarchy, as follows:

OID value	Used for
1	ISO
1.3	Organizations
1.3.6	US Department of Defense
1.3.6.1	Internet
1.3.6.1.2	IETF management
1.3.6.1.2.X	Management of related OIDs

To look up management-related OIDs, visit `http://www.alvestrand.no/objectid/1.3.6.1.2.1.html`.

▸ **Management Information Base (MIB)**: These are databases where objects are stored. MIB acts as translator that allows an SNMP server to query an object using a textual OID instead of a numeric one. For example, to retrieve a device name through SNMP queries, we can use OIDs `1.3.6.1.2.1.1.5.0` or `SNMPv2-MIB::sysName.0` respectively. Both will give the exact same result. However, the textual OID's purpose is easier to understand than a numeric OID's. We can compare MIB to OID as a domain name to an IP address. Some manufacturers provide their own MIB since they do not exist in standard MIB. It is important to know that when configuring MIBs, they are not supported devices by monitoring tools. There are a numbers of MIBs ready to be downloaded. Proxmox does not install an MIB by default. It has to be installed manually.

> For more details on MIBs, visit `https://en.wikipedia.org/wiki/Management_information_base`.
>
> There are three versions of SNMP currently available. Before implementing an SNMP infrastructure, it is important to know which version to use. The three versions are as follows:
>
> ▸ **SNMP version 1**: This is the oldest SNMP version that only supports 32-bit counters and has no security at all. A community string is sent as plaintext in this SNMP.
>
> ▸ **SNMP version 2**: This has all the features of version 1 with added features to support 64-bit counters. Most devices nowadays support version 2.
>
> ▸ **SNMP version 3**: This has all the features of version 1 and 2 with the added benefit of security. Both encryption and authentication are added to counters. If security is the biggest concern, this is the SNMP version that should be used.

How to do it...

SNMP is not installed by default in Proxmox. The following steps show how to install SNMP in Proxmox and configure it:

1. Run the following commands to install SNMP on the Proxmox nodes:

```
#apt-get update
#apt-get install snmpd snmp
```

2. Add the following repository in `/etc/apt/sources.list` of the Proxmox node. This is to add a repository to install SNMP MIBs:

   deb http://http.us.debian.org/debian/wheezy main non-free

3. Run the following commands to install SNMP MIBs:

   #apt-get update

   #apt-get install snmp-mibs-downloader

4. Open the `/etc/snmp/snmpd.conf` SNMP configuration file using an editor.

5. Ensure that the following line is uncommented. You can specify the node IP address. SNMP listens on port `161`. Change it here if required:

   agentAddress udp:127.0.0.1:161

6. Add the following line in the SNMP configuration file:

   rocommunity <secret_string> <IP/CIDR>

   In our example we have added the following line:

   rocommunity SecretSNMP 172.16.0.0/24

7. Save the file and exit the editor.

8. Restart SNMP using the following command:

   #service snmpd restart

9. To verify that SNMP is up and running, run the command as shown in the following screenshot. It also shows the expected result:

```
root@pmx1:/# snmpwalk -c SecretSNMP -v2c 172.16.0.71 SNMPv2-MIB::sysName.0
SNMPv2-MIB::sysName.0 = STRING: pmx1
root@pmx1:/# 
```

Monitoring a Ceph cluster with the Ceph dashboard

There are several options to monitor a Ceph cluster graphically. They are as follows:

Monitoring tools	Links
Calamari	`https://ceph.com/category/calamari/`
Kraken dash	`https://github.com/krakendash/krakendash`
Ceph dashboard	`https://github.com/Crapworks/ceph-dash`

All three of these are viable options to monitor a Ceph cluster. However, due to their simplicity and effectiveness, in this chapter, we are going to see how to install the Ceph dashboard.

Getting ready

The Ceph dashboard can be installed on any Ceph node or the *Proxmox+Ceph* node in the cluster. So long as it can read the `ceph.conf` file, it will function just fine. The Ceph dashboard does not require any web server or any other service to function. It is also a one-way monitoring system, meaning, we can read data but never write to the cluster.

How to do it...

1. Install `git` using the following command if it is not installed in the monitoring node:

   ```
   # apt-get install git
   ```

2. Clone the Ceph dashboard GitHub repository using the following command:

   ```
   # git clone https://github.com/Crapworks/ceph-dash
   ```

3. Go to the `/path/ceph-dash` Ceph dashboard directory.

4. Enter the following command to start the dashboard:

   ```
   # ./ceph_dash.py
   ```

5. To see the Ceph cluster dashboard, open a browser and type the URL with the format as `http://10.0.0.5:5000`. The Ceph dashboard listens on port `5000`.

The following screenshot shows our example cluster in a healthy status:

How it works...

The Ceph dashboard displays the following information about a Ceph cluster:

- ▶ Ceph cluster key
- ▶ Overall health status
- ▶ Monitor status
- ▶ OSD status
- ▶ Placement Group (PG) status
- ▶ Storage utilization percentage
- ▶ Total available space and used space
- ▶ Write speed per second
- ▶ Read speed per second
- ▶ Operations per second

Refer to the *Ceph storage* subsection under the *Introduction* section in *Chapter 6, Storage Configurations*, for information on Ceph components, such as MON, OSD, PG, and so on. All the data is automatically updated at regular intervals. During any faults within the cluster, the dashboard will show related information in a color-coded format as shown in the following screenshot:

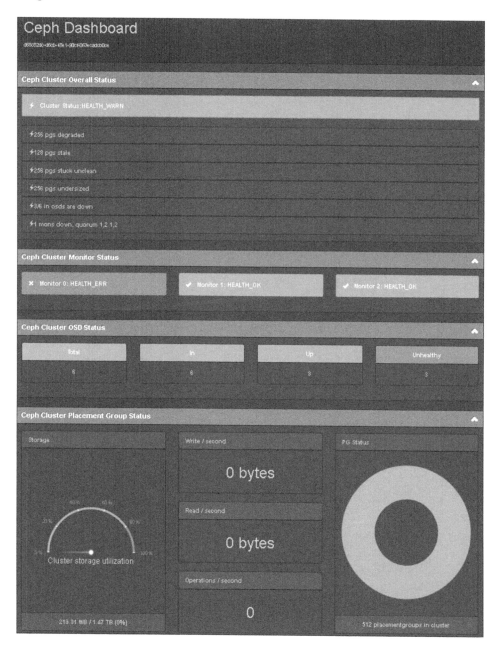

The previous screenshot shows our example cluster in distress with one node down along with three OSDs. These caused the PGs to degrade and the entire cluster to start rebalancing data.

Using the port forwarding in the firewall, we can also monitor a Ceph cluster remotely.

There's more...

It is possible to connect the Ceph dashboard with **Icinga monitoring service** to create visual graphs from the collected data. For details on how to add a graphing capability to the Ceph dashboard, visit `https://github.com/Crapworks/ceph-dash` and `https://github.com/Crapworks/check_ceph_dash`.

10

Advanced Configurations for VMs

In this chapter, we will see some advanced configuration options for virtual machines in Proxmox. The following configuration topics will be covered in this chapter:

- ▸ Configuring sound in a KVM VM
- ▸ Configuring a PCI passthrough
- ▸ Configuring a PCI Express/GPU passthrough
- ▸ Configuring a USB passthrough
- ▸ Configuring a hotplug
- ▸ Nesting virtual machines
- ▸ Isolating multiple subnets

Introduction

The features of a virtual machine can be extended beyond the basics through advanced configurations, such as adding sound devices, passthroughs, hotplugging, nested virtual clusters, and so on. These advanced configurations fully depend on different environments and requirements. Virtual machines will work even without these. Due to the nature of these configurations, it is advisable to implement these in a test environment first before deploying them in a real production environment.

Configuring sound in a KVM VM

In this section, we are going to see how to add the sound support to a KVM-based VM.

Getting ready

By default, the sound feature is not added to a VM. A newly created VM will not have a sound device. In order for the VM operating system to start the sound service, some arguments must be added to the VM configuration file.

When using a virtual desktop infrastructure, such as RDP, the sound is automatically added to remote virtual desktops on the client side. However, when using the SPICE protocol, a sound device must be added to the VM. As of Proxmox VE 3.4, it is not possible to add a sound interface through the GUI. However, there is a plan to add this feature in later versions of Proxmox.

How to do it...

The following steps will add a sound device to a VM:

1. Log in to the Proxmox node through SSH or directly through the console.
2. Navigate to the `/etc/pve/nodes/<node_name>/qemu-server/<vm_id>.conf` VM configuration directory.
3. Open the VM configuration file with your desired editor. Add the following argument based on the suggested OSes.

    For Windows 7 and later Windows-based VMs, add the following argument:

    ```
    Args: -device intel-had,id=sound5,bus=pci.0,addr=0x18 -
    device hda-micro,id=sound5-codec0,bus=sound5.0,cad=0 -
    device had-duplex,id=sound5-codec1,bus=sound5.0,cad=1
    ```

    For Windows XP-based VMs, add the following argument:

    ```
    Args: -device AC97,addr=0x18
    ```

4. Save the configuration file and exit the editor.
5. Power cycle the VM to activate the sound device.

Configuring a PCI passthrough

In Proxmox, it is possible to passthrough PCI devices directly into a VM. In this section, we will see how to configure and verify a PCI passthrough.

How to do it...

The following steps describe how to enable and configure the PCI passthrough in Proxmox:

1. Log in to the Proxmox node through SSH or directly through a console.

2. Open the grub configuration file by using an editor:

   ```
   # nano /etc/default/grub
   ```

3. Make changes to the GRUB_CMDLINE_LINUX_DEFAULT="quiet" line by using these suggestions.

   For Intel CPUs, make the following change:

   ```
   GRUB_CMDLINE_LINUX_DEFAULT="quiet intel_iommu=on"
   ```

   For AMD CPUs, make the following change:

   ```
   GRUB_CMDLINE_LINUX_DEFAULT="quiet amd_iommu=on"
   ```

4. Save the changes and exit the editor.

5. Run the following command to update grub:

   ```
   # update-grub
   ```

6. If you're using an AMD CPU, add the following line in the /etc/modprobe.d/kvm_iommu_map_guest.conf configuration file:

   ```
   options kvm allow_unsafe_assigned_interrupt=1
   ```

    Ensure that the VM is not set to auto start after a reboot, then power cycle the Proxmox node.

7. Locate the PCI device address in the form of xx:xx.x by using this command:

   ```
   # lspci
   ```

8. Enter the following line with the PCI device ID in the VM configuration file:

   ```
   hostpci0: xx:xx.x
   ```

9. Power up the VM.

10. Verify the PCI device by entering the following command in the VM monitor:

    ```
    info pci
    ```

11. The command will display the PCI information of the VM as shown in the following screenshot:

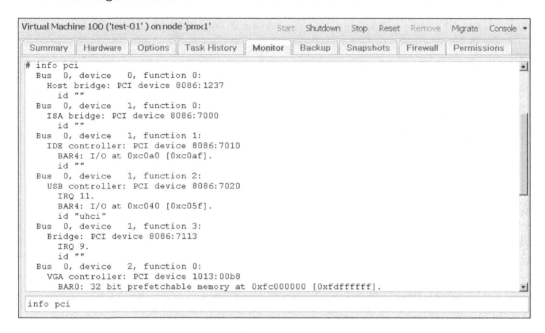

12. Install the necessary drivers for the PCI device in the VM operating system.

Configuring a PCI Express/GPU passthrough

In this section, we will see how to configure a PCI Express device and video adapters to be used directly in a VM.

Getting ready

PCI Express devices, such as a video adapter card support, was added in Proxmox since version 3.3. To enable this passthrough, the Proxmox node must have pve-kernel 3.10. The latest 3.10 kernel is only available for testing purposes through the pve test repository. In order to configure the PCI Express passthrough, the kernel 3.10 must be installed through a test repository. Note that there is no OpenVZ container support in kernel 3.10 and it is only in release candidate status. Before proceeding with this section, install the new kernel 3.10 on a test cluster. We can only add the PCI express and GPU passthrough to a VM from a CLI by adding arguments in the VM configuration file.

How to do it...

The following steps show how to enable standard non-GPU PCI Express devices, GPU-based devices, and GPU devices with embedded audio devices to a VM:

1. Open the VM configuration file in an editor.

2. Locate the PCI Express device ID by following the steps in the previous recipe using the `#lspci` command.

3. Add the following lines depending on the type of PCI Express device being added.

   For standard non-GPU PCI Express devices, add these lines:

   ```
   machine: q35
   hostpci0: xx:xx.x,pcie=1,driver=vfio
   ```

   For GPU PCI Express video adapters, add these lines:

   ```
   machine: q35
   hostpci0: xx:xx.x,pcie=1,x-vga=on,driver=vfio
   ```

   For GPU PCI Express video adapters with embedded sound devices, remove `.x` from the end of the PCI device address as follows:

   ```
   machine: q35
   hostpci0: xx:xx,pcie=1,x-vga=on,driver=vfio
   ```

4. Save the configuration file and power cycle the VM.

5. Install the necessary drivers within the VM operating system.

There's more...

Note that for a GPU passthrough, Intel-based integrated graphic adapters currently do not work with kernel 3.10. The Radeon series 5xxx, 6xxx, and 7xxx and Nvidia Geforce series 4xx, 5xx, 6xx, 7xx, 7, and 8 work with the GPU passthrough.

Configuring a USB passthrough

Like PCI devices, we can also pass USB devices directly into a virtual machine without power cycling a VM. We can connect varieties of USB devices, such as flash drives, webcams, scanners, and so on, directly into the VM. In this section, we are going to see how to passthrough a USB device into a KVM-based VM and OpenVZ container.

Although a USB passthrough works, there have been many incidents of device errors when this passthrough has been used. Commit extensive tests over several days to ensure that it works in a test lab before deploying it in a production cluster. In some cases, an entire node needed to be rebooted to clear out errors due to a USB passthrough.

How to do it...

For a KVM-based VM, a USB passthrough can be configured through the Proxmox GUI. However, for OpenVZ containers, it can only be configured through a CLI.

The following steps describe how to configure a USB passthrough for a KVM-based VM:

1. Log in to the Proxmox GUI and select the VM.
2. Click on **Monitor** from the tabbed menu.
3. Type the following command to get a list of the available USB devices in the host where the VM is hosted:

   `# info usbhost`

   It will display all the USB devices currently attached to the host. We are going to add the Patriot USB flash drive into the 100 VM, as shown in the following screenshot:

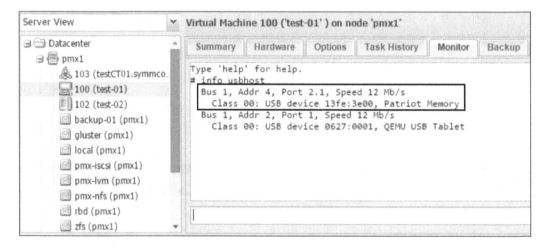

4. From the list, we can see that the device vendor ID is 13fe and the product ID is 3e00. We are going to attach the USB device by using the following command:

   `device_add usb-host,id=patriot,vendorid=0x13fe,vendorid=0x3e00`

5. Type the following command to verify that the USB device is now added to the VM:

   `# info usb`

   The following screenshot shows the new device that has been added to the VM:

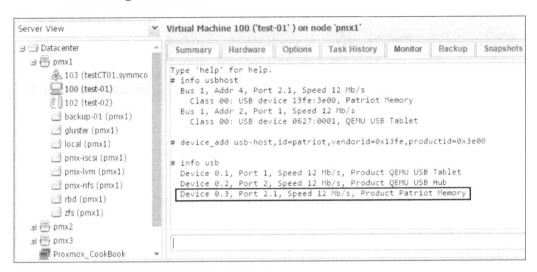

6. Install the necessary driver inside the VM to activate the USB device.

> To delete the USB device from the VM, run the following command:
>
> `device_del <device_id>`
>
> For our example, we named the USB device, `Patriot`, when we added the USB passthrough. Removing the device the command would look like this:
>
> `device_del patriot`

The following steps describe how to add a USB passthrough for OpenVZ containers:

1. Log in to the Proxmox node through SSH, Shell, or directly through the console.

2. Run the following command to see the list of USB devices. We only need to know the bus ID and device ID of the USB device:

   `#lsusb`

The following screenshot shows the USB device list. The bus ID and device ID is marked. These IDs will help us to determine the directory path of the USB device in the node:

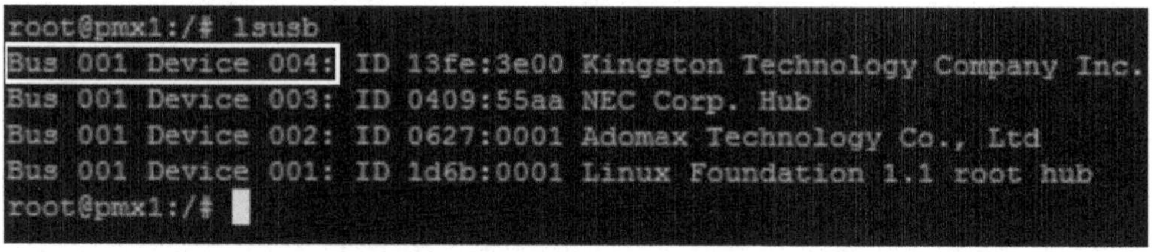

```
root@pmx1:/# lsusb
Bus 001 Device 004: ID 13fe:3e00 Kingston Technology Company Inc.
Bus 001 Device 003: ID 0409:55aa NEC Corp. Hub
Bus 001 Device 002: ID 0627:0001 Adomax Technology Co., Ltd
Bus 001 Device 001: ID 1d6b:0001 Linux Foundation 1.1 root hub
root@pmx1:/#
```

3. The USB device is located at /dev/bus/usb/001/004. Ensure that this is the right path for the USB device by using the following command:

   `#lsusb -D /dev/bus/usb/001/004`

4. Power off the container.

5. Run the following command to add the USB device into the containers with read/write access:

   `#vzctl set <vm_id> --devnodes <bus_path>:rw --save`

   For our example container, 103, the command will appear as follows:

   `#vzctl set 103 --devnodes bus/usb/001/004:rw --save`

6. Power up the container and install the necessary driver for the USB device.

Configuring a hotplug

In this section, we will see how to configure a hotplugging option in Proxmox virtual machines. Using the hotplugging feature, we can add and remove devices from a VM without restarting or power cycling the VM.

Getting ready

There are four device types that we can hotplug in a VM:

- Disk
- Network Interface Card (NIC)
- CPU
- Memory

As of Proxmox 3.4, we can only hotplug the CPU and memory, but cannot unplug them. Both the disk and **Network Interface Card** (**NIC**) can be hotplugged and unplugged. The following table shows the device types that are supported in different operating systems:

Device	Kernel support	Hotplug/unplug	OS
Disk	All	This is available for both OSes.	This is available for all versions of Linux/Windows.
NIC	All	This is available for both OSes.	This is available for all versions of Linux/Windows.
CPU	> 3.10	Hotplug is available only for Windows, whereas, both hotplug and unplug are available for Linux.	This is available for all versions of Linux and Windows Server 2008 and above.
Memory	> 3.10	Hotplug is available only for Windows, whereas, both hotplug and unplug are available for Linux.	This is available for all versions of Linux and Windows Server 2008 and above.

While the main configuration to enable hotplugging for Proxmox should be done through the CLI, we can enable a hotplug device by navigating to the Proxmox GUI | **Options** tab menu, as shown in the following screenshot:

Virtual Machine 100 ('test-01') on node 'pmx1'		Start	Shutdown	Stop	Reset

| Summary | Hardware | Options | Task History | Monitor | Backup | Snapshots |

Edit   Revert

Name	test-01
Start at boot	No
Start/Shutdown order	order=any
OS Type	Linux 3.X/2.6 Kernel (l26)
Boot order	Disk 'virtio0', CD-ROM, Network
Use tablet for pointer	Yes
Hotplug	Disk, Network, CPU
ACPI support	Yes
SCSI Controller Type	Default (LSI 53C895A)
KVM hardware virtualization	No
CPU units	1000
Freeze CPU at startup	No
Use local time for RTC	No
RTC start date	now
SMBIOS settings (type1)	uuid=02b61d3c-cd67-4eeb-b5d5-f5e9315c609f

How to do it...

We need to prepare a Linux-based VM first before hotplugging can be used. Two modules must be loaded to enable hotplugging. We can load the modules by using the following commands:

```
#modprobe acpiphp
#modprobe pci_hotplug
```

To load the modules during the boot process automatically, we can add them into `/etc/modules`.

We also need to create a new udev rule file in the `/lib/udev/rules.d/80-hotplug-cpu-mem.rules` file and add the following lines:

```
SUBSYSTEM=="cpu",ACTION=="add",TEST=="online",ATTR{online}=="0",AT
TR=={online}="1"
SUBSYSTEM=="memory",ACTION=="add",TEST=="state",ATTR{state}=="offl
ine",ATTR=={state}="online"
```

A VM needs to be power cycled or restarted to activate the modules and rules.

For a Windows-based VM, hotplugging does not need any additional preparation. Disk and NIC hotplugs work for all versions of Windows Server 2003 and above. The CPU and memory hotplug work for all Windows OSes above Windows Server 2008.

The following steps describe how to enable hotplugging for a VM through the GUI:

1. Log in to the Proxmox GUI.

2. Select a VM for which hotplugging needs to be enabled, then click on the **Options** tabbed menu.

3. Select the hotplug line item, then click on **Edit** to open a dialog box as shown in the following screenshot:

4. Select one or more devices to be hotplugged using the drop-down menu.

5. Click on **OK** to enable.

To add a new device to a VM, go to the **Hardware** tabbed menu and click on the **Add** button. As of Proxmox 3.4, we can only add the disk image, NIC, and CD/DVD drive by navigating to the **Hardware | Add** button, as shown in the following screenshot:

To add a new vCPU into the VM, run the following command from the Proxmox node CLI:

```
# qm set <vm_id> -vcpus 2
```

The preceding command will add a total of two vCPUs into the VM.

The following steps show how to enable a memory hotplug for a VM:

1. NUMA must be enabled before memory can be hotplugged. We can edit the VM configuration file in /etc/pve/qemu-server/100.conf and add the following argument:

    numa: 1

2. Restart the VM.

3. Edit the amount of allocated memory through the GUI under the **Hardware** tabbed menu.

The following screenshot shows the final configuration of our example VM with two vCPUs and NUMA enabled:

```
GNU nano 2.2.6                    File: 100.conf

balloon: 256
bootdisk: virtio0
cores: 1
hotplug: disk,network,cpu
ide2: none,media=cdrom
kvm: 0
memory: 512
name: test-01
net0: virtio=BA:9B:41:C9:43:2B,bridge=vmbr0
numa: 1
vcpus: 2
ostype: l26
parent: Clean_VM
smbios1: uuid=02b61d3c-cd67-4eeb-b5d5-f5e9315c609f
sockets: 1
virtio0: local:100/vm-100-disk-1.qcow2,format=qcow2,size=20G
```

Nesting virtual machines

It is possible to create a virtual cluster using a Proxmox hypervisor on top of an existing Proxmox cluster. Due to the performance drop of a nested hypervisor, the use case for a nested cluster is very limited. They can be used in, but are not limited to, the following scenarios:

- ▶ Practice clusters in a classroom
- ▶ Test clusters to test the latest software releases before applying them to real environments
- ▶ Proof of concept clusters to test new configuration ideas

In this section, we will see how to enable the nested feature in Proxmox.

Getting ready

Deploying a nested virtual cluster is very different from deploying on true hardware. Make sure to plan ahead if the nested virtual cluster is going to be used on a physical Proxmox cluster. There must be adequate resources, such as CPU and memory available to support the actual and virtual nested clusters. The nested virtual host can quickly be starved of resources in such an environment since there is a lot overhead due to a hypervisor on top of another hypervisor.

In order to have close to native performance of a hypervisor, the virtual machine must have access to some hardware features that leverage virtualization. These features are known as **hardware-assisted virtualization extensions**.

 For detailed information on hardware-assisted virtualization, visit `https://en.wikipedia.org/wiki/Hardware-assisted_virtualization`.

The nested hypervisor must have access to these extensions in order to be able to perform well enough for nested virtual machines. The nested feature seems to work flawlessly with AMD CPUs. Proxmox nodes with Intel CPUs tend to be touch and go when it comes to nested virtualization. If enabling a hardware-assisted extension is not possible, then the **KVM hardware virtualization** feature must be turned off for a VM before it can be used inside a nested environment, as shown in the following screenshot:

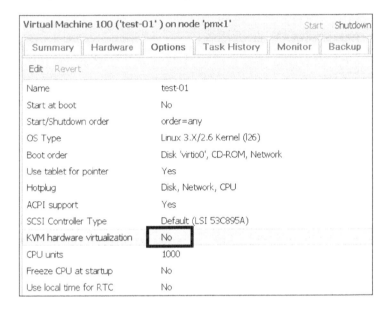

The KVM virtualization option is turned off by default for all VMs. If the option is not turned off when trying to start a nested VM, an error message similar to the following screenshot will be displayed:

User name	Description	Status
root@pam	Shell	OK
root@pam	VM 100 - Start	OK
root@pam	VM 100 - Start	Error: No accelerator found!
root@pam	Start all VMs and Containers	OK

How to do it...

The following steps show how to enable and configure the nested feature in the Proxmox node:

1. Load a module for nesting and enable it by using the following commands that are based on the different CPUs as listed:

   For Intel CPUs, use the following commands:

   ```
   # modprobe kvm-intel
   # echo "options kvm-intel nested=1" > /etc/modprobe.d/kvm-intel.conf
   ```

   For AMD CPUs, use the following commands:

   ```
   # modprobe kvm-amd
   #echo "options kvm-amd nested=1" > /etc/modprobe.d/kvm-amd.conf
   ```

2. To load the KVM module automatically during the reboot process, add the module to `/etc/modules`.

3. Verify that the module has been loaded and enabled by using the following command:

   ```
   # cat /sys/module/<kvm_intel or kvm_amd>paramters/nested
   ```

   The command should either display `Y` or `1` if the module is enabled

4. Change the CPU type for the VM to `host` through the GUI.

5. Add the following argument into the VM configuration file through a CLI:

   ```
   args: -enable-kvm
   ```

6. Power cycle the VM and install Proxmox as the hypervisor or any other hypervisor of your choice.

Isolating multiple subnets

In a virtual environment, it is possible to configure multiple subnets or networks on the same platform. It is a very useful configuration to keep all the networks separated from each other. This type of configuration is much more prevalent in a multitenant virtual environment, where multiple customers can coexist on the same platform while sharing hypervisor resources. It is a rather simple concept to isolate each subnet with its own virtual bridge. Basically, the idea is to create bridges without any physical interface attached to them. Each bridge acts as an individual virtual switch. In this section, we are going to see how to isolate the subnets using virtual bridges.

Getting ready

For our example, we are going to create two virtual networks for two clients. The entire configuration can be done from the Proxmox GUI or through the CLI by editing the network configuration file in /etc/network/interfaces for the Proxmox node where the VMs will reside. The entire process can be summarized through the following steps:

1. Create virtual bridges.
2. Create virtual machines.
3. Assign the bridges to respective virtual machines.

If the VMs do not need internode communication, then the virtual bridges do not need any network ports assigned. We can leverage VLAN to create multiple virtual networks spanned over multiple Proxmox nodes.

How to do it...

Create virtual bridges, as shown in the following screenshot, without any network ports:

```
auto vmbr101
iface vmbr101 inet manual
        bridge_ports none
        bridge_stp off
        bridge_fd 0

auto vmbr102
iface vmbr102 inet manual
        brideg_ports none
        bridge_stp off
        bridge_fd 0
```

We can also configure the virtual bridges with VLAN as network ports so that traffic can go out of the Proxmox node as shown in the following screenshot:

```
auto vlan101
iface vlan101 inet manual
        vlan_raw_device eth1

auto vlan102
iface vlan102 inet manual
        vlan_raw_device eth1

auto vmbr101
iface vmbr101 inet manual
        bridge_ports vlan101
        bridge_stp off
        bridge_fd 0

auto vmbr102
iface vmbr102 inet manual
        bridge_ports vlan102
        bridge_stp off
        bridge_fd 0
```

To isolate the subnets even further, we can create a virtual firewall for each subnet and connect the VMs to the firewall by using their respective bridges only. In this scenario, the virtual firewall will have two network interfaces: one for Internet and the other for the VMs in the subnet. The following screenshot shows the configuration of a virtual firewall with one of the virtual bridges, vmbr101, we created in the previous section:

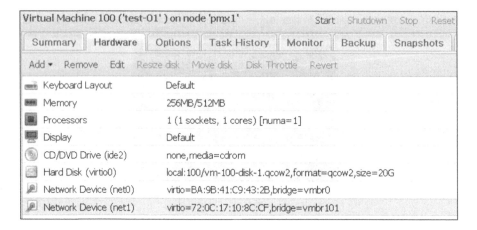

Virtual Machine 100 ('test-01') on node 'pmx1'					Start	Shutdown	Stop	Reset

Summary	Hardware	Options	Task History	Monitor	Backup	Snapshots

Add ▼   Remove   Edit   Resize disk   Move disk   Disk Throttle   Revert

Keyboard Layout	Default	
Memory	256MB/512MB	
Processors	1 (1 sockets, 1 cores) [numa=1]	
Display	Default	
CD/DVD Drive (ide2)	none,media=cdrom	
Hard Disk (virtio0)	local:100/vm-100-disk-1.qcow2,format=qcow2,size=20G	
Network Device (net0)	virtio=BA:9B:41:C9:43:2B,bridge=vmbr0	
Network Device (net1)	virtio=72:0C:17:10:8C:CF,bridge=vmbr101	

There's more...

The following screenshot shows a fictitious network diagram of a cloud service provider company, leveraging a virtual bridge to create a complex multitenant virtual environment:

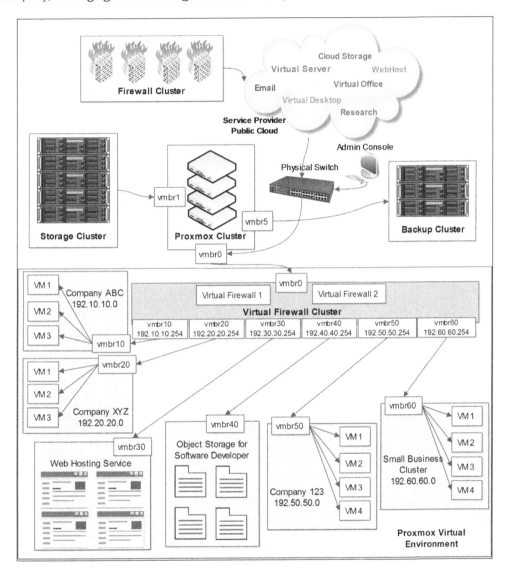

In the example network diagram, six separate isolated virtual networks have been created by leveraging the virtual bridge and virtual firewall, thus creating a complex cloud virtual environment. Analyze the preceding diagram to understand how each component is related to the other to design your own environment.

11

The CLI Command Reference

In this chapter, we will look at a list of commands for managing Proxmox storages entirely through a CLI. The commands are categorized as follows:

- ▶ Proxmox commands
    - ❑ Node-related commands
    - ❑ Cluster-related commands
    - ❑ Storage-related commands
    - ❑ KVM-based VM-related commands
- ▶ OpenVZ container-related commands
- ▶ Ceph commands
- ▶ Gluster commands
- ▶ ZFS commands

Introduction

The command list presented in this chapter is by no means a complete list of all the available commands. Only the most commonly used ones are shown here to get you started. There are many more command options available in the official Proxmox documentation for the categories mentioned here.

Proxmox commands

In this section, we will look at the commands for performing various tasks in Proxmox through a CLI.

How to do it...

In the following sections, we will explore some of the following commands:

- ▸ Node-related commands
- ▸ Cluster-related commands
- ▸ Storage-related commands
- ▸ KVM-based VM-related commands

Node-related commands

This section shows CLI commands that pertain to individual nodes only. These commands are run on specific nodes to perform various tasks, such as checking version numbers, performance status, upgrading packages, and so on:

1. To check the currently installed versions of the Proxmox packages in a node, use the following command:

   ```
   #pveversion -v
   ```

   The preceding command is useful when trying to compare versions with installed and released updated packages before installing them

The following screenshot shows the typical output of the command with the installed package list and version information:

```
root@pmx4:~# pveversion
pve-manager/4.0-16/a7dc5694 (running kernel: 3.19.8-1-pve)
root@pmx4:~# pveversion -v
proxmox-ve: 4.0-3 (running kernel: 3.19.8-1-pve)
pve-manager: 4.0-16 (running version: 4.0-16/a7dc5694)
pve-kernel-3.19.8-1-pve: 3.19.8-3
lvm2: 2.02.116-pve1
corosync-pve: 2.3.4-2
libqb0: 0.17.1-3
pve-cluster: 4.0-13
qemu-server: 4.0-12
pve-firmware: 1.1-5
libpve-common-perl: 4.0-8
libpve-access-control: 4.0-5
libpve-storage-perl: 4.0-11
pve-libspice-server1: 0.12.5-1
vncterm: 1.2-1
pve-qemu-kvm: 2.3-5
pve-container: 0.7-2
pve-firewall: 2.0-3
pve-ha-manager: 1.0-4
ksm-control-daemon: 1.2-1
glusterfs-client: 3.5.2-2
lxc-pve: 1.1.2-1
lxcfs: 0.9-pve1
cgmanager: 0.37-pve1
root@pmx4:~#
```

2. To upgrade a Proxmox node, use the following command:

`#pveupgrade`

The preceding command is a custom script by Proxmox, which is a wrapper around the `apt-get dist-upgrade` command

The benefit of using the preceding command is that it shows a little more information through the upgrade, such as whether or not a reboot is required not due to the kernel upgrade

3. To use the interactive custom shell, type the following command:

   `#pvesh`

   The preceding command exposes the entire line of the REST API in an interactive way. Type `quit` and press *Enter* to exit the shell.

   The following screenshot shows the API shell prompt:

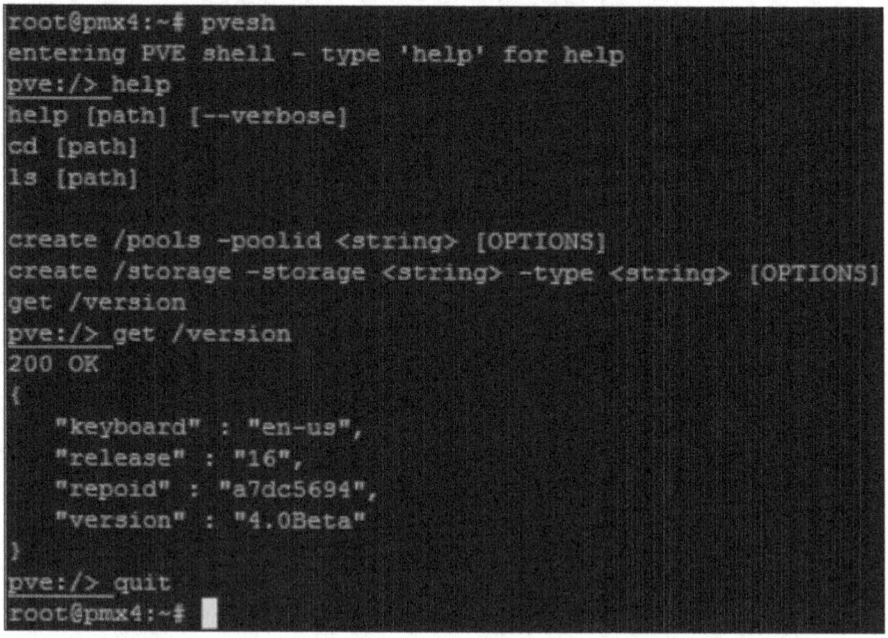

```
root@pmx4:~# pvesh
entering PVE shell - type 'help' for help
pve:/> help
help [path] [--verbose]
cd [path]
ls [path]

create /pools -poolid <string> [OPTIONS]
create /storage -storage <string> -type <string> [OPTIONS]
get /version
pve:/> get /version
200 OK
{
    "keyboard" : "en-us",
    "release" : "16",
    "repoid" : "a7dc5694",
    "version" : "4.0Beta"
}
pve:/> quit
root@pmx4:~#
```

4. To check the Proxmox node's performance, use the following command:

   `#pveperf`

   The preceding command is a quick way to check the CPU and hard drive performance of a node. This is useful for comparing the CPU and HDD performance between nodes.

The following screenshot shows the output of the command for one of the example nodes in our cluster:

```
root@pmx4:~# pveperf
CPU BOGOMIPS:       13600.08
REGEX/SECOND:       1340573
HD SIZE:            11.93 GB (/dev/dm-0)
BUFFERED READS:     98.14 MB/sec
AVERAGE SEEK TIME:  22.78 ms
FSYNCS/SECOND:      166.46
DNS EXT:            0.97 ms
DNS INT:            0.36 ms (domain.com)
root@pmx4:~#
```

5. To manage the subscription key for a node, use the following command:

```
#pvesubscription
```

The preceding command is useful when the Proxmox GUI becomes inaccessible for any reason and you need to apply, get, or update the subscription key

The following screenshot shows the output of the possible options for using the command:

```
root@pmx4:~# pvesubscription
ERROR: no command specified
USAGE: pvesubscription <COMMAND> [ARGS] [OPTIONS]
       pvesubscription get
       pvesubscription set <key>
       pvesubscription update [OPTIONS]

       pvesubscription help [<cmd>] [OPTIONS]
```

Cluster-related commands

This section shows the CLI commands related to basic Proxmox cluster management:

1. Use the following command to create a new cluster:

```
#pvecm create <cluster_name>
```

The preceding command can be run on any node in Proxmox that is going to be a part of the cluster

2. Use the following command to check the Proxmox cluster status:

`#pvecm status`

The preceding command can be run from any member node in the cluster

The following screenshot shows the output of a cluster status command:

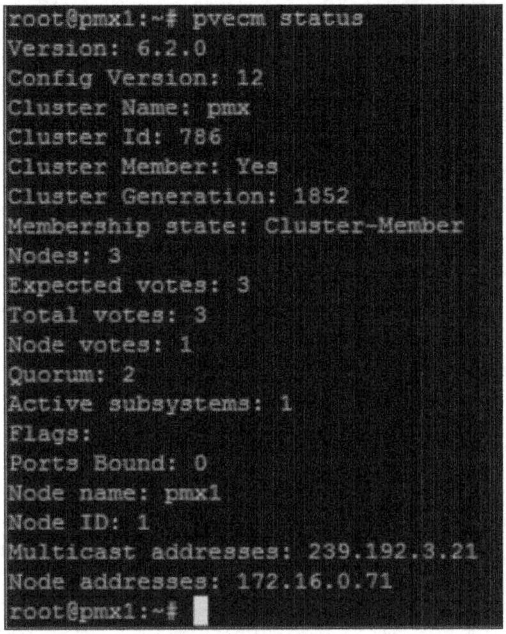

```
root@pmx1:~# pvecm status
Version: 6.2.0
Config Version: 12
Cluster Name: pmx
Cluster Id: 786
Cluster Member: Yes
Cluster Generation: 1852
Membership state: Cluster-Member
Nodes: 3
Expected votes: 3
Total votes: 3
Node votes: 1
Quorum: 2
Active subsystems: 1
Flags:
Ports Bound: 0
Node name: pmx1
Node ID: 1
Multicast addresses: 239.192.3.21
Node addresses: 172.16.0.71
root@pmx1:~#
```

3. Use the following command to add a node to the Proxmox cluster:

`#pvecm add <ip_of_existing_node>`

The preceding command needs to be run on a node that is not a member of the cluster yet, whereas, `<ip_of_existing_node>` is the IP address of any member node of the cluster

4. Use the following command to see a list of Proxmox nodes:

`#pvecm nodes`

The preceding command shows a list of all the member nodes in the cluster along with their hostnames and the date and time when they were added to the cluster

The following screenshot shows the list of member nodes in our example cluster:

```
root@pmx1:~# pvecm nodes
Node   Sts   Inc    Joined                  Name
   1    M    1840   2015-07-19 14:45:49     pmx1
   2    M    1848   2015-07-19 17:59:10     pmx2
   3    M    1852   2015-07-19 17:59:14     pmx3
root@pmx1:~#
```

5. Use the following command to change the expected vote of a node to re-establish a quorum:

    ```
    #pvecm expected <numeric_value>
    ```

    The preceding command is useful when quorum establishment is not possible due to failure of nodes or network connectivity issues. The Proxmox cluster is based on corosync, which is a democratic system and requires a majority vote of nodes to create a quorum. When the quorum is absent, the cluster filesystem becomes inaccessible to prevent data corruption. The preceding command tells the Cluster Manager (CMAN) of new and expected votes.

    For example, in a four node Proxmox cluster, a quorum will be established with a minimum of three votes from three nodes. If two nodes fail at the same time, then only the remaining two nodes can vote, which is not majority vote. In this scenario, by running the preceding command with an expected value of 1, we can tell CMAN to expect only one vote to establish the quorum.

6. Use the following command to regenerate a security certificate for the nodes:

    ```
    #pvecm updatecerts
    ```

    The preceding command generates all necessary files or directories for Proxmox self-signed SSL certificates to ensure that all the nodes have the same SSL

    To forcefully recreate new self-signed SSL certificates, use the following command with the `force` option:

    ```
    #pvecm updatecerts -force
    ```

7. Use the following commands and execute them in order to restart the Proxmox GUI if it becomes inaccessible:

    ```
    #service pvedaemon restart
    #service pveproxy restart
    #service pvestatd restart
    ```

8. Use the following command to remove a node from the cluster:

    `#pvecm delnode <hostname>`

    The preceding command removes a member node from the cluster

9. Rejoining the same node to a Proxmox cluster with the same IP address is useful when a node needs to be taken out of the cluster due to an issue and needs to be rejoined to the same cluster with with the same IP address. For our example, we have two Proxmox nodes in the cluster where the second node failed:

    ❑   `Node1:172.16.0.71`=pmx1

    ❑   `Node2:172.16.0.72`=pmx2 (failed node)

    On pmx1, run the following command to remove the faulty node:

    `#pvecm delnode proxmox2`

    On pmx2, run the following commands in this order:

    ❑   Create a backup of the `/etc/pve` directory by using the following command:

        `#cp -a /etc/pve /root/pve_backup`

    ❑   Stop the cluster service by using the following command:

        `#service pve-cluster stop`

    ❑   Unmount the pve directory by using the following command:

        `#umount /etc/pve`

    ❑   Stop the cluster manager by using the following command:

        `#service cman stop`

    ❑   Remove the cluster configuration file by using the following command:

        `#rm /etc/cluster/cluster.conf`

    ❑   Remove the cluster package by using the following command:

        `#rm -rf /var/lib/pve-cluster/*`

    ❑   Start the Proxmox cluster service by using the following command:

        `#service pve-cluster start`

    ❑   Re-add the node to the cluster by using the following command:

        `#pvecm add proxmox1`

10. Use the following command to create a new corosync cryptographic key:

    `#pvecm keygen <output_file>`

Storage-related commands

This section looks at command-related storage management in Proxmox:

1. Use the following command to see a list of attached storages with Proxmox:

   `#pvesm status`

   The preceding command lists the status of all the storages, including the storage name, storage type, and so on. This is a quick way to see the name of the attached storage.

   The following screenshot shows the status of storages attached to our example cluster:

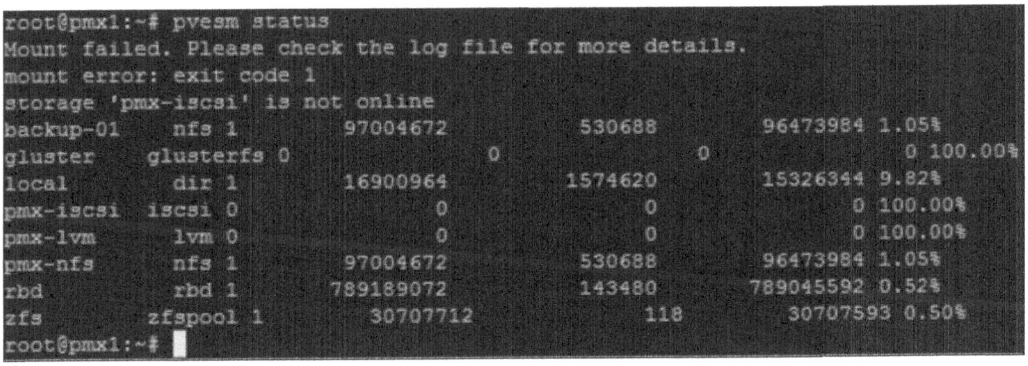

```
root@pmx1:~# pvesm status
Mount failed. Please check the log file for more details.
mount error: exit code 1
storage 'pmx-iscsi' is not online
backup-01    nfs 1         97004672           530688         96473984 1.05%
gluster      glusterfs 0                 0                 0         0 100.00%
local        dir 1         16900964          1574620        15326344 9.82%
pmx-iscsi    iscsi 0              0                0                0 100.00%
pmx-lvm      lvm 0                0                0                0 100.00%
pmx-nfs      nfs 1         97004672           530688         96473984 1.05%
rbd          rbd 1        789189072           143480        789045592 0.52%
zfs          zfspool 1      30707712              118         30707593 0.50%
root@pmx1:~#
```

2. Use the following command to attach a new storage with Proxmox:

   `#pvesm add <storage_name> -type <storage_type>`

3. Use the following command to detach a storage from a cluster:

   `#pvesm remove <storage_name>`

4. Use the following command, to see a list of stored files in a particular storage:

   `#pvesm list <storage_name>`

   The preceding command displays a list of all the files stored in a particular storage

The following screenshot shows a list of backup files stored in the `backup-01` storage:

```
root@pmx1:~# pvesm list backup-01
backup-01:backup/vzdump-openvz-101-2015_06_01-12_28_24.tar.lzo  tar.lzo        1016
backup-01:backup/vzdump-openvz-103-2015_07_04-00_00_16.tar.lzo  tar.lzo   182711184
backup-01:backup/vzdump-openvz-103-2015_07_07-00_00_13.tar.lzo  tar.lzo   182711175
backup-01:backup/vzdump-openvz-103-2015_07_21-00_00_13.tar.lzo  tar.lzo   182739726
backup-01:backup/vzdump-qemu-102-2015_06_27-00_00_15.vma.lzo    vma.lzo      71129
backup-01:backup/vzdump-qemu-102-2015_07_04-00_00_02.vma.lzo    vma.lzo      71144
backup-01:backup/vzdump-qemu-102-2015_07_21-00_00_02.vma.lzo    vma.lzo      71139
root@pmx1:~#
```

5. Use the following command to see a list of the available Gluster volumes in a remote Gluster node:

    `#pvesm glusterfsscan <gluster_node_ip or hostname>`

    The preceding command is useful for retrieving the volume list from the Proxmox node without logging into the Gluster node

    The following screenshot shows the volume list for one of our example Gluster nodes with two volumes:

```
root@pmx1:~# pvesm glusterfsscan 172.16.0.72
iso-win
gfs-isolnx01
root@pmx1:~#
```

6. Use the following command to see a list of available NFS shares on a remote node:

    `#pvesm nfsscan <nfs_node_ip or hostname>`

    The preceding command is useful for retrieving the NFS share list without logging into the NFS server node. The list also shows the IP address or subnet that is allowed to access the share.

    The following screenshot shows the NFS share list for one of our example NFS server nodes with one share:

```
root@pmx1:~# pvesm nfsscan 172.16.0.74
/mnt/pmx-nfs 172.16.0.0
root@pmx1:~#
```

7. Use the following command to see a list of LVMs on the current Proxmox node:

    `#pvesm lvmscan`

    This cannot retrieve the LVM list from the remote node

KVM-based VM-related commands

This section shows commands for performing KVM-based VM-related tasks:

1. Use the following command to a see list of all the VMs in a node:

   ```
   #qm list
   ```

   The list shows the running status of a VM along with the allocated memory amount, boot disk image size, and PIDs. The preceding command only shows the VM list of the node where the command is run.

   The following screenshot shows the VM list for the pmx1 node:

   ```
   root@pmx1:~# qm list
       VMID NAME                    STATUS    MEM(MB)    BOOTDISK(GB)  PID
        100 test-01                 running   512              20.00  754763
        102 test-02                 stopped   512               1.00  0
   root@pmx1:~#
   ```

2. Use the following command to start a powered-off VM:

   ```
   #qm start <vm_id>
   ```

3. Use the following command to clone a VM:

   ```
   #qm clone <existing_vm_id> <new_vm_id> -format
   [qcow2|raw|vmdk] -storage <destination_storage_ID> -target
   <destination_node>
   ```

4. Use the following command to take a snapshot of a VM:

   ```
   #qm snapshot <vm_id> <snapshot_name>
   ```

 Note that this is not a LVM snapshot, but rather a live snapshot, which simply preserves the state of the VM. Live snapshots can only be performed on a VM with a **qcow2** disk image, or it can store the disk image of any format on a storage that supports live snapshots, such as NFS, RBD, and more. A VM with a large allocated memory will take longer to create snapshots.

5. Note that all live snapshots are ignored during a full backup of the VM. Use the following command to roll back to a previously created snapshot:

   ```
   #qm rollback <vm_id> <snapshot_name>
   ```

6. Use the following command to remove a snapshot of a VM:

   ```
   #qm deletesnapshot <vm_id> <snapshot_name>
   ```

7. Use the following command to remove a VM:

   ```
   #qm destroy <vm_id>
   ```

Note that this action is irreversible and will permanently remove the VM.

8. Use the following command to migrate a VM:

   `#qm migrate <vm_id> <destination_node> -online`

   The preceding command will move a VM from one node to another. If the VM is powered on and you need to migrate it without powering it down, use the `-online` flag along with the command or else it is not necessary.

9. Use the following command to forcefully reset a VM:

   `#qm reset <vm_id>`

   The preceding command is equivalent to the resetting of a physical node

10. Use the following command to stop a VM:

    `#qm stop <vm_id>`

    The preceding command is equivalent to pushing the power button or pulling out the power cord of a physical node

11. There are no direct commands for getting a list of all disk image files for a VM, but we can access the VM through the QEMU monitor, and then retrieve the device list. The following screenshot shows the command chain for retrieving the disk image list from our example VM, `100`:

```
root@pmx1:~# qm monitor 100
Entering Qemu Monitor for VM 100 - type 'help' for help
qm> info block
drive-ide2: [not inserted]
    Removable device: not locked, tray closed

drive-virtio0: /var/lib/vz/images/100/vm-100-disk-1.qcow2 (qcow2)
    Detect zeroes:    on
qm> quit
root@pmx1:~#
```

From our example, we can see that the `100` VM has one VirtIO disk image with the qcow2 format. Now, let's discuss other commands that allow the resizing of a virtual disk image, suspending a VM, creating a template from a VM, and more things:

1. Use the following command to resize a virtual disk image:

   `#qm resize <vm_id> <virtual_disk> <size_in_gb>`

    As of Proxmox 3.4, it is only possible to increase the size of a virtual disk, and not to decrease it. For the `<virtual_disk>` option, use the ID of the disk image and not the entire disk image file name; for example, `ide0`, `ide1`, `scsi0`, `virtio0`, `virtio1`, `virtio2`, and so on.

2. Use the following command to suspend a VM:

   `#qm suspend <vm_id> -skiplock`

3. Use the following command to create a template from a VM:

   `#qm template <vm_id> -disk [ide0|ide1|virtio0 etc.]`

4. Use the following command to unlock a VM:

   `#qm unlock <vm_id>`

   Before committing the backup of a VM, Proxmox locks the VM to prevent another node from backing up the same VM. If the backup fails due to an error, the lock remains and the VM does not get unlocked. This will prevent the VM from powering up or any future backups. This command manually unlocks the VM.

There's more...

A comprehensive list of KVM commands can be found at `https://pve.proxmox.com/wiki/Manual:_qm`.

OpenVZ container-related commands

This section shows commands for performing OpenVZ container-based VM-related tasks.

How to do it...

Let's start using OpenVZ container-related commands by working through the following steps:

1. Use the following command to see a list of all the containers in a node:

   ```
   #pvectl list
   ```

   The preceding command only shows the list of containers that are hosted in the node where this command is issued. Pvectl is a wrapper from Proxmox around the original OpenVZ `vzctl` command.

   The following screenshot shows a list of containers in the example `pmx1` node:

   ```
   root@pmx1:~# pvectl list
          VMID NAME                         STATUS      MEM(MB)     DISK(GB)
           103 testCT01.symmcom.com running     512         4.00
   root@pmx1:~# 
   ```

2. Use the following command to start a container:

   ```
   #pvectl start <ct_id>
   ```

3. Use the following command to stop a container:

   ```
   #pvectl stop <ct_id>
   ```

   The preceding command is equivalent to pushing the power button or unplugging the power cord of a physical node

4. Use the following command to shut down a container gracefully:

   ```
   #pvectl shutdown <ct_id>
   ```

5. Use the following command to restart a container:

   ```
   #pvectl restart <ct_id>
   ```

   The preceding command is equivalent to pushing the reset button of a physical node

6. Use the following command to remove a container:

   ```
   #vzctl destroy <ct_id>
   ```

Note that this action is irreversible. The preceding command will remove the container permanently.

7. Use the following command to migrate a container to another node. Use the `-online` option flag only when live-migrating it:

```
#pvectl migrate <ct_id> <target_node> -online
```

8. Use the following command to check the status of a container:

```
#vzctl status <ct_id>
```

The following screenshot shows the status of the example `103` container:

```
root@pmx1:~# vzctl status 103
CTID 103 exist mounted running
root@pmx1:~#
```

9. Use the following command to change the number of CPU cores in a running container:

```
#pvectl set <ct_id> -cpus <numeric_value>
```

The following screenshot shows that we have added a second CPU core in the example `103` container:

```
root@pmx1:~# pvectl set 103 -cpus 2
Setting CPUs: 2
CT configuration saved to /etc/pve/openvz/103.conf
root@pmx1:~#
```

10. Use the following command to change the virtual disk size of a container:

```
#pvectl set <ct_id> -disk <numeric_value_in_GB>
```

The following screenshot shows that we have increased our disk image size from the existing 4 GB to 8 GB for the example `103` container:

```
root@pmx1:~# pvectl set 103 -disk 8
CT configuration saved to /etc/pve/openvz/103.conf
root@pmx1:~#
```

11. Use the following command to change the swap storage size on a running container:

```
#pvectl set <ct_id> <numeric_value_in_MB>
```

12. Use the following command to gain access into the container as root. The recommended method of accessing the container is SSH. This command is only useful for accessing the container from the host node:

```
#vzctl enter <ct_id>
```

The following screenshot shows that we have accessed the example `103` container from the host node by using the preceding command, and then we have checked the storage space and exited back to the host node:

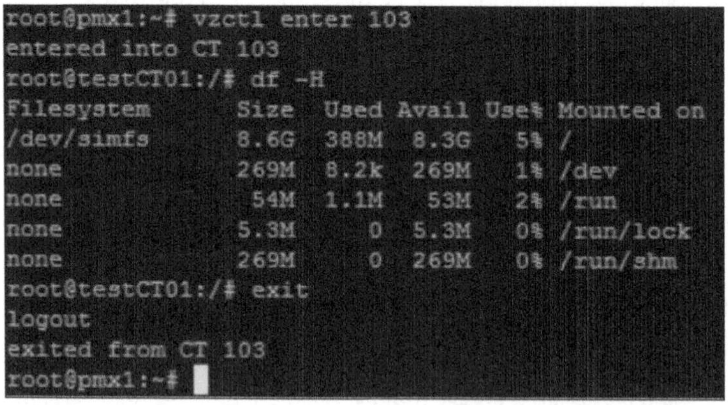

```
root@pmx1:~# vzctl enter 103
entered into CT 103
root@testCT01:/# df -H
Filesystem        Size  Used Avail Use% Mounted on
/dev/simfs        8.6G  388M  8.3G   5% /
none              269M  8.2k  269M   1% /dev
none               54M  1.1M   53M   2% /run
none              5.3M     0  5.3M   0% /run/lock
none              269M     0  269M   0% /run/shm
root@testCT01:/# exit
logout
exited from CT 103
root@pmx1:~#
```

13. Execute the following command inside the container directly from the host node without accessing the container:

```
#vzctl exec <ct_id> <command>
```

The following screenshot shows that we have executed a command from the Proxmox host to check the storage space inside the example `103` container:

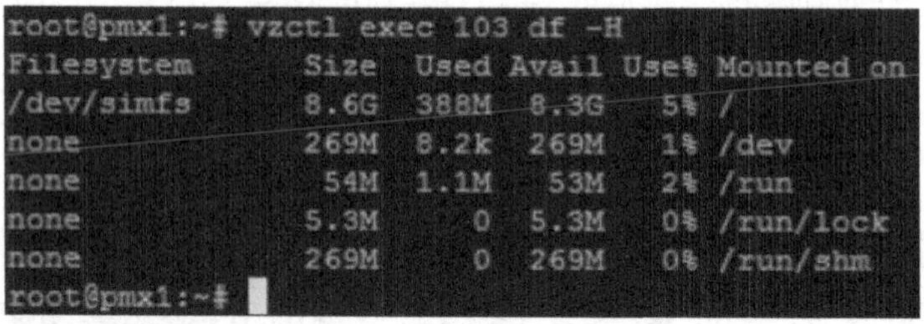

```
root@pmx1:~# vzctl exec 103 df -H
Filesystem        Size  Used Avail Use% Mounted on
/dev/simfs        8.6G  388M  8.3G   5% /
none              269M  8.2k  269M   1% /dev
none               54M  1.1M   53M   2% /run
none              5.3M     0  5.3M   0% /run/lock
none              269M     0  269M   0% /run/shm
root@pmx1:~#
```

There's more...

A detailed list of the available container-based commands can be found at `https://pve.proxmox.com/wiki/Vzctl_manual` and `https://pve.proxmox.com/wiki/Pvectl_manual`.

Ceph commands

In this section, we will look at commands for performing various tasks for a Ceph cluster in Proxmox.

How to do it...

The following steps demonstrate the commands used to perform certain tasks for a Ceph cluster:

1. Use the following command to check the Ceph cluster's health summary:

   ```
   # ceph -s
   ```

   The following screenshot shows our example Ceph cluster with a warning:

   ```
   root@pmx1:~# ceph -s
       cluster d68c82dc-d6cb-48e1-90cf-063ecadcb0ce
        health HEALTH_WARN 1 requests are blocked > 32 sec
        monmap e3: 3 mons at {0=172.16.0.71:6789/0,1=172.16.0.72:6789/0,2=172.16.0.73:6789/0}
        osdmap e508: 6 osds: 6 up, 6 in
         pgmap v14325: 512 pgs, 2 pools, 3240 kB data, 811 objects
               273 MB used, 1504 GB / 1505 GB avail
                    512 active+clean
   ```

2. Use the following command to check the Ceph cluster's health details with errors:

   ```
   # ceph health detail
   ```

   The following screenshot shows the warning details that tell us whether or not one of the OSDs is experiencing any problems:

   ```
   root@pmx1:~# ceph health detail
   HEALTH_WARN 1 requests are blocked > 32 sec; 1 osds have slow requests
   1 ops are blocked > 8388.61 sec
   1 ops are blocked > 8388.61 sec on osd.3
   1 osds have slow requests
   ```

3. Use the following command to see an OSD map:

   ```
   # ceph osd tree
   ```

   The preceding command shows a list of all the member nodes of the Ceph cluster, and the OSDs in each node. This is a quick way to see which OSD is located in a particular node and the ID of each OSD.

The following screenshot shows the OSD tree of our example cluster:

```
root@pmx1:~# ceph osd tree
# id     weight   type name        up/down reweight
-1       1.44     root default
-2       0.72         host pmx1
0        0.24                      osd.0    up      1
1        0.24                      osd.1    up      1
2        0.24                      osd.2    up      1
-3       0.72         host pmx2
3        0.24                      osd.3    up      1
4        0.24                      osd.4    up      1
5        0.24                      osd.5    up      1
root@pmx1:~#
```

4. Use the following command to prevent unnecessary rebalancing during node maintenance:

   ```
   # ceph osd [set|unset] noout
   ```

   The preceding command is helpful during regular maintenance when a node or OSD needs to be taken offline temporarily. This prevents the cluster from redistributing data among the other OSDs, thus causing a significant slowdown. After the maintenance is done, be sure to `unset` the option.

5. Use the following command to check the Ceph configuration during runtime:

   ```
   # ceph daemon osd.X config show | grep <string>
   ```

   The preceding command is very useful to see which configuration is currently applied to all OSDs. For the `<string>` parameter, we can enter any possible string and it does not need to be the exact configuration name.

   The following screenshot shows an example to check the number of threads currently assigned for different features:

```
root@pmx1:~# ceph daemon osd.1 config show | grep threads
    "osd_op_threads": "2",
    "osd_disk_threads": "1",
    "osd_recovery_threads": "1",
    "osd_op_num_threads_per_shard": "2",
    "filestore_op_threads": "2",
    "keyvaluestore_op_threads": "2",
    "internal_safe_to_start_threads": "true"}
root@pmx1:~#
```

6. Use the following command to inject a configuration in running the Ceph cluster. This is extremely useful for changing the configuration value on the fly without restarting an entire Ceph cluster:

```
# ceph tell osd.* injectargs '--<string> <value>'
```

The following screenshot is an example of changing the OSD operation thread value into a running Ceph cluster from 2 to 4:

```
root@pmx1:~# ceph tell osd.* injectargs '--osd-op-threads 4'
osd.0: osd_op_threads = '4'
osd.1: osd_op_threads = '4'
osd.2: osd_op_threads = '4'
osd.3: osd_op_threads = '4'
osd.4: osd_op_threads = '4'
osd.5: osd_op_threads = '4'
root@pmx1:~#
```

We can confirm that the value has been changed by running the following command:

```
#ceph daemon osd.1 config show | grep osd_op_threads
```

7. Use the following command to create a new OSD:

```
# pveceph createosd /dev/sdX –fstype ext4
```

If there is an existing partition on the drive, remove it using **fdisk**. Change the – fstype flag to use different filesystems, such as ext3, btrfs, and so on.

8. Use the following command to repair damaged PGs:

```
# ceph pg repair <pg_id>
```

It is normal for a few months old running Ceph cluster to develop inconsistent PGs. In almost all cases, this inconsistency can be repaired without any issues at all. This command tells the cluster to find all the pieces of the PG and repair it. Note that as soon as an inconsistency in the PG is detected, it should be repaired. If it is left for an extended period of time, data loss may occur.

To get the exact name of the PG, run the detailed health command as follows:

```
#ceph health detail
```

9. Use the following command to the see real-time Ceph log:

```
# ceph –w
```

The preceding command shows a running log on the screen for the Ceph cluster. The log shows information, such as the total PGs, the PG status, the total cluster storage used, read/write operations per second, and so on. Press *Ctrl + W* to stop the scrolling of the log.

The following screenshot shows the running log of our example Ceph cluster:

```
root@pmx1:~# ceph -w
    cluster d68c82dc-d6cb-48e1-90cf-063ecadcb0ce
     health HEALTH_OK
     monmap e3: 3 mons at {0=172.16.0.71:6789/0,1=172.16.0.72:6789/0,2=172.16.0.73:6789/0}, elect
ion epoch 542, quorum 0,1,2 0,1,2
     osdmap e557: 6 osds: 6 up, 6 in
      pgmap v14652: 512 pgs, 2 pools, 1032 MB data, 2379 objects
            1335 MB used, 1503 GB / 1505 GB avail
                512 active+clean

2015-07-23 12:08:14.911972 mon.0 [INF] pgmap v14652: 512 pgs: 512 active+clean; 1032 MB data, 133
5 MB used, 1503 GB / 1505 GB avail
2015-07-23 12:08:57.463090 mon.0 [INF] pgmap v14653: 512 pgs: 512 active+clean; 1032 MB data, 133
5 MB used, 1503 GB / 1505 GB avail; 98493 B/s rd, 0 op/s
2015-07-23 12:08:58.494971 mon.0 [INF] pgmap v14654: 512 pgs: 512 active+clean; 1032 MB data, 133
4 MB used, 1503 GB / 1505 GB avail; 610 kB/s rd, 0 op/s
2015-07-23 12:08:59.578328 mon.0 [INF] pgmap v14655: 512 pgs: 512 active+clean; 1032 MB data, 133
2 MB used, 1503 GB / 1505 GB avail; 44525 kB/s rd, 35 op/s
2015-07-23 12:09:03.090742 mon.0 [INF] pgmap v14656: 512 pgs: 512 active+clean; 1032 MB data, 133
2 MB used, 1503 GB / 1505 GB avail; 27951 kB/s rd, 18 op/s
2015-07-23 12:09:04.125790 mon.0 [INF] pgmap v14657: 512 pgs: 512 active+clean; 1032 MB data, 133
2 MB used, 1503 GB / 1505 GB avail; 32657 kB/s rd, 15 op/s
```

10. Use the following command to create a Ceph monitor on a Proxmox node:

    ```
    # pveceph createmon
    ```

    The preceding command creates a Ceph monitor or MON on the Proxmox node where this command was issued

11. Use the following command to check a Ceph cluster's usage:

    ```
    # ceph df
    ```

    The preceding command shows the cluster-wide storage consumption and the consumption by each pool in the Ceph cluster

    The following screenshot shows the storage usage information in our example Ceph cluster:

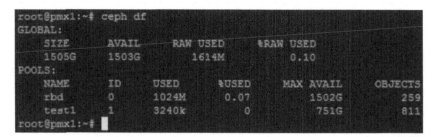

12. Use the following command to benchmark the Ceph OSD:

```
# ceph tell osd.* bench
```

The preceding command is the Ceph built-in performance testing command for testing the read/write performance of all OSDs in the cluster. This command checks each OSD separately. So, depending on the number of OSDs in the cluster, the benchmark may take a while to complete.

The following screenshot shows the benchmark output for all six OSDs in our Ceph cluster:

```
root@pmx1:~# ceph tell osd.* bench
osd.0: { "bytes_written": 1073741824,
  "blocksize": 4194304,
  "bytes_per_sec": "29405936.000000"}
osd.1: { "bytes_written": 1073741824,
  "blocksize": 4194304,
  "bytes_per_sec": "29533376.000000"}
osd.2: { "bytes_written": 1073741824,
  "blocksize": 4194304,
  "bytes_per_sec": "27558497.000000"}
osd.3: { "bytes_written": 1073741824,
  "blocksize": 4194304,
  "bytes_per_sec": "21596766.000000"}
osd.4: { "bytes_written": 1073741824,
  "blocksize": 4194304,
  "bytes_per_sec": "19828580.000000"}
osd.5: { "bytes_written": 1073741824,
  "blocksize": 4194304,
  "bytes_per_sec": "27186012.000000"}
root@pmx1:~#
```

13. Use the following command to reweight an OSD:

```
# ceph osd crush reweight osd.X <num_value>
```

The preceding command is useful when adding or removing an OSD in the Ceph cluster. Whenever an OSD is added or removed, the cluster goes into rebalancing mode, causing significant bandwidth consumption. By reweighting an OSD incrementally or decrementally, we can slow down the rebalancing, thus causing fewer interruptions.

If we want to add a 2 TB HDD to the Ceph cluster as an OSD, Ceph will assign the weight of 2 automatically and rebalance it accordingly, thus trying to move a large amount of data. However, if you reweight incrementally, for example, 0.25, 0.5, 1.0, and so on, the impact on the cluster will be significantly less. Based on this example, our command will look as follows:

```
#ceph osd crush reweight osd.11 0.25
```

When issuing the preceding command, Ceph will commence rebalancing in smaller chunks, and when rebalancing is finished, we can reissue the command with a weight value of 0.5 and have the process start all over again.

14. Use the following command to see a list of Ceph pools:

```
# rados lspools
```

The following screenshot shows the pool list for our example Ceph cluster:

```
root@pmx1:~# rados lspools
rbd
test1
root@pmx1:~#
```

15. Use the following command to benchmark a Ceph pool for write performance:

```
# rados bench -p <pool_name> -t <threads> -b <blocksize>
<seconds> write --no-cleanup
```

The following screenshot shows that the write performance has commenced on our Ceph cluster for the pool named `test1` with one thread and a block size of 4096 for 10 seconds. The `--no-cleanup` flag will keep the benchmark file so that we can run the read test. Without the flag, the benchmark file would be deleted automatically:

```
root@pmx1:~# rados bench -p test1 -t 1 -b 4096 10 write --no-cleanup
 Maintaining 1 concurrent writes of 4096 bytes for up to 10 seconds or 0 objects
 Object prefix: benchmark_data_pmx1_612405
   sec Cur ops   started  finished  avg MB/s  cur MB/s  last lat    avg lat
     0       0         0         0         0         0         -          0
     1       1        80        79  0.303975  0.308594  0.005317  0.0127906
     2       1       276       275  0.533021  0.765625  0.0041720.00732583
     3       1       436       435  0.563475     0.625  0.0056180.00692675
     4       1       578       577  0.561276  0.554688  0.0566150.00692347
     5       1       714       713  0.555277   0.53125  0.0047250.00702627
     6       1       871       870  0.564909  0.613281   0.01668 0.0069037
     7       1      1033      1032  0.574579  0.632812  0.0049410.00679413
     8       1      1186      1185  0.577444  0.597656  0.0056950.00676162
     9       1      1301      1300  0.563215  0.449219  0.0044370.00684887
    10       1      1308      1307  0.509708 0.0273438  0.0523250.00722716
 Total time run:        10.107682
Total writes made:     1309
Write size:            4096
Bandwidth (MB/sec):    0.506

Stddev Bandwidth:      0.250724
Max bandwidth (MB/sec): 0.765625
Min bandwidth (MB/sec): 0
Average Latency:       0.00771908
Stddev Latency:        0.0230002
Max latency:           0.588967
Min latency:           0.003353
root@pmx1:~#
```

16. Use the following command to benchmark a Ceph pool for read performance:

```
# rados bench -p <pool_name> -t <threads> -b <blocksize>
<seconds> seq
```

Before we perform the read performance test, we have to ensure that the cache is cleared by using the following command to get accurate test results. The command needs to run on all member nodes of the Ceph cluster:

```
#echo 3 | tee /proc/sys/vm/drop_caches && sync
```

The following screenshot shows the sequential read benchmark result that is performed using one thread and a block size of 4096 for 10 seconds:

```
root@pmx1:~# echo 3 | tee /proc/sys/vm/drop_caches && sync
3
root@pmx1:~# rados bench -p test1 -t 1 -b 4096 10 seq
   sec Cur ops    started   finished   avg MB/s   cur MB/s   last lat    avg lat
     0        1          1          0          0          0          -          0
     1        1        944        943     3.6752    3.68359  0.000649 0.00105634
 Total time run:          1.257334
Total reads made:        1309
Read size:               4096
Bandwidth (MB/sec):       4.067

Average Latency:          0.000955656
Max latency:              0.118269
Min latency:              0.000499
root@pmx1:~#
```

Gluster commands

In this section, we will look at the commands for performing various tasks for GlusterFS in Proxmox.

How to do it...

The following steps demonstrate the various commands that are used to perform various tasks for GlusterFS in Proxmox:

1. Use the following command to create a Gluster volume in a replicated mode:

```
# gluster volume create <name> replica [count]
<destination_brick 1> <destination_brick 2> <...>
```

Creating a Gluster volume named `testgfs` with two replicas would be as follows:

```
#gluster volume create testgfs replica 2
172.16.0.72:/mnt/gfs/testgfs 172.16.0.73:/mnt/gfs/testgfs
```

The following screenshot shows the output of the Gluster volume creation process:

```
root@pmx2:/mnt# gluster volume create testgfs replica 2 172.16.0.72:/mnt/gfs/testgfs 172.16.0.73:/mnt/gfs/testgfs
volume create: testgfs: success: please start the volume to access data
root@pmx2:/mnt#
```

2. Use the following command to see a list of Gluster volumes:

   `# gluster volume list`

3. Use the following command to start and stop the Gluster volume:

   `# gluster volume [start|stop] <volume>`

4. Use the following command to check the status of Gluster peer nodes:

   `# gluster peer status`

5. Use the following command to attach nodes to a Gluster peer:

   `# gluster peer probe <hostname>`

6. Use the following command to detach a node from the Gluster peer:

   `# gluster detach <hostname>`

7. Use the following command to see a list of all the nodes in a pool:

   `# gluster pool list`

   The preceding command shows the UUID of each volume and the location of the nodes they are in

   The following screenshot shows the output of the command in our example Gluster cluster:

```
root@pmx2:/mnt# gluster pool list
UUID                                       Hostname        State
b94a55c8-cc6d-4226-afba-3d13901e0a81       172.16.0.73     Connected
739a0bdf-bc28-41ee-8500-71b69ad90001       localhost       Connected
root@pmx2:/mnt#
```

8. Use the following command to see a list of all the available Gluster commands:

   `# gluster help`

There's more...

A detailed list of Gluster commands can be found at http://www.gluster.org/community/documentation/index.php/Gluster_3.2:_gluster_Command.

ZFS commands

In this section, we will look at the commands for performing various tasks for ZFS on Proxmox.

How to do it...

1. Use the following command to create the `raidz` ZFS pool:

```
# zpool create <pool_name> raidz -m <mountpoint> </dev/sdX> </dev/sdX> <...>
```

The command to create a `zpool` named `testzfs` in the `/mnt/zfs1` mount point with three drives looks like this:

```
#zpool create testzfs raidz -m /mnt/zfs1/ /dev/vdf /dev/vdg /dev/vdh
```

The following screenshot shows the output of the `zpool` list to verify that our pool is created:

```
root@pmx1:~# zpool list
NAME       SIZE   ALLOC   FREE    CAP   DEDUP   HEALTH   ALTROOT
testzfs    298G   259K    298G    0%    1.00x   ONLINE   -
root@pmx1:~#
```

2. Use the following command to delete the ZFS pool:

```
# zpool destroy <pool_name>
```

This action is irreversible. Once the pool is deleted, it is permanently removed.

3. Use the following command to list all the ZFS pools and storage space:

```
# zpool list
```

4. Use the following command to see the status of all the drives for the ZFS pool:

```
#zpool status
```

The preceding command is useful for checking if any drives are offline or approaching failure by checking the read/write or checksum error count

The following screenshot shows the pool status for the example `testzfs` pool, which comprises three drives with no errors:

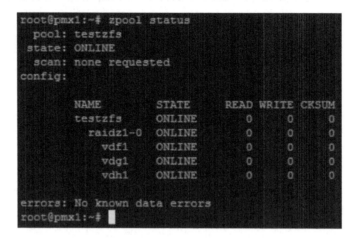

```
root@pmx1:~# zpool status
  pool: testzfs
 state: ONLINE
  scan: none requested
config:

        NAME           STATE     READ WRITE CKSUM
        testzfs        ONLINE       0     0     0
          raidz1-0     ONLINE       0     0     0
            vdf1       ONLINE       0     0     0
            vdg1       ONLINE       0     0     0
            vdh1       ONLINE       0     0     0

errors: No known data errors
root@pmx1:~# 
```

5. Use the following command to initiate `scrub` on the ZFS pool:

    ```
    # zpool scrub <pool_name>
    ```

    Scrubbing ensures the data integrity of the ZFS pool. Be sure to perform `scrub` during off hours or when usage is the lowest since scrubbing will slow down the pool significantly.

6. Use the following command to upgrade the ZFS pool after applying a newer release:

    ```
    # zpool upgrade
    ```

    After each major upgrade of the ZFS package, the pool needs to be manually upgraded to the latest version to activate new features. Pools are not automatically upgraded during package updates.

7. Use the following command to see a list of ZFS datasets:

    ```
    # zfs list
    ```

8. Use the following command to create a new ZFS dataset:

    ```
    # zfs create -o mountpoint=<filesystempath> <name>
    ```

9. Use the following command to set the mount point for a ZFS dataset:

    ```
    # zfs set -o mountpoint=<filesystempath> <name>
    ```

    The preceding command is useful for moving the mount point from one directory to another. Be sure to unmount the dataset first, and then remount it after changing the mount point.

10. Use the following command to mount all the ZFS pools:

```
# zfs mount -a
```

The preceding command will automount all the pools if they are not currently mounted

11. To mount a specific pool or dataset, simply issue the command with the name of the pool or dataset as follows:

```
#zfs mount testzfs
```

12. Use the following command to unmount the ZFS dataset or pool:

```
#zfs umount <mountpoint_path>
```

If we wanted to unmount the example testzfs1 pool, which is in mountpoint /mnt/zfs1, the command would appear as follows:

```
#zfs umount /mnt/zfs1
```

13. Use the following command to remove the ZFS dataset:

```
# zfs destroy <name>
```

The preceding action is irreversible. Once the command is issued, the dataset is removed permanently.

14. Use the following command to rename the ZFS dataset:

```
# zfs rename <old_filesystem_name> <new_filesystem_name>
```

There's more...

For a comprehensive list of ZFS commands in greater detail, visit http://thegeekdiary. com/solaris-zfs-command-line-reference-cheat-sheet/.

Index

Thank you for buying
Proxmox Cookbook

About Packt Publishing

Packt, pronounced 'packed', published its first book, *Mastering phpMyAdmin for Effective MySQL Management*, in April 2004, and subsequently continued to specialize in publishing highly focused books on specific technologies and solutions.

Our books and publications share the experiences of your fellow IT professionals in adapting and customizing today's systems, applications, and frameworks. Our solution-based books give you the knowledge and power to customize the software and technologies you're using to get the job done. Packt books are more specific and less general than the IT books you have seen in the past. Our unique business model allows us to bring you more focused information, giving you more of what you need to know, and less of what you don't.

Packt is a modern yet unique publishing company that focuses on producing quality, cutting-edge books for communities of developers, administrators, and newbies alike. For more information, please visit our website at www.packtpub.com.

About Packt Open Source

In 2010, Packt launched two new brands, Packt Open Source and Packt Enterprise, in order to continue its focus on specialization. This book is part of the Packt open source brand, home to books published on software built around open source licenses, and offering information to anybody from advanced developers to budding web designers. The Open Source brand also runs Packt's open source Royalty Scheme, by which Packt gives a royalty to each open source project about whose software a book is sold.

Writing for Packt

We welcome all inquiries from people who are interested in authoring. Book proposals should be sent to author@packtpub.com. If your book idea is still at an early stage and you would like to discuss it first before writing a formal book proposal, then please contact us; one of our commissioning editors will get in touch with you.

We're not just looking for published authors; if you have strong technical skills but no writing experience, our experienced editors can help you develop a writing career, or simply get some additional reward for your expertise.

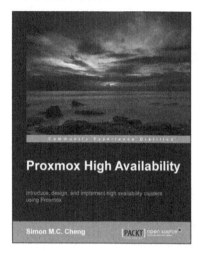

Proxmox High Availability

ISBN: 978-1-78398-088-8   Paperback: 258 pages

Introduce, design, and implement high availability clusters using Proxmox

1. Learn to use Liferay tools to create your own applications as a Java developer, with hands-on examples.

2. Customize Liferay portal using the JSR-286 portlet, extension environment, and Struts framework.

3. Build your own Social Office with portlets, hooks, and themes and manage your own community.

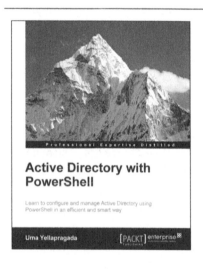

Active Directory with PowerShell

ISBN: 978-1-78217-599-5   Paperback: 230 pages

Learn to configure and manage Active Directory using PowerShell in an efficient and smart way

1. Create and manage domains, organization units, sites, and IP subnets using PowerShell.

2. Learn advanced operations in Active directory such as promoting, demoting active directory domain controllers, recovering AD objects, and working with replication using PowerShell.

3. A complete guide that will unleash the power of automation in Active Directory environment.

Please check **www.PacktPub.com** for information on our titles

VMware vCenter Cookbook

ISBN: 978-1-78355-397-6   Paperback: 302 pages

Over 65 hands-on recipes to help you efficiently manage your vSphere environment with VMware vCenter

1. Learn how to increase availability and scalability of your virtual environment.

2. Improve efficiency and optimize resource usage in your virtual infrastructure.

3. Explore new vCenter features and discover best ways to implement them using proactive examples.

OpenStack Essentials

ISBN: 978-1-78398-708-5   Paperback: 182 pages

Demystify the cloud by building your own private OpenStack cloud

1. Set up a powerful cloud platform using OpenStack.

2. Learn about the components of OpenStack and how they interact with each other.

3. Follow a step-by-step process that exposes the inner details of an OpenStack cluster.

Please check **www.PacktPub.com** for information on our titles

Made in the USA
Middletown, DE
04 January 2020